DESIGN EDUCATION
FOR THE
MIDDLE YEARS

A Teachers' Guide

D. M. Shaw
J. M. Reeve

FROM THE LIBRARY OF

Bridget Egan

HODDER AND STOUGHTON

LONDON   SYDNEY   AUCKLAND   TORONTO

The Authors

D. M. SHAW

David Shaw is an educational adviser for schools to the Coventry LEA. For a number of years he was a senior lecturer in the Education Unit of Lanchester Polytechnic where he was responsible for in-service teacher courses in craft, design and technology. Previously he had been a head of department and had taught for many years in a number of secondary schools. He has written and lectured widely on design and technology education in schools and is well known for his work in developing the uses of plastics as educational media. Mr Shaw was for some years a chief examiner for the CSE and is now a moderator/assessor for design and technological studies. His previous publications include the following:

> *Principles and Practice of Woodwork for G.C.E. Students*, Hodder and Stoughton, 1963.
>
> *Woodwork, Design and Practice*, Hodder and Stoughton, 1973.
>
> *Technology Module No. 6—Plastics*, NCST, 1976.

J. M. REEVE

John Reeve is responsible for design studies at Abbot's Farm Middle School, Rugby. Before entering the teaching profession he was a marine engineer in the Merchant Service. He later gained further qualifications in electrical engineering whilst employed in the electricity supply industry. Mr Reeve then studied fine art and crafts at a college of art and later underwent teacher training. Subsequently he has spent a number of years teaching in junior and middle schools and has lectured on the teaching of art and design.

First published 1978
Reprinted 1981, 1983
Fourth impression 1987

Printed and bound in Great Britain for Hodder and Stoughton Educational, a division of Hodder and Stoughton Ltd, Mill Road, Dunton Green, Sevenoaks, Kent by Biddles Ltd, Guildford and King's Lynn

British Library Cataloguing in Publication Data

Shaw, David Malcolm
    Design education for the middle years.
    1. Design—Study and teaching (Elementary)
    2. Design—Study and teaching (Secondary)
    I. Title   II. Reeve, J. M.
    745.4'07'1   NK1170

    ISBN 0-340-22367-7

Contents

Preface v

Acknowledgements v

Section A
Design Studies within the School Curriculum

1. Design Education 1
   The role of design education within the general education of pupils in the middle years of schooling (8-14 years).

2. The Scope of the Subject 7
   The design/problem-solving process; case histories.

3. Design as a Social Study 29
   Health and the physical and cultural environments as contexts for design-based learning.

Section B
Requirements and Resources—the Teacher's Role

4. Planning the Course as a Major Curriculum Activity 35
   Course objectives, their production and classification.

5. The Detailed Construction of a Design-Based Course 49
   Course structuring and related factors.

6. The Recording and Evaluation of Pupils' Performance 59
   Course-work record-keeping systems; measuring and recording pupil achievement.

7. Resources for Design Education 71
   Teaching staff; physical provision; timetabling.

8. Display Techniques   78
    Educational uses and essential techniques of display in schools.

Section C
The Provision of Design Experience in Two and Three Dimensions

9. Visual Communication   90
    *The wider implications of visual communication and its relationship to
    personal and external factors.*

10. Visual Communication: Experience in Two Dimensions   101
    *The provision of two-dimensional experiences; elements and organisation
    of two-dimensional space and modes of two-dimensional expression.*

11. Experience in Three Dimensions   117
    *The development of spatial perception. The environment; natural and
    man-made objects. Three-dimensional materials, their manipulation and
    uses.*

12. Constructional Techniques for the Middle Years   124
    A basic approach to teaching materials manipulation.

Bibliography   134

Summary Index   138

Preface to Second Printing

However defined and interpreted the purposes of design education in schools remain largely misunderstood by many teachers. The Schools' Council 'Design and Craft Education' project and the more recent DES sponsored Royal College of Art 'Design in General Education' project have promoted and advanced developments in this area of the curriculum.

School examinations at GCE 'O' and 'A' levels, the CSE and experimental CEE in design and associated studies now exist and courses leading to these examinations are growing in number. The GCE 'A' level design examination is accepted for entrance purposes by an increasing number of university and polytechnic faculties.

However, serious concern is currently being expressed that where design-based courses exist in the lower part of secondary schools, in middle schools and in the upper forms of junior schools a number of them lack cohesion and real educational purpose.

The DES Inspectorate's survey *Primary Education in England* (HMSO, 1978), expressed concern about the comparative neglect of three-dimensional constructional work and suggested that both boys and girls should undertake work with resistant materials and the tools and techniques associated with them. The need to provide experimental science was also expressed.

To set before teachers examples of good practice in this field the DES published *Craft, Design and Technology—Some Successful Examples* (HMSO, 1980).

Further positive support for such curricular activity is given in *Design Education at Secondary Level*, a Design Council consultative report published in 1979 and by the RSA supported statement on *Education for Capability* (1980) signed by many leading politicians, industrialists and educationalists.

Many teachers are therefore seeking positive guidance, not only on the content of design-based programmes of work, but even more importantly, on the professional requirements for establishing and successfully implementing such activity at all levels in schools.

As the foundations of sound design-based learning programmes lie in the experiences provided for the pupils in their middle years of schooling (8-14), this book provides specific guidance on how teachers might relate their work to the aims and objectives of design in education on the one hand and the very real difficulties of transforming them into meaningful pupil activities on the other.

Because it has been written to stimulate discussion on development in this area of the curriculum this book may, in parts, be considered somewhat controversial. It is hoped that the advice it offers will be found of value to both specialist and non-specialist trained teachers at a time when the educational debate is calling for a searching review of the purposes and practices of education as a whole.

Acknowledgements

The authors gratefully acknowledge the encouragement and assistance they have received from all those who have been associated with the production of this book. In particular they wish to record their thanks to the staff and pupils of St Mark's Middle School, Rugby, for their help and forbearance.

Section A Design Studies within the School Curriculum
Chapter 1 Design Education

1.1 What is Design Education in Schools?

The word 'design' is capable of many interpretations, but it can be defined quite simply as the conception and realisation of an idea which will satisfy a particular need or purpose. In this broad context of human activity, in which everyone is involved, design embraces activities as diverse as shaping a piece of pottery, weaving a tapestry, preparing a meal, making furniture or constructing a house, as well as the high-order thinking involved in civil, mechanical, electrical and environmental engineering, such as the planning and execution of a television network or of a traffic system for a large urban conurbation.

Design education can also be interpreted in a variety of ways. In schools it is largely concerned with providing experiences through activities, studies, or courses which encourage a wide ranging and balanced approach to two and three dimensional design involving the pupil's physical, intellectual and emotional participation.

It is the purpose of this book to develop this broad concept, in the context of design education in the middle years of schooling. Traditionally art and crafts, aspects of work in home economics, applied science and other relevant disciplines have been taught almost entirely in isolation. Design education in schools can be identified as an integrating factor which brings together studies which, whilst sharing many common objectives and much overlapping content, have previously been presented as quite separate independent subjects.

Within the interdisciplinary framework of design education this work is examined in relation to developments taking place in primary and secondary schools, but more specifically in the middle years of schooling, and to the function of such education in contemporary society.

Careful attention is given to patterns of child development in these formative, transitional years, during which the emphasis is placed on the development of attitudes and the acquisition of learning techniques.

The term 'middle years of schooling' covers pupils in the age range of 8-14 years, of whom approximately one-third are currently in middle schools, most of which cater for 8-12-year-olds. The remainder are in the upper classes of primary or the lower forms of secondary schools.

Because of the wide variation in educational provision for these children it is not possible to be specific in overall recommendations as to detailed organisation and content of design-based studies. However, general guidelines are offered as a stimulus for discussion with regard to the organisation, facilities, course content, methodology and day-to-day work in this field.

Contemporary western culture depends upon the ability to operate a complex technological society and maintain economic and political stability. In these circumstances the arts and crafts have been treated as peripheral activities, of relatively minor value compared to the business of maintaining that society. This attitude is reflected in the British educational system, which aims in primary schools mainly to make children literate and numerate. In the secondary and further education fields a major aim is to equip the student with qualifications in specialised areas of knowledge.

The traditional concept of art and craft, as relating only to painting, modelling, sculpture, pottery etc., continues to exist. It is perpetuated mainly by certain teachers whose outlooks and experience rarely extends beyond the confines of the academically biased educational world, or the classrooms in which they operate. In secondary schools in particular this attitude frequently results in the imposition of artificial subject/timetable barriers betwen 'art' (painting, drawing, modelling, printing) and the closely associated expressive activities such as drama, dance and music, or of the crafts of pottery, wood, metal or fabrics. Hardly ever are these related to technology or science. Despite the fact that we live in a world of advancing technology and that this country's economic survival depends upon its capacity and expertise as a manufacturing nation, the overwhelming majority of candidates sitting the advanced level GCE examinations are entered for the humanities, pure sciences and mathematics. Only a significant minority are entered for the applied disciplines such as engineering science or design and technology.

People are subjected daily to a barrage of visual images through television, advertising, magazines, instruction booklets, signs and the like. What is their impact upon the individual? How does he interpret them? How does he respond? Are schools as concerned about 'visual literacy' as they are about the skills of reading and numeracy, vitally important as they are? If not, should they be?

At work, during leisure, in the home or travelling, people continually use electrical, electronic or mechanical equipment which are the inventions and products of our age. How are we disposed towards them? How do we utilise or maintain them? What could happen if these devices fail us? What is our practical or moral response to the uses and abuses of science and technology, the home, the environment, or the dwindling resources of raw materials? Can we, or our children, perceive interactions and relationships between things and situations, of cause, effect, or consequence? How well are children equipped to sift through the immense and growing volume of information, data, or conflicting evidence, to extend their enquiry or experience in relevant directions to attain some coherent solution to their individual problems?

The acceptance and establishment of a major cohesive role for design education will help to create a unifying agency with a potential for linking the related disciplines in this area of the curriculum. This does not imply the necessary abolition or abandonment of 'subjects' which, though traditional in name, are, in content, of undisputed importance in general education and development of children. Thus, both the knowledge and skills involved in such subjects as mathematics and English, and the practice of arts and crafts are of intrinsic value. Rather the case is to suggest that 'action-based' approaches to learning and to the context in which the subject matter appears are complementary but no less vital and important.

Developments already taking place in many primary schools provide a seminal basis for design education. From the way in which this aspect of the curriculum is presented can be distilled three distinct but related roles which are capable of adoption, adaptation and development in their application to curriculum organisation. These can be identified as *central, core* and *supporting* roles (Fig. 1.1).

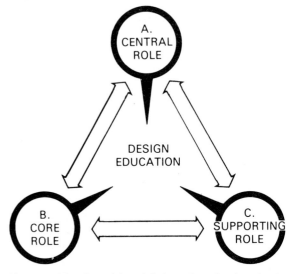

Fig. 1.1   The three roles of design education in schools.

1.2   The Central Role

There exists what may be termed the 'central role' of art/craft activities which closely corresponds to aspects of what is felt to be the traditionally accepted meaning of art, i.e., the urge of man to express in visual form his emotionally charged thoughts and feelings; the creative/manipulative activity which is experienced and enjoyed for its own sake. The practice of arts and crafts is now recognised, particularly in primary schools, as a vital element in the spiritual and emotional development of children and a valuable agency in learning. Nevertheless, thinking and feeling, and actually producing some 'thing' are still afforded inferior status by many teachers rooted in the traditional system of classical, and in recent years, science-based, education. However it is through the tactile-motor-visual experiences that a child comes to terms with himself and his surroundings, and his approach to them is enhanced. A child often expresses his thoughts more easily by visual and tactile means than verbally, and the emotional satisfaction so experienced can rarely be gained in any other way. Teaching by such means has, or may have, therapeutic value, as well as providing a means of personal expression through a third form of language.

Tactile, spatial and visual experience all extend the young pupil's emotional growth and these three elements of the central role need to be widely explored. The emphasis varies from one experience to another, but the growth of total emotional awareness can only develop if carefully cultivated.

The middle years of schooling are, for the pupil, a period of change. The spontaneity of the 8-year-old gives way to the questioning of the young teenager, and it is therefore important that the teacher or teachers concerned modify their approach and the experiences provided to suit the intellectual and emotional age of the individual pupil. This is at least as important as his physical age, as the rate of maturation varies widely. Though generalisations can often obscure the wide range of variation in attitude and emotional and intellectual maturity, it is most usual for the 8-year-old to participate in the creative experience without questioning, but with an imaginative approach unhampered by the realities of the everyday world as might be seen by the 12-14-year-old. Maturity in this sense brings with it constraints, or at least the awareness of constraints, which do not hamper the younger child.

Fig. 1.2 'A Lorry'. Painting by an eight-year-old boy. A spontaneous approach where the child represents what he knows. Note the placing of the wheels 'under' the body, the plan view of the road and the driver in the cab.

The degree of realism, actuality and accuracy required in any given situation depends heavily upon the degree of maturity of the child. The highly imaginative approach of the 8-year-old can turn cotton bobbins into tractor wheels which to the 13-year-old will still only be cotton bobbins. The desire for realism and accuracy and that mechanical things should work is a sign of the growing maturity which materially affects the teacher's reaction to the suggestion of topic choice or treatment.

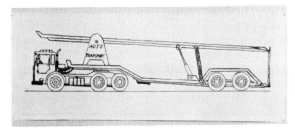

Fig. 1.3 'A Lorry'. Drawing by a twelve-year-old boy. Note the attention not only to overall proportions but also to fine detail, e.g., each wheel is located by eight nuts.

Some children, given a free choice, work or apparently 'play' in a limited range of materials with which they have achieved a degree of success. Others, quite possibly of a more extrovert nature, will take up and utilise anything which comes to hand, with little thought regarding its suitability or the degree of skill required to employ it.

The development of what is often termed 'visual literacy' — the emotional awareness of the environment coupled with the ability to express personal attitudes towards it through two- and three-dimensional modes of expression — is the most important, though too often the most under-rated and least understood facet of the whole study. Underlying this development is the need of children and many adults to express themselves in visual and concrete terms. Words are often found inadequate to describe their feelings.

Personal enquiry into materials, their handling and tooling capability is carried out by the younger child for its own sake; later it becomes more purposeful. The teacher's role in this situation is difficult: when to guide, when to support and when to leave well alone; how far to direct or suggest alternative lines of approach to a topic or the means of expression. Only experience coupled to a careful study of each child's abilities, aptitudes and attitudes will provide the answers.

Side by side with the growth of emotional maturity comes social development. The 8-9-year-old, whilst usually preferring to work alongside a friend, will nevertheless tend to work as an individual with little positive thought as to his co-workers' role, though occasionally he will be inclined to copy. By the age of 14 the ability to recognise and evaluate the role of each member of a team is more widespread.

1.3 The Core Role

Basing an education on the belief that knowledge is not fragmented, it follows that other areas of study and activity can stem directly from the central art-craft experience. Thus a second role, the 'core role' can be defined; i.e., where work in other areas stems from that based within the art-craft experience. Mention has been made of the close associations between activities in the expressive arts of music, painting, sculpture, dance and drama. From these it is a short step to the studies of language, history or the humanities. In these fields, too, emotions and feelings play no less a part than does the intellect. They should not be ignored if the total educational experience is to be realised.

As an example of this interplay of activities the Puppet Theatre (see p. 64) may be cited. This involves designing and constructing puppets and marionettes, scenery, and indeed the structure of the theatre itself. The puppets and marionettes, based on the human form, are made proportionate. Thus we have initially an investigation into the form of the human body and its necessary articulations. Costumes may be historical in character; this too calls for some research. Sets, however simple, offer scope for scaling up of original sketches whilst the planning and construction of the theatre itself carries overtones of structures and architectural studies. The production of scripts, of music and indeed of making simple musical instruments, can all stem from such a wide-ranging topic. Without the art-craft basis however, the core of the exercise would be stillborn and lack cohesion.

The investigations into materials properties which relate to design requirements open up wide avenues of developmental possibilities. 'Will a particular material "do?" is a starting point for pupil-centred science activities. Schools Council Science 5-13 Project publications, particularly those dealing with wood, metal and plastics, offer many exciting and related activities: indeed the building of simple science equipment, itself a test in design/problem solving, can stem from questions arising in the art-craft situation. Deciding which glue can be used for 'outside work' is the sort of

problem which leads to many such experimental procedures. Spontaneous pupil interest in, for example, mechanical devices, if properly handled, might open up links not only with science but with mathematics, geography and English, so that such topics, initially craft centred, spread across disciplinary boundaries.

All too often pupils will request permission to make something which the teacher considers to be too difficult in terms of craft technique, levels of skills required and so on. Whilst this may be true it is important always to ascertain exactly what the pupil has in mind and, if necessary, to discuss and modify. The whole question of whether skills should be developed in anticipation of a need or in response to such a need is a complex one. As with any contradiction the essence of success lies in compromise. (Course content is further considered in Chapters 4 and 5.)

Clay work and pottery is an example of an essentially craft-based activity from which could develop closely related studies. Clay is used as a plastic medium in creative work at all levels. Searching for material, digging it up in its natural state and preparing it for use can relate to the study of minerology, geography and science. The diverse and ancient methods of firing and glazing relate to historical and cultural studies, whilst the handling of clay can afford valuable material for creative writing and language development. The art-craft basis of these and many similar examples form a core for the exercise, stimulating development and establishing positive links between its many facets.

1.4 The Supporting Role

The third role of design education here may be termed the 'supporting role'. It is where two- and three-dimensional work complement and enhance the work and experiences in other disciplines. The part it plays in the pupil's learning is to enable him to explore, realise, communicate and express. Too often secondary schools which maintain traditional approaches underplay the service or supportive role of the discipline. In Infant, Junior, Middle and enlightened Secondary schools however, the service role can be shown to be much more than a mere extension of hand-based activity but an integrating factor in its own right.

The form or subject teacher too often fails to capitalise on the potential for pupil involvement.

4

How many teachers in the non-design-based disciplines deliberately plan and prepare for two- and three-dimensional activities to be an intrinsic part of their pupils' work within their disciplines? In the majority of cases no such activity is conceived by the formal subject teachers. Some of the reasons for this lack of vision may be:

(1) The teacher is unaware of the missed educational value of the joint experience and feels that the time spent on such activities is a dilution or diminution of the time spent on his or her subject.
(2) The teacher, for personal reasons, has not taken the initiative in approaching colleagues with design expertise, to discuss such possibilities.
(3) Design department staff, especially in secondary schools, have failed to offer their facilities and explain the value of the department's potential contribution to other members of the school staff.
(4) Design departments have been too pre-occupied with an inward-looking approach to the role of their disciplines and have tended to put off approaches, when made, from other departments.

It is self-evident that teachers should work more closely with colleagues in other disciplines.

Examples of the supporting role of two- and three-dimensional art and craft work are many. The making of mathematical models in expanded polystyrene, the production of models, pictures and charts for history and geography, visual expression of written and oral work in English and social studies, are just a few possibilities.

Fig. 1.5 Two- or three-dimensional modelling helps to develop spatial perception and can aid the acquisition of concepts associated with physical geography.

Fig. 1.6 'The owl and the pussy cat . . .'

One very real problem which such collaboration poses is that associated with trying to achieve a balanced on-going programme of creative studies. Fitting the three roles within the framework of the school and specialist timetables calls for discussion, planning and a great deal of goodwill between all concerned. Specialist trained teachers and form teachers alike must appreciate the value of such joint activity before they can be expected to offer active co-operation and tolerate the pin-pricks and inconveniences which will inevitably accompany it.

The contemporary tendency to categorise affects teachers as much as any other group in society. Once an area of activity or branch of knowledge has been sifted out of a mainstream there is a tendency to invest or develop around it a set of approaches, treatments or language. In time these create an insulative effect restricting transference of thought and promoting conditioned attitudes. Over-specialisation of curriculum subjects can foster

Fig. 1.4 When pupils make three-dimensional geometrical models this enhances the learning situation through physical involvement in their production.

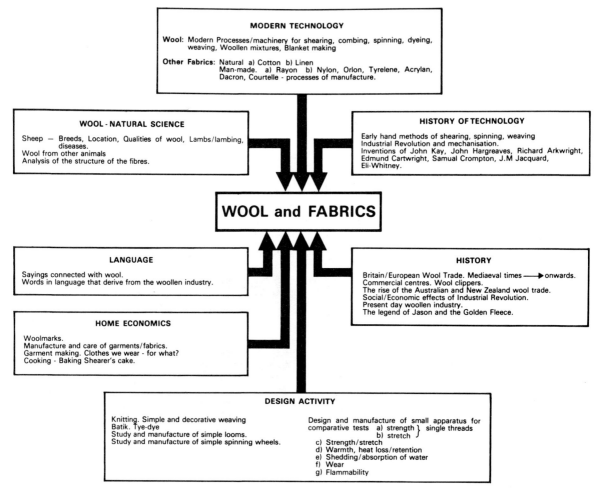

MODERN TECHNOLOGY

Wool: Modern Processes/machinery for shearing, combing, spinning, dyeing, weaving, Woollen mixtures, Blanket making

Other Fabrics: Natural a) Cotton b) Linen
Man-made. a) Rayon b) Nylon, Orlon, Tyrelene, Acrylan, Dacron, Courtelle - processes of manufacture.

WOOL - NATURAL SCIENCE

Sheep — Breeds, Location, Qualities of wool, Lambs/lambing, diseases.
Wool from other animals
Analysis of the structure of the fibres.

HISTORY OF TECHNOLOGY

Early hand methods of shearing, spinning, weaving
Industrial Revolution and mechanisation.
Inventions of John Kay, John Hargreaves, Richard Arkwright, Edmund Cartwright, Samual Crompton, J.M Jacquard, Eli-Whitney.

WOOL and FABRICS

LANGUAGE

Sayings connected with wool.
Words in language that derive from the woollen industry.

HISTORY

Britain/European Wool Trade. Mediaeval times ——→ onwards.
Commercial centres. Wool clippers.
The rise of the Australian and New Zealand wool trade.
Social/Economic effects of Industrial Revolution.
Present day woollen industry.
The legend of Jason and the Golden Fleece.

HOME ECONOMICS

Woolmarks.
Manufacture and care of garments/fabrics.
Garment making. Clothes we wear - for what?
Cooking - Baking Shearer's cake.

DESIGN ACTIVITY

Knitting. Simple and decorative weaving
Batik. Tye-dye
Study and manufacture of simple looms.
Study and manufacture of simple spinning wheels.

Design and manufacture of small apparatus for comparative tests a) strength } single threads
b) stretch }
c) Strength/stretch
d) Warmth, heat loss/retention
e) Shedding/absorption of water
f) Wear
g) Flammability

Fig. 1.7 A typical project on 'wool and fabrics' which whilst centred on environmental studies involved design activity.

these attitudes amongst children. The activities in a P.E. lesson may be seen as unconnected with work in drama, although elements of both lessons are concerned with the expressive use and control of the body. Although three roles have been defined for design education, this is done to provide a basis upon which a policy for their implementation can be devised and to help to identify the nature of activities undertaken, not to fit activities specifically into one category or another. Any such rigid classification could harden and become reinforced, and if applied in the schools, would become an antithesis of the fundamental argument. Clearly there exist intermediate zones where the three overlap.

Chapter 2 The Scope of the Subject

2.1 The Design/Problem-solving Process

Problems are an inescapable part of everyday life, whether they assume global proportions or are experienced at a personal level. It is within the capacity of most people to devise some form of approach to a task with the hope of arriving at a satisfactory solution. The approach that they adopt may be crystallised into a routine, learned possibly through trial and error, but it is the one they find to be the most effective way of achieving their particular objective. The harmony of family life may rely heavily upon individual family members performing duties or procedures agreed amongst themselves. Should sickness or any unusual event occur, new procedures have to be devised; adjustments are made or fresh roles assumed. The more complex the task the more necessary it becomes to approach it in a systematic way. Procedures at different levels of sophistication are required, for example, in locating and mending a faulty domestic electrical fuse, stripping an engine to locate a defect, designing a production system, and solving an economic crisis. But whatever the magnitude of the problem account has to be taken on the one hand of those factors which offer help in its solution, and on the other of those which have a constraining effect. The success of any solution is judged by its effectiveness in solving the problem.

There is no single infallible approach to the solution of a given problem since each individual has a unique psychological and temperamental make-up. Approaches differ. Indeed the clear separation of an ill-defined problem from a possible, though vaguely conceived solution is, for many adults, as well as for children, quite impossible. Problem-solving in designing may therefore consist of equating a progressively more clearly defined problem with an acceptable solution. This has been termed 'the problem-solving interactive couple'. Edward de Bono's work in the study of problem solving is well known. Reference should be made to his *Children Solve Problems* (Penguin Educational), *The Five-day Course in Thinking* (Penguin Books), and other works.

A 'linear' approach, which is rather more logical and systematic in character, is often used in design problem solving. It takes the form of a procedural 'path' which begins with the awareness and identification of a problem and ends, ideally, with a successful solution to it. This critical path can be broken down into a developmental sequence of four related areas of activity (Fig. 2.1).

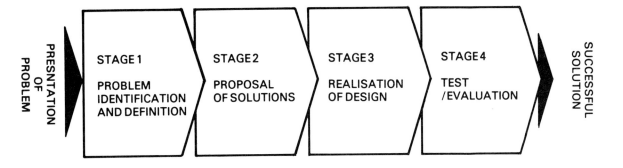

Fig. 2.1   Essential stages in the linear design process.

The Linear Design Problem-solving Approach

Whilst the linear approach should not unilaterally be employed in design-based activities/studies, nevertheless it serves as a useful model or 'tool' in helping both teachers and pupils to appreciate the resources and constraints which are involved in designing.

Upon becoming aware of, or being presented with, a problem or assignment, it is essential that a pupil is clear in his mind exactly what its true nature is, or what has to be achieved. As part of a project on sport, two boys conducted a school survey to find what was the 'favourite sport' of pupils and staff. They realised with some frustration that 'favourite' had a number of interpretations: 'the one I watch', 'the team I support', 'the one I play'; it also raised questions such as 'is horse-riding a sport?'. They suspended the questioning and retired to construct a questionnaire more specific in the information required. Doctors, teachers, engineers and others are frequently presented with patterns of behaviour which are symptomatic of causes that are not obvious. A successful outcome is unlikely in the long term if only the symptoms are treated. Causes must be diagnosed and dealt with at source.

Investigation is an element of the initial 'problem identification and defining' stage (see Fig. 2.2). Research into the nature of the problem involves the collection of relevant information which, if the final objective is constructional, could involve a number of tests or investigations. If the objective is 'investigational', e.g., to find the average height of children of a given age, this preliminary activity might involve the construction of various pieces of experimental equipment, e.g., a rule for measuring the height of children, made by children, for use by children in a classroom situation.

It can be seen that the main problem-solving line could contain secondary lines of design activity stemming from it but directly related to it (see Fig. 2.3).

Through investigating and collecting information it is possible to separate that which is relevant to the problem from that which is not. The problem can be correctly identified and criteria established against which the final solution can be measured for its efficiency or effectiveness. Also at this stage it may be possible to compile a design brief that can be employed which provides for alternative solutions, i.e., that the object or system will have to satisfy certain requirements or perform a range of functions. The brief may evolve from the problem identification/defining stage, or may constitute the assignment/problem itself (for example, see the description of the abacus project on p. 21), thereby stimulating investigation.

Once the problem has been defined and comprehended at an appropriate level, and the relevant data has been assembled, the next logical step is to propose ways of solving it (see Fig. 2.4).

Traditional aspects of the educational system continue to concentrate on the transmission of bodies of absolute knowledge, values or solutions. A pupil's or student's success is still largely measured by his ability to memorise and restate them. The value of this material must not be underrated, but it must be treated as a means rather than an end. Advances in science and technology in the last few decades have brought social, economic and cultural changes at a rate and diversity unprecedented in history. The obvious implication for education is

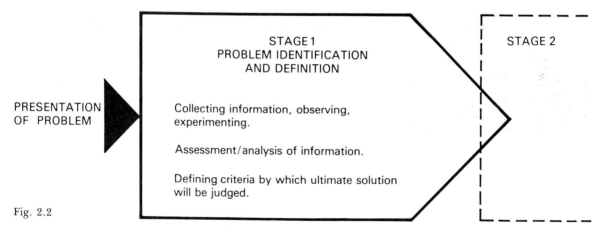

PRESENTATION OF PROBLEM

STAGE 1
PROBLEM IDENTIFICATION
AND DEFINITION

Collecting information, observing, experimenting.

Assessment/analysis of information.

Defining criteria by which ultimate solution will be judged.

STAGE 2

Fig. 2.2

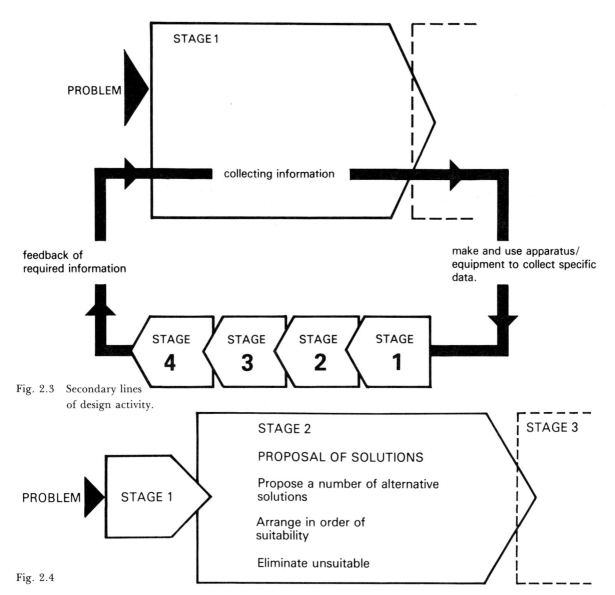

STAGE 1

PROBLEM

collecting information

feedback of
required information

make and use apparatus/
equipment to collect specific
data.

| STAGE 4 | STAGE 3 | STAGE 2 | STAGE 1 |

Fig. 2.3   Secondary lines
of design activity.

STAGE 2

PROPOSAL OF SOLUTIONS

Propose a number of alternative
solutions

Arrange in order of
suitability

Eliminate unsuitable

STAGE 3

PROBLEM   STAGE 1

Fig. 2.4

that its systems cannot remain static and inflexible. Knowledge in many areas continuously expands and values are constantly questioned. There may be a concensus of agreement about a final objective, but there are inevitably many ways of attaining it.

One of the main educational features of the **design/problem-solving approach is that it extends** a creative capacity by encouraging the pupil — who in the middle years is particularly inventive — to think 'laterally' in devising a number of alternatives as probable solutions. The concept of lateral thinking suggests that there is value in investigating

the non-positive as well as the positive idea to prevent or postpone for as long as possible the exclusion of alternatives, ridiculous though they may appear to superficial or practical judgement. This phenomenon has frequently featured in many areas of human advance; that metal could 'float' in the form of a ship was ridiculed at one time.

A group of 12-year-old children made a request to erect a set of cricket stumps on a playground for use at breaktimes. Constructional and other problems prevented them from doing this by what they conceived as the only method available, so they were encouraged to abandon their activities in favour of a more systematic approach as defined by the problem-solving approach.

The problem/assignment (design brief)
To put three standard wooden cricket stumps on the playground in an upright position for games of cricket.

Their lively discussions at stage 1 produced the following data and criteria:

Stage 1 Analysing the problem
(A) The stumps
(1) We have three standard wooden stumps with points on. We can cut the points off if we wish. The stumps can take a reasonable shock or blow without breaking.
(2) The stumps must be set up in the traditional way; i.e. evenly spaced in a line, 225 mm between outside stumps, and on a level to carry bails.
(3) The stumps must not be dislodged, fall in any direction or be a nuisance in this sort of way. They must be upright and fairly firm to withstand pressures from the wind or accidental knocking from behind.
(4) Only tennis balls can be used in the playground. The stumps must move back or fall over, but not too easily when they have been struck by the ball. The batsman must be seen to have been bowled out or to have struck his wicket, to avoid arguments. The stumps must operate independently.
(5) The bails must fall off when the stumps are hit.

(B) The playground
(1) The playground is made of tarmac, is hard and level. Perhaps we could break part of it up to fit in wickets, perhaps not. We would have to get permission.
(2) There are some buildings on two sides of the playground and grass on the other two. A tree branch overhangs the playground.
(3) At breaktimes all the boys and girls in the school use the playground. They are bound to play or wander across the area where the game is being played and might knock the wicket over if it were not stable.

(C) The players
(1) The presence of a wicket keeper is optional.
(2) Girls and boys of all ages will play the game.

This investigation of the problem was not exhaustive but it served the purpose of focusing the children's attention, and stimulating a more thorough analysis of it compared with their original treatment. Some helpful, as well as constraining factors, were discovered at this stage, which might, and did, arise during their initial attempts. These could have incurred possible wastage of time, energy, materials, and have therefore created frustration at points later in the execution of the project. Being therefore discovered earlier they were taken into consideration in proposing possible design solutions.

Following the first stage of the design process the children were encouraged to 'invent' as many solutions to the problem as they cared to make, no great regard being made at this stage to the technical operational detail possibilities. The 'fantastic' was to be acceptable within the terms of lateral thinking.

The following proposals represent a sample of possible solutions that were submitted and later discussed by the children.

Example (A) (Fig. 2.5)
The stumps, which are attached to hinges at their points are secured to the bottom of a stout but small trolley which is mounted on wheels or castors. The trolley is fitted with a rubber solution/compound which keeps the stumps upright, but allows them to 'give' when taking an impact in any direction.

Example (B) (Fig. 2.6)
The stumps are set into strong rubber (tennis) balls which, in turn, are set in 'special stuff' in the playground. The balls will keep the stumps upright, 'right' them if they get a slight knock, but will swivel in the 'stuff' if they get a hard one. The stumps could then be moved upright again.

Example (C) (Fig. 2.7)
The stump points are hinged on spring-loaded clips which have an adjustable trip mechanism which can be set to release at the desired pressure on the stumps. The stumps fall back on impact to strike other springs which shoot them back upright to re-set the clips. The stumps and mechanisms are set on a solid base which gives the wicket stability.

Example (D) (Fig. 2.8)
A steel bar which acts as an axle passes through the stump at a fulcrum sited to enable the stump to

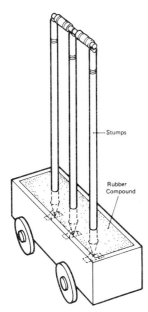

Fig. 2.5   Cricket stumps holder proposed, solution A.

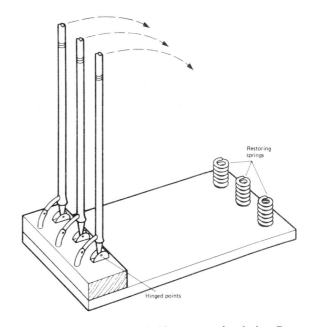

Fig. 2.7   Cricket stumps holder proposed, solution C.

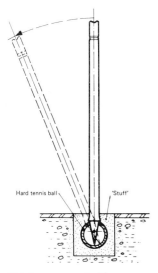

Fig. 2.6   Cricket stumps holder proposed, solution B.

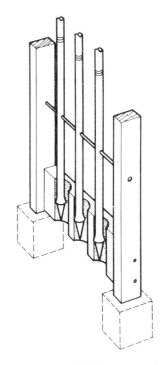

Fig. 2.8   Cricket stumps holder proposed, solution D.

swing back and over at the required pressure from the ball upon impact. The axle forms the top cross-bar of a gantry, the uprights of which locate into special sockets sited in the playground. The stumps are normally maintained in an upright position by the points, which are located in shaped recesses carved into the wooden bottom cross-bar, which also acts as an extra support giving stability to the structure. The stumps can operate independently.

These examples may lack technical refinement, appear clumsy or too elaborate, but they represent 'first-shot', hypothetical solutions conceived at child-level, with knowledge, experience and inventiveness appropriate to that level. Further investigations and experimenting could naturally develop from this point, the critical assessment of which would lead to the ordering of the solutions in a list of envisaged suitability.

As indicated, children at this age, when enthusiasm coupled with energy is running high, are prone to take their first idea and implement it regardless of considering the possibility of the many alternatives. It therefore becomes important to restrain this urgent impulsiveness and encourage wider-ranging, deeper and more comprehensive thought. It must also be explained that the chosen 'solution' will not automatically be the 'best' one, as developments along the critical design/line path may prove. (There may well be more than one acceptable solution to any problem.)

Up to this point in the process the pupil's thinking has been 'divergent', i.e., he has purposefully set out from the initial awareness of the problem to gather as much relevant data to the problem as possible, investigated freely and devised a variety of alternatives. Having made a decision upon what, in his opinion, is the system, approach, or device most likely to bring about success, he will then focus his mind on the development of this idea. Thereafter thinking can be said to be 'convergent'.

The chosen solution is then translated into a prototype or model, i.e., the system, device, approach, or apparatus is proposed. 'Realisation of the design' is the third stage of the process (see Fig. 2.9).

By subjecting the prototype, system or artifact to test conditions, an evaluation can be made of its efficiency, effectiveness or otherwise. The criteria against which it is compared are those drawn up in the first stage of the process.

It may be that at this point, the 'test evaluation' stage (see Fig. 2.10), the proposed solution may not entirely meet the standards required. Two lines of action could be taken in this case: (1) to extend the proposed solution by modifications to the original, or (2) to devise ancillary equipment or system. If this fails and the performance falls well below requirements, then the approach may be abandoned and a fresh attempt made at a solution by reverting to the list of alternatives compiled in stage 2 and selecting the second possibility (see Fig. 2.10). Once into the area of aesthetics however, evaluation of an end product becomes based more on personal preferences, tastes or fashion. Criteria for evaluation in such a case needs to be less rigid and to take into account these vagaries.

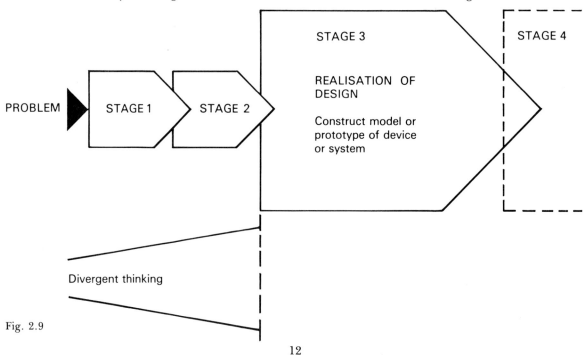

Fig. 2.9

12

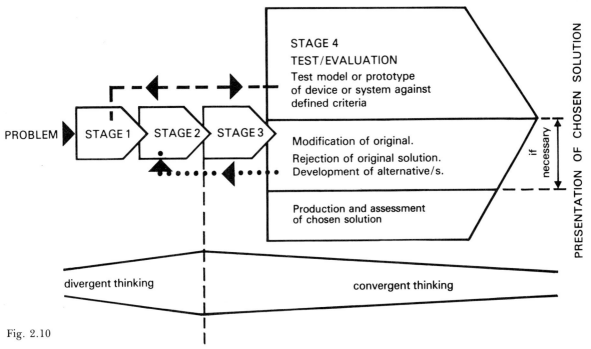

STAGE 4
TEST/EVALUATION
Test model or prototype
of device or system against
defined criteria

Modification of original.
Rejection of original solution.
Development of alternative/s.

Production and assessment
of chosen solution

PROBLEM ▶ STAGE 1 ⟩ STAGE 2 ⟩ STAGE 3 ⟩

if necessary

PRESENTATION OF CHOSEN SOLUTION

divergent thinking   convergent thinking

Fig. 2.10

Too frequently pupils see their success or failure at school in terms of whether they, or their work, is right or wrong, is approved or disapproved. Standards are not their own and appear to be arbitrarily dictated by adults. The evaluation stage in the problem-solving approach dispenses with this and directly involves the child in forming judgements and defining opinion. Standards are established by the pupil or the group as a result of their direct involvement in the process. Their efforts are unique and of their own devising. There is a greater likelihood of pupils knowing what they wish to achieve whether they have accomplished it or not, why they have failed if this is so, and how they may improve performances. This personal evaluation of the solution becomes in a sense self-evaluation, and plays a critical part in the development of sound judgements. The process as a whole also offers scope for personal creativity/inventiveness and the exercise of individual abilities.

From the presentation of the problem through to its solution the pupil will be aware of factors exercising a considerable influence upon progress. On the one hand they assist, and on the other they retard or maybe prevent. These may be termed 'resources' and 'constraints' respectively. Fig. 2.11 illustrates and lists the influence of some of these factors upon the process.

In society at large there is a growing awareness that the products of science and technology are a mixed blessing. Atomic power has a potential for good or ill. Artificial fertilisers, pesticides and modern farming methods may have increased food production but may damage the delicately balanced ecocycles of nature upon which health, growth and the quality of the natural environment ultimately depend. In evaluating the possible worth of an effective solution the pupil's attention needs to be drawn to wider contextual implications. Although the solution is primarily designed to benefit or facilitate in some way, it may contain an adverse, counter-productive element (see Fig. 2.12). Such facets of design-based studies link naturally with aspects of the humanities and environmental studies.

Not all design-based activities necessarily adhere rigidly to the critical path flow. It may have been inferred from the foregoing that if a mistake is made anywhere along the line all is lost. This is not so. Lateral approaches suggest that if options are left open, even the apparently unsound ones, they can often help overcome difficulties or apparent failures. Pupil involvement could extend through all four stages or be concerned with only one, two or three of them, depending upon the educational aim of the activity. Should this aim be to develop a particular skill or reach a specific point, the pupil

13

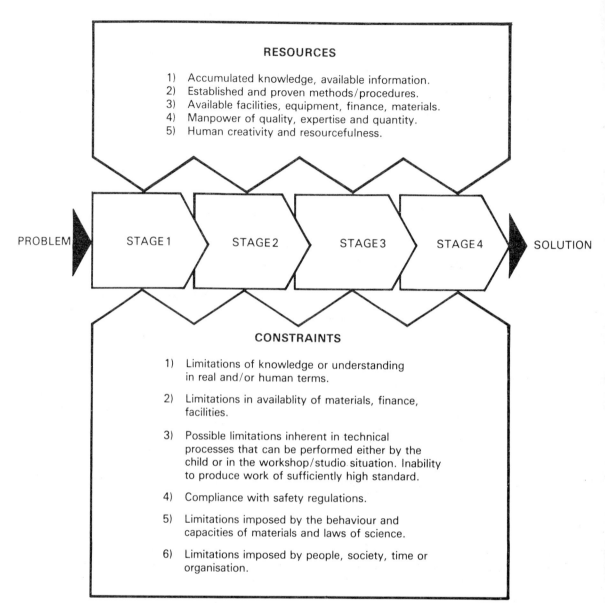

RESOURCES

1) Accumulated knowledge, available information.
2) Established and proven methods/procedures.
3) Available facilities, equipment, finance, materials.
4) Manpower of quality, expertise and quantity.
5) Human creativity and resourcefulness.

PROBLEM   STAGE 1   STAGE 2   STAGE 3   STAGE 4   SOLUTION

CONSTRAINTS

1) Limitations of knowledge or understanding in real and/or human terms.

2) Limitations in availablity of materials, finance, facilities.

3) Possible limitations inherent in technical processes that can be performed either by the child or in the workshop/studio situation. Inability to produce work of sufficiently high standard.

4) Compliance with safety regulations.

5) Limitations imposed by the behaviour and capacities of materials and laws of science.

6) Limitations imposed by people, society, time or organisation.

Fig. 2.11 The linear design process—resources and constraints.

may be required to adhere strictly to instructions given to him by a teacher or followed in a book. Conversely, involvement may only extend to the designing of solutions without necessarily executing them.

A child who lacks confidence, or is of limited ability, is likely to respond to the security of knowing what he is going to make, or being told exactly what to do.

The objective may be to evaluate pieces of work devised and constructed by other people. These may include the pupils' own contemporaries or the work of artists and craftsmen, architects and engineers (see Fig. 2.13).

It is not unknown for ancillary activities so to change the course of a project that they become in themselves the main line of enquiry. This may be quite different from the original, but in certain circumstances should be encouraged rather than quashed.

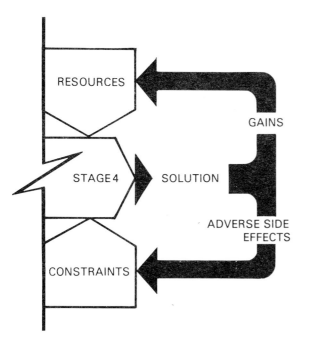

Fig. 2.12 Positive and negative effects of design solutions.

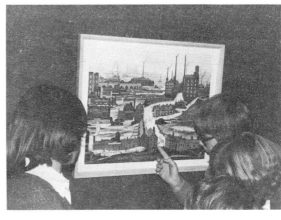

Fig. 2.13 Children discussing a Lowry painting.

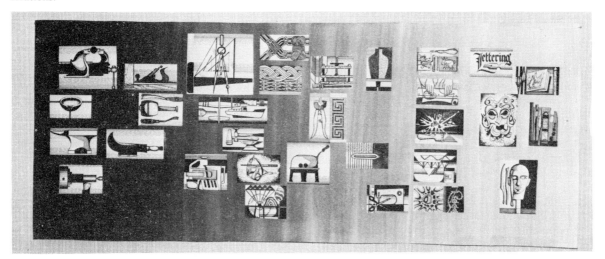

Fig. 2.14 Design activity extends over the whole range of arts and crafts, and beyond.

The design/problem-solving approach is presented as a guide for conducting design-based activities. Its inherent flexibility facilitates its adaptation to individual children's abilities, the type of project in which they are involved, and the educational aims being pursued by the teacher. It can be employed in classroom or studio/workshop and utilised by individual pupils or groups.

2.2 The Design Process and Art/Craft Activities
In the context of pupil activity, design processes are directly related to a wide range of traditionally disparate areas of study. Where these include the arts and crafts the situation is the same, extending from the traditional 'heavy' crafts of wood and metal to the 'fine' two-dimensional arts of painting and drawing. Fig. 2.14 exemplifies this range but is

15

not exclusive. Activities generally grouped under the subject title Home Economics also have a positive relationship which should not be ignored.

2.3 The Design/Problem-solving Process—Case Histories

The operation of the design/problem-solving approach can be illustrated by describing several examples.

Example 1

Age/ability range	10/11 years, mixed ability, Middle School.
Group size	20, with sub-grouping.
Type of design activity	Supporting role (for definition see Chapter 1).
Situation	The pupils in the year group had noticed a wide variety of 'strangers' visiting the school, looking lost and enquiring for different locations within the building. It was decided to treat the problem as a design activity.

Stage 1 Problem identification and definition. The design brief was: 'To devise a system for directing about the school building people who may be unfamiliar with its layout.'

By discussion amongst themselves and by conducting a survey amongst other pupils, members of the teaching and non-teaching staff and people visiting the school (Fig. 2.15), the children were able to compile the following information relative to the problem:

(1) That a surprising variety of people did in fact visit the school, other than the normal school population. They could be roughly classified as follows:

   (a) County (L.E.A.) education personnel
   H.M. Inspectors, local area officers, doctors, nurses, etc. peripatetic teachers of musical instruments and remedial reading and dance, audio/visual technicians, etc.

   (b) Other educational personnel
   Teachers from other schools, lecturers from establishments of further education, students, travelling dramatists and demonstrators. Managers of the school, etc.

   (c) Tradespeople
   Fuel and grocery deliverymen, technical equipment manufacturers and maintenance staff, materials and equipment demonstrators, salesmen. A variety of building trades workmen. Engineers, piano tuners, etc.

   (d) Miscellaneous
   Representatives of all the public services including fire, police, road safety, British Rail, Post Office, etc. Missionaries and representatives of the Church and charitable organisations. Members of the public using the building privately or visiting on school functions. Parents, job applicants, ex-teachers, the relatives of teachers and guests of the school (old people, etc).

   (e) Other children
   Children about to join the school, pupils from other schools in sports teams, etc. groups such as guides, Sunday school classes, etc., past scholars, etc.

(The list could have been extended indefinitely.)

(2) That the visitor coming into the school or moving about it and searching for where they wanted to go did so with certain attitudes and in different manners. Some were impatient, anxious, casual, impressionable, in a hurry, rather arrogant, over-awed, bemused or timid. Others were intelligent or had an instinctive capacity to find their way about the building or were embarrassed at 'troubling' anyone, whilst at the other extreme some expected or needed to be 'led by the hand' to where they wanted to be.

(3) That places where people wanted to get were, for example: Main Hall, cloakrooms and toilets, administrative offices, classrooms, annexes and practical unit, boiler room and cellars, greenhouse, etc.

(4) That although it was a principle of staff and pupils of the school to help visitors, and that the main entrance was in good vision of the headteacher's and secretary's office, it was noted that:

   (a) people could be in the building at, literally, almost any hour of the day or night and at weekends when the normal school population were not about;

THIRD YEAR DESIGN PROJECT:

Brief:

To devise a system for directing about the school people who may be unfamiliar with its layout.

QUESTIONNAIRE for the project

Who are the people who visit the school and would require directions?

Doctors
School dentist
School nurse
Educational officials
Teachers of dance, music and remedial reading.
Psychologist
County (l.e.a.) technicians

Tutors and lecturers
Inspectors
Teachers from other schools
Dramatists and musicians
School managers
Students and student helpers

Technical equipment salesmen, demonstrators, and repairmen.
Builders, plumbers, electricians
Boiler maintenance men, roof repairers, glaziers
Engineers, chimney sweepers
Piano tuner

British Rail staff
Postmen, Firemen, Post Office telephone staff, Water Board staff
Missionaries, clergymen, representatives from charitable organisations
Parents, relatives of children and teachers, guests of the school (e.g. old people)
Womens' Institute, churchpeople, voters

New pupils, children from visiting teams, children of the Sunday school, past pupils.

Fig. 2.15   The questionnaire: 'Who visits the school — and why?'

Notices must gain people's attention, but people are not always in the mood to look at them, or if they do so possibly not very carefully. This problem must be overcome. What moods or attitudes could people have upon entering or moving about the building?

intelligent	casual
nervous	hurried
anxious	illiterate
bored	angry or in a temper
excited	distressed
embarrassed	over-awed
self-conscious	dreamy or vague
happy	familliar with the layout but not with recent
arrogant	changes
impressionable	

What are the entrances and exits of the school?

Entrances from the playground — (a) into the cloakroom (b) into the main corridor

The main front door
Entrance from the playing field — (a) by the flag pole (b) at the end of the side path

Kitchen door
'Fourth year' classroom block entrance
The three entrances into the practical unit
Boiler room entrance

What are the places that people would wish to go to?

The classrooms	Ladies and girls' toilets
The main hall	The kitchen
The secretary's office	The playground
The deputy head's office	The practical unit work-shop
Mens and boys' toilets	The playing field
The headmaster's office	The cloakrooms and showers
The games store	The costume room
The science area	The caretaker's/cleaners' room
The staff room	The library

(b) the headteacher and secretary were quite often away from their normal physical location in the building attending to business elsewhere;

(c) visitors could, and did, enter the building anywhere and at any time — on one occasion firemen came in through a trap-door in the cellars;

(d) on various occasions certain doors were locked or blocked and people familiar with one entrance/exit would have to try another unfamiliar one;

(e) that people not only sought direction upon entering the building but required guidance once they were in it and moving around it.

(5) The main building had six access and exit doors in frequent use but certain categories of people would use certain doors more than others (e.g., kitchen deliveries and certain domestic business funnel in through two doors to one side of the building, visiting teams used the playground entrances). The practical unit had three main doors, the fourth year annex one.

Stage 2 Proposal of solutions. Having amassed information the pupils discussed it collectively and proposed several alternative solutions.

(1) That all doors be locked except the main ones and 'Information Centres' be set up at those points.
The advantages would be that a good directional system could be established at places where people would be bound to go.
The disadvantages of this idea were:

(a) that it did not necessarily provide for people already in the building;

(b) people already familiar with the school could get annoyed or frustrated by finding their way obstructed;

(c) it would be too disruptive to normal school life;

(d) it would present a fire hazard.

(2) Print out labelled plans of the school in leaflet form and place them in boxes at strategic points for use by visitors.
The advantages would be that detailed information was being made available and that people could look at their plans wherever they were in the building.

The disadvantages would be that:

(a) this system would involve expense and time to produce the plans/leaflets;

(b) people might not wish to bother with pieces of paper. They might not keep them if they did and throw them away. This would be wasteful;

(c) younger children might not be able to interpret the plan;

(d) although employed in society this method is not a familiar way of directing the general public, although the idea of a central layout plan has something to commend it.

(3) A system of written signs (Fig. 2.16).
This was seen as an efficient and familiar way of directing people. Signs could be produced quite easily.
The disadvantages could be that:

(a) as children were the main users of the school their ages and stages of development might be such that they were unable to read the words on the notices;

(b) where a number of directional signs were together they would take up a lot of wall space and/or present many words which the observer would have to read to discover the one he required.

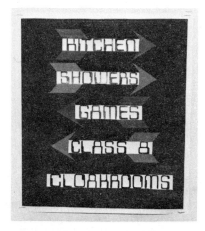

Fig. 2.16 Simple verbal signs.

(4) A system of pictorial signs.
This was regarded as an efficient means of visual communication in which children had, through design activity, received some practice.

18

Picture signs could take up less space proportionately than verbal ones. They would also be 'read' faster. This alternative also offered scope for further experience in techniques of visual communication.
The disadvantages were thought to be that:

(a) people interpret 'words' better than 'pictures' since it is part of a common language that we all understand and use. There is not a common symbolic pictorial language throughout society, although the use of traffic and other signs was steadily developing one;

(b) some of the pictures would be difficult to think up.

(5) A number of pupil 'guides' stationed at major entrance/exit points in the building to conduct people about.
This idea gave the 'personal' touch in welcoming and helping visitors. It would be appreciated and give a good impression. It would also give pupils experience in developing social skills. There was also a very good chance

of the visitor arriving where he wanted to be. But there were disadvantages:

(a) pupils were only in the building approximately between 8.30 a.m. and 4.30 p.m., for five days a week;

(b) pupils could not be stationed at places in the hope that people would just 'turn up' to be shown. Children would get bored with this and 'mess about';

(c) pupils would also miss their lessons which would do them 'no good in the long run'.

During this stage of problem solving pupils explored the possibilities or otherwise of each alternative. Once this was complete the phase of 'lateral thinking' was terminated and pupils had to exercise their minds to focusing on one alternative and developing it. They thus passed onto Stage 3.

Stage 3 Realisation of design. Selection of the alternative to be employed was by ballot amongst the group of pupils themselves. The results were presented on a block chart (Fig. 2.17) which also

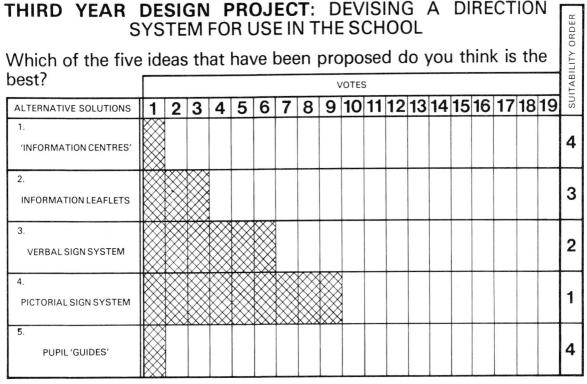

THIRD YEAR DESIGN PROJECT: DEVISING A DIRECTION SYSTEM FOR USE IN THE SCHOOL

Which of the five ideas that have been proposed do you think is the best?

ALTERNATIVE SOLUTIONS	VOTES																			SUITABILITY ORDER
	1	2	3	4	5	6	7	8	9	10	11	12	13	14	15	16	17	18	19	
1. 'INFORMATION CENTRES'																				4
2. INFORMATION LEAFLETS																				3
3. VERBAL SIGN SYSTEM																				2
4. PICTORIAL SIGN SYSTEM																				1
5. PUPIL 'GUIDES'																				4

Fig. 2.17 The result of the ballot suitability ratings.

showed a 'suitability order' of the various alternatives.

Having selected alternative 4, i.e., the pictorial-sign method, the pupils set about developing and implementing the idea. Further particularised information was obtained:

(1) Listing the places to which people would wish to go in roughly assessed order of priority. This would give some idea of the range and quantity of particular signs needed.

(2) Producing a flow diagram of people moving from likely places through to most likely locations, e.g., children flowed from playground to staff room door and branched out, visitors mostly used main entrance and sought the Secretary's office, everyone needed to know where the toilets were, and so on.

For this survey the pupils produced a plan of the school and marked the information upon it (Fig. 2.18).

(3) From (1) and (2) it was decided which signs were to be located where. This information was also entered upon the 'master' plan.

Concurrent with the above activities pupils were invited to devise designs for the signs. This followed further class discussion on aspects of visual communication. In particular the role of colour in a coding system, e.g., 'follow the blue to the changing rooms and showers', was seen to be of considerable advantage. Individual contributions were gathered together and displayed and the most suitable system was selected by a small committee of staff and pupils (Fig. 2.19).

To test the effectiveness of the proposed systems, temporary signs were made from card and paint (Fig. 2.20), and placed in position (Fig. 2.21). A 'mini-survey' was taken for their effectiveness. This mainly took the form of observing and questioning. From it was seen that the signs tended to be too small, and above the direct line of vision of smaller

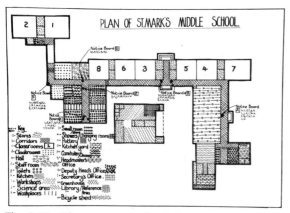

Fig. 2.18   The annotated school plan.

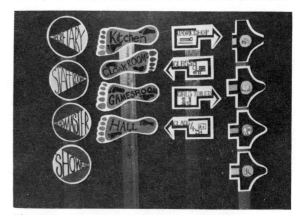

Fig. 2.20   Temporary signs.

Fig. 2.19   A selection of proposed direction indicators.

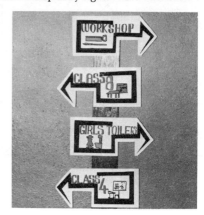

Fig. 2.21   A 'sign post' in position.

children, particularly a group of First School pupils who were having an introductory tour around the building before 'coming up'. Adjustments were therefore made and permanent signs made from hardboard and enamel paints.

Stage 4 Test/Evaluation. The effectiveness or otherwise of the signs was assessed in two ways over a period of two terms:

(1) Did the new pupils voluntarily refer to the signs to find their way about the building? This information was obtained through observation and questioning by the older pupils.
(2) Visitors were also asked by pupils and teaching and non-teaching staff if they had noticed the signs and, if so, did they think they were necessary, or effective. A questionnaire was also drawn up to this effect and presented to those who were willing or who had time to fill it in.

Pupils also fed back their observations of people's behaviour at large gatherings at school functions, e.g., concerts, open days, and parents' evenings. The general conclusion was that the system had gone a long way towards solving the difficulty, although the signs continued to be ignored by some people. Could this have been due to some inadequacy? For example, were the ciphers not striking enough, or the colours not bold enough, etc.? Could people have ignored the signs or have been indifferent to them because there were simply so many to contend with nowadays? Pupils were, on the whole, satisfied with the system that they had produced. It had served its educational and social purpose. Although it could have been improved further they saw little real benefit in doing so.

Example 2

Age/ability range	11/12 years, mixed ability; Secondary School.
Group size	Initially class of 30. Giving way to development groups of 2.
Type of design activity	Supporting role.
Situation	A class of children was engaged in studying number bases other than 10. Arising from discussion it was suggested that apparatus could be used to transmit

number values, of any base, without employing arabic symbols. Several pupils were keen to produce such a device.

Stage 1 Problem identification and definition. The design brief was: 'To design and make an abacus with a number base of one's own choice between two and nine (inclusive).'

In order to assist the pupils compile their own individual source of data they were issued with a set of questions which acted as a transitional link between their existing knowledge and design criteria. The questions were:

Section A. Mathematical/Theoretical
(1) What number base will the abacus serve?
(2) How many columns of values will be displayed?
(3) What will be the decimal value equivalent of the columns on your abacus?

Section B. Human/Social
(1) What will be (a) the age, and (b) the level of mathematical knowledge and understanding of (i) the operative, (ii) the observer receiving information from the abacus?
(2) Do users have any special or unusual characteristics, e.g., are they disabled, blind? How may this affect the design of the apparatus?
(3) Who are the people who are likely to use the apparatus, how will they use it, and in what situations? For example, will it be sited on the wall, used as a pocket-device, or be a desk model? How is it likely to be handled — carefully or otherwise? How will these factors influence the design?

Section C. Technical
(1) How can digit values be transmitted to the user, avoiding arabic symbols if possible?
(2) What mechanism would be employed?
(3) Of what materials is the apparatus to be made?

The vocabulary employed in these questions was, of course, appropriate to the age and ability of the children to whom they were given; account being taken as well of the terms that had previously been explained to them in the building up of a mathematical language.

Stage 2 Proposal of solutions. Although primarily intended as a personal project several children expressed the wish to work in pairs and throughout the group there was informal collaboration and co-operation. This resulted in a variety of possible solutions to the design problem, a number of which were influenced by mutual exchanges of ideas or information. Some improbable inventions were argued out of existence at the paper stage, but discussion in depth, even of the most unlikely possibilities, was a most fruitful experience, as the children considered a much wider range of ideas than would have been the case had they worked individually and exclusively.

Stage 3 Realisation of design. From a number of devices produced we can select a binary abacus made by a boy to exemplify the design/problem-solving approach in operation with regard to this project. His response to the questions were as follows:

A(1) The number base will be 2 — The binary system.

A(2) There will be four columns of values.

A(3)

column	4th	3rd	2nd	1st
decimal equivalents	8's	4's	2's	1's

B(1) This apparatus will be used for teaching small groups of children my own age (11), the binary system, or for giving someone a binary number, say, on a control panel. The children would know a little about place values and the adults would know a lot. The person operating the abacus would be very knowledgeable about the binary system. The people using and observing would be normal.

This corresponds exactly to the situation in which the boy found himself.

B(2) The apparatus would need to be large enough to enable about ten people to see it at once. It must be operated easily by an instructor and be transportable. It should be suitable for use on a desk.

C(1) Only two digits are registered on each column of binary values — zero and one. There are only two alternatives, which could be given as 0 and 1, or black and white, sound and no sound, off and on, light and no light. I choose light and no light.

C(2) A lighting system would involve bulbs which could be switched on or off separately. This means there will be an electrical circuit.

C(3) The electrical circuit and the bulbs would need to be mounted on a base which could be made of wood, metal or plastics.

At this point several salient features emerge.
(1) The child is operating from a social situation with which he is familiar, in which he is comfortable, and from his own level of mathematical knowledge and understanding.
(2) He has made personal decisions.
(3) He has constructed a brief as a basis for the development of the design.
(4) He is aware, at his level of mental understanding, what the problem is and what he wishes to achieve.

It might be argued that he has not developed a number of alternative proposals, but these were provided within the context of individual participation and discussion in a group activity. A variety of solutions were developed and his acceptance or rejection of them was largely unconscious and in this case did not warrant inclusion in his written brief. We must not expect material accruing from the design process necessarily to be expressed in tangible form, nor that the development proceed logically in clearly defined steps. Some people, more than others, possess the ability to memorize data and reason probabilities in their mind without recourse to concrete aids. Obstacles or failures may require reversions to previous stages whilst certainties may permit leap-frogging of certain stages.

In order to produce the prototype shown (Fig. 2.22) it is necessary for the boy to:

(1) Gain information about simple electrical circuits which he did on his own initiative.
(2) Devise and construct a circuit relating the positioning of bulbs to the columns of number values.
(3) Conduct an interim test for the device's effectiveness amongst 'critical' fellow pupils. From this arose the problem of right to left orientation of increasing column values between operator and observers facing each other.

Having confirmed the workability of the basic idea, the prototype was incorporated into a design for a more efficient product. Again the boy was involved in decision making, design and constructional activity. He decided:

Fig. 2.22 The binary abacus completed.

(1) That because of his limited range of tool skills the apparatus would predominantly be made of wood (although plastics and metal were used in detail fittings).

(2) The console would have the form illustrated (see Fig. 2.22). This had the advantages of:

  (a) Presenting a red screen to the viewer which could be illuminated from behind with light from bulbs beamed on to it. Both screen and bulbs to be carried on the upright upon which edge could be hinged the lid.

  (b) Carrying on the lid, and convenient to finger control, a uniform bank of on/off switches labelled to give right-to-left orientation of ascending values, the same as on the screen.

  (c) Being able to contain with easy access the electrical circuit and power source.

  (d) Being durable, yet at the same time pleasing in appearance and economic in the use of materials.

  (e) Being transportable.

To manufacture the cabinet/console involved the pupil in a variety of woodworking skills and techniques including cutting and shaping, marking out, joining and finishing.

The fitting of the electrical system entailed the mounting of lights and switches, installation of distribution boxes and the grouping of wires.

Stage 4 Test/evaluation. Rigorous test/evaluation was applied by fellow pupils, headmaster and a visiting HM Inspector! The apparatus was pronounced satisfactory for the purpose it was designed to serve.

With this particular example the craft experience predominated in the use of wood for construction. Science, craft and mathematics were linked and 'art and craft' performed a supportive role.

This worked example represents the product of a well-motivated 12-year-old boy of a good average ability, having an interest in science/craft activities, but not a great deal of previous experience in design/problem-solving. As such it illustrates the standards that can be attained through this approach.

Example 3

Age/ability range	10 + years, mixed ability. Middle School.
Group size	Year group of 70 pupils divided into two teaching groups of 35. Working group size 1-5.
Type of design activity	Central.
Situation	It was decided to involve the year group in an extended study on the theme of 'form'. They had not systematically explored this area of art activity previously and had negligible experience in design/problem-solving activity, but they had received a previous year's experience in a mixed-media studio/workshop situation. It was hoped that the project would wean pupils from total teacher dependence to a more self-reliant approach to their work through use of the 'design process'.

The project also illustrates how the 'design process' may be effectively applied to 'art activities', traditionally considered almost totally subjective and therefore completely outside the apparent constraints of logic.

Cognisance of these factors had to be taken into account in planning the proposed activities which aimed to achieve the following educational aims:

(1) To encourage the children to move gradually

from dependence on teacher-direction towards self-directed independent, resourceful activity in the art/craft workshop/studio situation.

(2) To extend previous experience in a range of materials with associated techniques.

(3) To enable children to realise that creative ideas may be expressed in a variety and combination of materials.

(4) To teach children the fundamental concept of form but to relate it to qualities of texture, shape, colour, etc. To be aware of man-made and natural forms in the environment.

(5) To develop the ability to create two- and three-dimensional expressive designs from the study of natural and man-made forms.

(6) To establish inter-active links between two- and three-dimensional work.

(7) To introduce the design/problem-solving approach at a point and a rate suitable to the intelligence, abilities, and capabilities of individual children within the context of a large, mixed ability group.

These aims were to be pursued within the resources available and constraints imposed by the situation in the particular Middle School. The constraints were experienced mainly in terms of materials, equipment, staffing, finance and pressures upon time caused by other curricular activities.

A flow chart of developmental phases was drawn up and added to as the project/theme progressed. This acted as a reference for teachers and children on which a development and extension of theme-based activities could be traced.

These phases, preceded by the Introduction, are outlined together with a discussion at each stage as follows.

Stage 1 Problem identification and definition
Theme 'Form'
Introduction
(1) General talk by teacher.
(2) Film/slides and talk 'Functional forms'.
(3) Studio/workshop exhibition on 'Form' (Fig. 2.23).

This introduction served as an input of information and as a stimulus for future activity: also as a reference source to which children and teacher could refer back. As such it corresponds to Stage 1 in the design/problem-solving process (see p. 8-9).

This was a whole group activity where children were only looking, listening and discussing.

Stage 2 Proposal of solutions, and
Stage 3 Realisation of design
Developmental Phase A
Rectangular and Cylindrical Hollow Forms
(1) Individual children making rectangular and cylindrical forms out of cardboard to personal choice of size and colour.
(2) Pupils were given the choice of working singly or in small 'friendship' groups to construct three-dimensional compositions of (a) exclusively cylindrical forms, (b) exclusively rectangular forms, (c) combination of rectangular and cylindrical forms (Fig. 2.24).

The activities in this stage were predominantly teacher-directed. This was a familiar organisational pattern to the children and therefore the starting point for their activities. They worked with stiff card, which was also a material familiar to them.

Fig. 2.23 'Form'—a studio exhibition designed to stimulate pupil interest in this topic.

Fig. 2.24 Three-dimensional pupil compositions built up from a single form.

Choice/decision making extended to:

(1) Size of working group.
(2) Size and colour of units in the composition.
(3) The composition itself.

Experience, of a limited character appropriate to levels of knowledge and ability, was therefore given in Stages 2 and 3 of the problem-solving process, i.e., the proposal of various arrangements followed by selection and choice of construction. Further experience was also gained in measuring, cutting, shaping and joining, the fundamental mechanics of structure and three-dimensional composition.

Fig. 2.25 'A modern city'—the prototype model. Pupils aged eleven years.

The use of geometric forms in modern architecture arose in general class discussion. This stimulus suggested further investigation and was taken up by a trio of boys and developed into the project: 'To make a model of a proposed modern city'. The project constituted a complete design/problem-solving assignment. As a core-role activity it extended into aspects of environmental and social studies as well as providing experience in creating and arranging aesthetically pleasing yet functionally efficient forms.

Developmental Phase B
Creative Three-dimensional Studies Based on the Hand
The subject of the human hand was then introduced as a form that could be studied and represented in three and later two dimensions. Being an integral part of the body, its functions, qualities, structure and movements could be readily appreciated and conveniently examined. What was ordinary and taken much for granted was found by the children to hold interest and certain fascinations.

(1) An introductory talk was given by the teacher about natural forms; then various aspects of the hand were discussed: its anatomy and articulations, its role as the body's tool for, e.g., pushing, gripping, picking, its role in expressing, e.g., fear, loving, protecting, directing. This was followed by

(2) Individual assignments. Using the rectangular and cylindrical form as a basis for construction producing sculptures of the hand in gestures and material(s) of one's own choice. The materials available were wood, clay, expanded polystyrene, wire, cardboard, papier maché, and thermalite (see Fig. 2.26).

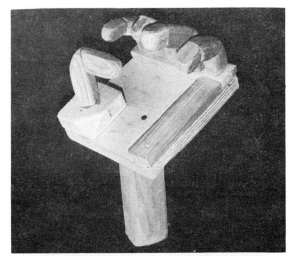

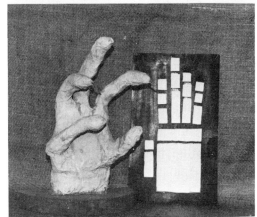

Fig. 2.26 Models of hands in different postures. Note the use of a variety of media.

25

As children proceeded from Stage 1 they took up the assignment which provided some experience, albeit still of a limited character, of all four stages of the design/problem-solving process. Their experience was extended by

(a) being given an assignment;
(b) being offered a choice/decision with regard to materials;
(c) expressing personal feelings/ideas with regard to the posture of the hand;
(d) discussing ideas, techniques and difficulties, etc., with the teacher;
(e) encountering and overcoming manipulative/ constructional problems associated with chosen materials;
(f) investigating properties/limitations of materials and use of tools.

Where it was thought profitable instruction was given to the whole group, as opposed to individuals, at (e) and (f).

Developmental Phase C
Two-dimensional Designing Projects
The purpose of this phase was to link three-dimensional to two-dimensional activity, utilising accumulated knowledge gained from Phases A and B.

(1) (a) Drawings in pencil, charcoal or crayon of a model hand (see Fig. 2.27);
    (b) expressive paintings/drawings of the hands.
(2) Study of the side view of the hand, concentrating on skeletal sections and articulations.

Fig. 2.27   A sketch which exhibits the value of close observation and involvement in modelling (see Phase B).

(3) Production of a series of line drawings of both hands held together in whatever posture. Shapes of main masses drawn as simple shapes (see Fig. 2.28).

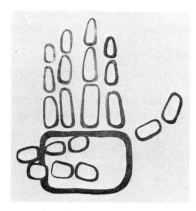

Fig. 2.28   The relationship of forms is highlighted in this composition by an eleven-year-old.

As well as introducing the idea of direct links between two- and three-dimensional activity in the minds of the children, the above activities encouraged close observation and examination of line and shape which they recorded in a conventional drawing manner. Scope, at (3), was given for personal expressive work, the line drawings becoming abstract and simplified records of the shapes seen; as such they provided the source from which a pictorial design could evolve. The children were encouraged to devise and draw a number of arrangements and to consider them critically.

Activity in this Phase C, closely linked and followed as it was by Phase D, provided a more 'in-depth' involvement in Stage 1 of the design/ problem-solving process.

Developmental Phase D
Two-dimensional Designing Projects
Utilising the sketches obtained from (3) in Phase C, or indeed from other inspirational sources, to create two-dimensional art works in a material or combination using one of the following processes:

(a) relief sculpture
(b) batik (Fig. 2.29)
(c) block-printing
(d) embroidery (Fig. 2.30)
(e) clay/plaster casting
(f) collage.

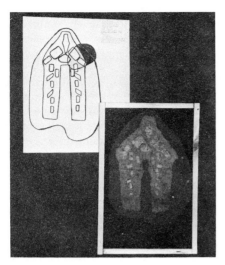

Fig. 2.29 Batik, with associated working drawing, by an eleven-year-old pupil of average ability.

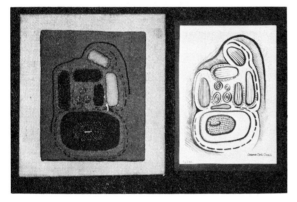

Fig. 2.30 Embroidery with associated working drawing.

(1) To prepare a number of sketches, from original ones (of Phase C Part (3)); then move towards the production of a master drawing on which the finished work would be based. Attention given to elements of composition, colour, size, line, shape, etc.

(2) Interpretation of master-design in the process and materials of one's choice.

Lecturettes were given to the whole class with film/slides on block printing, and the history and process of batik.

Activities at this phase continued to provide a greater in-depth involvement in Stages 2 and 3 of the design/problem-solving approach, i.e., the preparation of a wide variety of possibilities on designs, of making a choice and developing and interpreting it, again using a choice of materials or process.

By this point in the development of the theme, differences in rates of working, of abilities, of choices and personal approaches had diversified the range of activities being pursued in the studio/workshop. Children worked more independently in their personal work, yet co-operated to help one another over problems and discuss their work. In some cases, e.g., dyeing and batik, they were able to instruct and advise fellow pupils or refer to instructional books, pamphlets or manufacturers' directions. There was a general growth in confidence in operating the design line process.

Developmental Phase E
Three-dimensional Projects
Freedom was given to select stimulus/source, and to develop and execute a design in three-dimensional form under the following general headings:

(A) Natural forms
     For example, the human figure, the human head, animals, shells, etc.
(B) Man-made forms
     (1) Forms in the home
          Stools, key racks, book racks, salad servers, shoe cleaning boxes, cheese boards, etc.
     (2) Forms for sport
          Boomerangs, table tennis bats, hand bats, etc.
     (3) Forms for play
          Toys, go-karts, boats.
     (4) Forms for decoration
          Wall plaques, wood jewellery, plant holders.
     (5) Forms for the workshop
          Tool boxes, mallets, hammers.

At this point the design/problem-solving approach is the method by which individual children proceed to accomplish three-dimensional artifacts of their own choosing. The staffing team of two, the facilities and materials of the workshop/studio/reference area become the agencies through which the children realise their objectives.

At some points in Phase D and E of the theme the whole class received instruction in the theory and application of the design/problem-solving approach as a method of operation and organisation to attain objectives in the art/craft area of activities. It would have been inadvisable to introduce it earlier as the concept would be too abstract and they would have been unable to relate it to their practical experience.

The phases based on the theme were developed over a period of one or two terms with this particular group of pupils. Individual pupil progress, as well as being conditioned to a certain extent by the scale of the projects, was largely determined by those factors which constantly exercise themselves on children in the middle years; i.e., the wide variation and rates of development, individual approaches and style of working, and the widely different levels in maturation, ability and concentration. The activities were performed within the context of a studio/workshop situation which, whilst flexibly organised to provide multi-media choices, did not always offer individual pupils immediate working facilities or personal attention as and when required. Pupils were therefore encouraged to devise their own working arrangements which, with guidance, they were able to achieve to a satisfactory degree.

Stage 4 Test/evaluation. In this series of highly subjective situations, formal test/evaluation of the objective type exemplified in Examples 1 and 2 was inappropriate. There thus tended to be an immediacy of emotional reaction on the part of the pupil to his own work. However objective considerations of work in progress or accomplished did feature in informal discussions between teacher and individual pupils with regard to personal efforts.

The foregoing examples illustrate the incorporation of a few of the traditionally conceived arts and crafts practised in schools into a meaningful role within the context of the design/problem-solving approach and their relationship to other aspects of curriculum activity. The inherent flexibility of the process enables its principles to be adapted to the function of art and craft in any of the three major roles defined in Chapter 1. It may be noted that the problem-solving approach is as useful to the teacher in determining his pattern of organisation with regard to projected school or classroom activities as it is to the pupil in developing his own self-motivated creative experiences.

Chapter 3   Design as a Social Study

The concepts traditionally associated with art and crafts and home economics as elements in the overall curriculum have in the past been restricted. Many of the pupil activities involved have been thought of largely in terms of studies and practical work mainly related to the production of food or of two- and three-dimensional objects or artifacts, made in the studio/workshop or elsewhere in the school. Such an 'introspective' approach to pupil activities in this area of the curriculum, while allowing a useful contribution to the general education of pupils has, nevertheless, tended to stunt its growth and development as a curricular area of major importance.

A reorientation in the educational viewpoint held by teachers concerned with these educational activities leads to a reappraisal of the possibilities for design education. The 'design and make' situation, though important, is but a component part of the overall potential of design education.

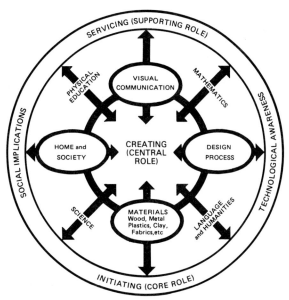

Fig. 3.2   Possible subject relationships inherent within design education.

Thus far in this volume the authors have been concerned mainly with design education as a means of aiding self expression, of stimulating creative thinking and of communicating ideas; of developing a critical awareness of problems, of rational and intuitive decision making, and of simplifying and rationalising a variety of creative though often disparate activities. The majority of these worthwhile activities can take place within the context and confines of the school, but this is not the totality of design education as outlined earlier.

Linking the spectrum of design education described above to that sector of the curriculum now generally known as Environment Studies is Social Design Studies. They are concerned with developing awareness of and personal involvement in the complex relationships which exist between design technology, society and the natural and man-made environment.

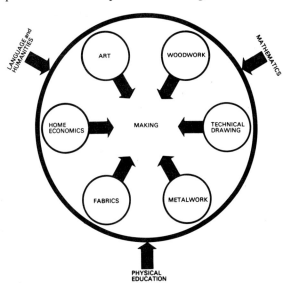

Fig. 3.1   A traditional view of art and crafts activities.

'Operation Front Door', a research/development study conducted as a part of the 1974-5 RCA research project Design in General Education, was concerned essentially with a visual study of the immediate environment and architecture which surrounded a London secondary school. This type of study, with its stress on 'looking outwards' emphasises the fact that design activity in the environment *is* worthy of pupil involvement within the general framework of a divergent approach to design education. Parallel activities in other areas of the curriculum serve a similar dual purpose of stimulation and personal involvement, and may be in fact closely related both in content and methodology to activities initiated from this starting point.

Social design studies can help the pupil, at appropriate levels of sophistication, to begin to understand the complexity of society. His researches and investigations, because of their positive links with 'real' situations, can reflect the reality of the world through its system of social organisation, and of the effects of design upon the environment.

Topics might for example include researches and possible solutions relating to the home, to local urban traffic problems such as are found in most town and city centres, pollution in a local stream or river, or the effects on the neighbourhood of building a new road, housing estate or factory. Such activities can also help in developing an understanding of the decision-making processes of society, and in nurturing the ability to record and re-order knowledge so that the same problem can be seen from a number of points of view.

The ways to which society organises and orders itself are manifested in a wide spectrum of service areas. These include, for example, *health*, involving the school nurse, doctors, health centres and hospitals, and *planning*, involving architects, engineers and environmental planners in a variety of activities, sharing a joint concern for almost every aspect of the physical environment, urban and rural, national and international.

A further important service area comprises the *social services*, including Church and clergy, social workers and the police who are concerned with our spiritual, emotional and physical needs in both personal and group identities — the cultural environment.

Some activities based on design or related to it which might be developed under these three headings are as follows.

3.1 Health as a General Topic for Design Activity

For all pupils the study of health can involve basic food technology and nutrition, and bodily and family care. It is also concerned with domestic living facilities and their organisation and maintenance, providing for the physical and emotional health of individuals, families and social groups or communities.

In secondary schools many excellent home economics courses, existing in their own right, have been built up around this vital area of human activity. Unfortunately, where home economics departments have been absorbed into larger design departments or faculties, the essential value of such pupil experience for boys and girls alike has too often been either overlooked or largly ignored because such work at first sight may not readily appear to fit into the pattern or philosophy put forward for the design department as a whole.

This quite naturally has resulted in a degree of antipathy being shown by many experienced home economics teachers who have felt that the importance of their discipline has been denigrated or at best considered peripheral rather than at the centre of the main stream of design education in schools.

If design education is to fulfil its potential role as a cornerstone of general education it is essential that:

(1) the importance and value of the home economics contribution is recognised by all teachers involved in design education, and
(2) when philosophy is formulated as aims and objectives, the values implicit in home economics are incorporated.

The old title 'domestic science', with its emphasis upon the scientific aspects of food technology, of hygiene and so on, tended to imply a certain lack of involvement in the aesthetic, artistic and cultural aspects of the domestic environment. Presently, because of the widespread but incorrect assumption that design education must be almost entirely art based, it would be equally wrong to anticipate that the home economics contribution to design studies should be concerned predominantly with those artistic, aesthetic and cultural aspects which previously were not emphasised.

In fact a balance between the two views is required, for to ignore the importance of either the cultural/aesthetic or technological aspects of domestic activity is to unnaturally and unnecessarily restrict the scope of the educational activities embodied within the discipline.

Pupils in the middle years should be involved in a variety of investigational and problem-solving situations associated with food, its sources, preparation, storage and nutritional qualities. Habits of eating, hygiene and all aspects of food technology provide numerous starting points for individual and group work using design/problem-solving approaches.

Experimental procedures devised to find out for example 'Why does stale food go mouldy?' or 'What does cooking do to food?', or 'How do we know if the water is fit to drink?', can be balanced by basic activities concerned for example with colour psychology and selection such as simple food or table decoration, or with practical problems such as the best shape for a scrubbing brush or jug, or simple food preparation and cooking, surely a necessity for all pupils. Starting with such a seemingly obvious question as 'How does a cooker work?' pupils can be led into a variety of design situations ranging across materials science, fuels, electrical theory and safety, ergonomics, aesthetics, functional efficiency, cookery theory (change of state of materials), maintenance, etc.

While on the surface such an open-ended approach might appear largely unstructured, all the activities exemplified above can be correlated to basic course objectives (e.g., pp. 36-7, objectives 1, 2, 4-9).

Certain aspects of the day-to-day organisation and running of a home, while too complex for younger members of this age range, are appropriate for the older pupils. Planning, whether it is concerned with buying clothes or kitchen equipment, preparing a meal, re-arranging a room or organising a budget, inevitably involves many aspects of design study and problem-solving. An approach of particular value as a design tool in these and similar circumstances, where planned sequential action is required, is the engineer's 'critical path' or network, the production of which to serve simple situations is well within the capacity of most children over the age of ten years (Fig. 3.3).

The use of line diagrams may also be used in conjunction with activity planning. Figure 3.4 shows a sketch plan to illustrate the bodily movements/stages required to make the cup of tea, corresponding to the critical path in Fig. 3.3.

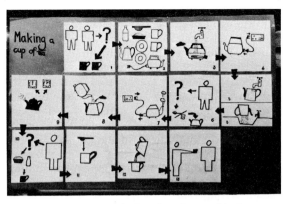

Fig. 3.3   A pupil's critical path to 'tea making'.

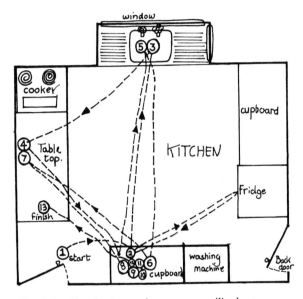

Fig. 3.4   'Routing' to make tea — a pupil's chart.

For all children, direct involvement with the health services through their officers and institutions is almost inevitable. However, extreme care is needed if young children are to be exposed through social aspects of design-based work to the emotional stress of trying to be of service to those suffering acute illness or disablement. Certain pupils in the upper middle range have shown a considerable capacity for helping the elderly and infirm as well as disadvantaged children suffering from temporary or permanent disablement. A useful activity is designing and making simple but effective equipment to help with simple tasks such as reading a book, opening a can or bottle, picking objects off

31

the floor and making games or variations of them to help strengthen or maintain digital dexterity, arm or leg muscles etc.

Working directly with hospital patients is best left until young people are emotionally more mature, but social services in devising and making equipment to help younger children in day nurseries, infant and junior schools is well within their scope, and can help inculcate a positive concern for the welfare of others.

However, young children should not be subjected to the attention of an ever-changing series of adults. Before initiating such activities therefore, teachers should consult their LEA advisory staff to obtain appropriate detailed guidance.

Such design activities, involving external factors, far from lessening the load on the teacher, in fact increase his responsibility. Prior teacher consultation with the staff concerned is essential to find out just what facilities/equipment may be needed in any given circumstance. Also it is vital that the staff of the institution concerned appreciate the educational objectives involved, and the limitations of time, ability, skills and resources which are available to the project(s). Timetabling such activities can in itself be a considerable disincentive, as from the recipient's point of view help is usually required as soon as the problem arises, and not on a time scale extending possibly into several months afterwards.

To meet this sort of external pressure may involve the teacher in splitting teaching groups or even in requesting design activity periods which extend over a period of days rather than hours. Where 'integrated day' approaches are in practice such difficulties are relatively easily overcome, but where a rigid timetable regime is in operation compromise is often difficult to attain, for other disciplines have equal claim on available teaching time.

Where design based or other studies call for travel outside the school, the practical problem of transport to the site of activity requires particular attention. What is accessible and 'local' to the school, i.e., within walking distance, can often determine how much of this work is undertaken. Schools may strain to provide the odd 'one-off' venture, but this can produce an unfair drain on school funds or parents' pockets, for bus fares, or unwarranted demands on the use of staff transport to support such curriculum activity. Additionally, in these circumstances teachers will be well advised to ensure that they and their pupils are fully insured

against any accidents which may arise.

Of particular value appear to be 'feed-back' situations where pupils provide educational toys or equipment for their former primary school or classes.

Personality problems are largely avoided because in this situation the children concerned know and are known by their former teachers. Thus a rapport is relatively easy to establish which is conducive to a successful outcome of the activity. In this connection a short 'handing over' ceremony with the officials and recipients of the assistance will help in creating an atmosphere in which further tasks of social service can fruitfully take place.

Whenever pupils are engaged in activities which take them outside school, particular problems arise for the teacher which call for special attention.

Firstly the need for adequate preparation of the pupils involved and of materials for their use. The pupils must be fully acquainted with the problem under investigation and fully aware too of their personal role in its solution and, equally importantly, prepared to carry out their work in a logical and thorough manner. The responsibility for this preparation lies with the teacher. Work sheets, questionnaires, partially drawn plans/sketches/maps, and guidance and appropriate source material must be on hand before the work is undertaken, though this of course does not preclude the development of further learning aids by teacher or pupils as the project develops.

Nevertheless, without such initial guidance and assistance, pupils of this age range — and others — either do not get off to a satisfactory start, or the project loses impetus through the inability of the pupil to direct his own activity.

In either case, apart from the total loss of a potentially rewarding educational experience, the pupil becomes almost certainly bored and disillusioned.

Secondly, there is the need for adequate supervision. Without a good personal relationship between pupil and teacher, personal discipline within the group is more difficult to maintain outside the classroom. Even where pupil involvement is high the teacher needs to maintain a firm though light rein on group and individual behaviour, for in these circumstances accidents are more likely to occur than in the normal classroom situation.

Finally, there must be adequate follow-up and feedback after the project has run to ensure that for the pupil educational gains are reinforced and that for the teacher further activities of a similar nature can be planned, improved and progressed in the light of the experience gained.

3.2 The Physical Environment

With certain exceptions man has in the past generally regarded environmental resources as being inexhaustible. It is only recently, because of the accelerated rate of technological development and massive increase in energy requirements by an increasing world population, that he has begun to appreciate the magnitude of the problems confronting him and future generations.[*]

Whilst in the past landscaping, fine architecture and art provided a visual man-made environment for the fortunate few which is now appreciated and enjoyed by many, the products of the Renaissance, the Classical, Romantic and other movements extending throughout Europe and elsewhere were largely overshadowed by the disastrous and contrasting visual and environmental side-effects of industrialisation during the nineteenth and early twentieth centuries. Such is the result of the application of technology without the constraints imposed by a comprehensive design study approach to its effects for ill as well as for immediate or apparent good.

Technological, cultural and environmental awareness in pupils can be fostered and linked effectively through the application of design approaches to social problems associated with the physical environment. Activities related to industrial archaeology[†] profitably link industrial and social history with an awareness of developing technology, with ecology and other areas of environmental study. Visits to museums, field work, personal research and making models of old equipment and industrial sites all help to link design studies to other curriculum areas and, in that sense, to link pupil experience.

Today as in the past, it is fashionable in certain quarters, to decry technological advance. Children, while being made aware of the inappropriate and unhappy effects of its wrong application, need nevertheless to come to terms with its enormous potential in the service of mankind. Man rather than technology is at fault when things go wrong.

[*]See B. Ward and R. Dubois, *Only one Earth*, Pelican, 1972.

[†]See Schools Council, *Industrial Archaeology for Schools*, Heinemann, 1973.

Fig. 3.5 Technological design projects can involve a wide range of science-based activities.

Thus social consciousness is not at variance with awareness of interest in and ultimately social control of technology. While much of the argument about the role and effects of technology in modern society is beyond the comprehension of younger pupils, basic issues can be raised through discussion and pupil involvement in related yet simple design projects. *Technology* by V. C. Hudson[‡] provides a useful source of discussion material on this most important topic.

In this sense architecture, planning, conservation of resources, etc., can be seen as technologies which are, or should be, concerned with maintaining or improving the quality of life. At basic levels children of this age can begin to decide for themselves whether such activities are justified or justifiable, not perhaps with the degree of sophistication of argument of the mature adult, but maybe with the clarity of perception of youth.

At this level the involvement of the teacher is critical. He must avoid inculcating personal views of a dogmatic nature, yet he needs nevertheless to steer the children's thinking and involvement towards those aspects of technology which would seem advantageous to society and to point out those aspects which are ultimately anti-social in effect whether immediate or long term. The ultimate value of prestigious feats of very costly engineering might be weighed against possible advances (which could be made for the same cost in man power and money) in alleviating starvation through, say, irrigation and water control. The ever-increasing range and quantity of consumer goods might be set

[‡]V. D. Hudson, *Technology*, Probe Series, SCH Press, 1971.

against the need to develop simple but adequate housing. Topics of such magnitude as these are, in their totality, beyond the comprehension of most children in this age range, but the seeds of concern must be sown and can be nurtured through involvement with the ideas involved. At the other end of the scale are the problems associated with the need, presumed or actual, for disposable bottles, cutlery and crockery; for elaborate packaging or electrical gadgetry.

How is this to be achieved? Certainly not by lectures, 'chalk and talk' and 'hard sell' approaches, but by pursuing a policy of involving pupils in design-based situations where such considerations will naturally arise. Making a model of a 'city of the future' (see p. 25) can lead to a critical appraisal of 'our town today'. This, in turn can be broken down into aspects of group living, group identity and social needs on the one hand, and the ways in which available technology can be used to serve those needs on the other.

'Design a temporary pre-fabricated town for an earthquake disaster area' at simplest levels of consideration can involve 8-14-year-olds in a wide range of social, environmental, and technological problems and investigations.

It is the personal and appropriate involvement in technological design activities of which the above is only one of many possible examples, which will help to bring about such awareness as is essential if tomorrow's adults are to live with and make positive use of technology and combine it with a real concern for the total environment.

3.3   The Cultural Environment

The truism 'Man does not live by bread alone' is often forgotten or ignored — as planners of high rise flats have found out. Close links exist between man's physical, social, emotional and spiritual needs, and to ignore any one whilst being involved exclusively with another has never proved wholly satisfactory.

The social implications of design activity need to be considered in relation to society's cultural and emotional well-being and the well-being of individuals within that society every bit as much as its implications for their physical state.

Such a context provides positive links with aspects of social and domestic history, sociology and religious education through design-based work centred on topics such as the provision of a domestic

water supply and disposal system, the social effects of the industrial revolution and its impact on the domestic life of the new factory work force. A project on church architecture should not stop at a study of the physical, the buildings themselves, but should extend to a realisation of the powerful emotional and spiritual forces which led to their construction.

The transistor, like atomic fission, can be put to man's service or his destruction. The development of the beginning of a scale of social values relating to technology and its applications can and maybe ought to start within the experiences provided by and through design education. Melville Harris* suggests that the skills involved are essentially

(a) the 'study skills', i.e., the ability to collect, to classify and experiment etc.,
(b) the basic skills of language, mathematics and art, and
(c) the use of social conduct, of attitudes to others and respect for the environment.

Equally these are also some of the basic skills acquired through and used in design education which, in its social role supplement, complement and enhance the educational possibilities of environmental and related studies.

In Chapter 1 the 'supporting' nature of design education was outlined. In social design studies design education has not only a 'supportive', but also a 'core' role to play.

The three service areas outlined above can thus offer many starting points for social design activities for pupils in the middle years.

To sum up, this chapter is concerned with 'caring'; within the widest possible curricular context and through social design studies children can be helped in various ways:

to understand and care for and about people;
to care about society and its relationship to the individuals within it;
to care for things, but not in a materialistic sense;
to care about the world in which they live, and
to care about the quality of life which they and others live — or might live.

*Harris, M., *Environmental Studies*, Macmillan, 1971.

Section B   Requirements and Resources—the Teacher's Role

Chapter 4   Planning the Course as a Major Curriculum Activity

Arriving at detailed course objectives

In Chapters 1 and 2 relationships between various facets of design education are outlined but an awareness of the potential scope of the study, whilst essential when reviewing this area of the curriculum, does not itself provide any detailed answers in terms of possible pupil activity.

The choice of topics and activities which go into any detailed course plan and the depth to which they are to be studied and experienced will depend ultimately upon the viewpoint, experience and expertise of the teacher or teachers directly concerned.

The classic approach to defining course content begins with the aims of the school, followed by their interpretation in terms of the aims for each disciplinary area. From this point major and subsidiary (or detailed) objectives would follow thus: —

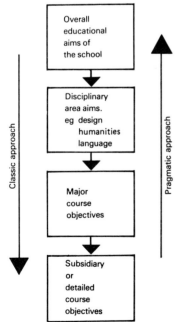

In relation to pupil development 'aims' may be defined as: 'the intention or "purpose" of the teacher or school to bring about design abilities or attitudes'.

Objectives by comparison are more precise statements that refer to 'intended levels of pupil performance or attitude', and they are most usefully defined in these terms.

In reality many teachers tend to be concerned more directly with what they want pupils to achieve in practice and in an assessment of pupils' ability levels. Starting from this practical standpoint, when deciding course content the classic approach referred to above can be reversed, the overall educational aims of the school stemming from detailed statements of objectives. Nevertheless in trying to relate such objectives to the aims of the curriculum as a whole it may be advantageous to redraft them in the form of aims to be sought for rather than objectives to be achieved.

Considering the potential scope of design activity we can see how broad is the range of objectives and how they might be realised through pupil experiences. A typical objective, to express ideas in pictorial form is a purpose readily understood by the teacher, but how is this, and other objectives, to be achieved? What strategies must the teacher use to help the pupil become interested, then involved and ultimately reasonably skilled in this or any other ability or technique?

A possible approach to answering these and similar questions might begin by hypothesising the ideal performance of an average child at the end of the course of study. From that end point we can work 'backwards' defining the programme of activities which is necessary to achieve such major course objectives. This way we can more easily define the steps required to progress logically from the beginning of the course to its conclusion.

This suggestion would seem to propose a

comprehensive but rigid course structure through which each pupil would proceed 'willy-nilly'. Nothing is in fact further from the authors' intention; we believe, on the contrary, that flexibility and equating of experience and performance levels to the abilities of individual pupils must override all other requirements. This apparent contradiction can be resolved by trying to ensure that each child receives a balanced diet of experiences: this need not be the same for the whole class but should fit into a prepared and programmed framework of experience (see Chapter 5).

Course objectives might be expressed at two or more levels to accommodate the wide differences in understanding and in pupil age, ability and experience say, those at the age of ten or fourteen years. Where this consideration is made the objectives could be arranged sequentially (see 'With Objectives in Mind', S.C. Project Science 5-13).

The total course content will be determined mainly by a combination of:

(1) Major course objectives described in terms of intended improvements in levels of
 (a) pupil performance in a range of mental/manual skills and techniques;
 (b) changes in pupil attitudes both individually and collectively.

(The examples which follow relate to (a) above. These can be termed 'performance' objectives. A similar group could be developed for (b) above, i.e., 'attitude' objectives.)

(2) The range and depth of expertise which can be provided by teaching staff combined with the provision of adequate facilities and teaching time.

Whilst obviously the factors under (2) considerably affect those under (1), the first need is to isolate these desired changes in pupil attitudes and behaviour. These should eventually be listed and grouped, but at first the teacher may list course objectives in random order (as they are identified). Such a random list of objectives, even though imperfectly expressed, might begin as follows.

That each child shall, at the end of the course,

(1) have a working knowledge and experience of wood, clay, metals (thin sheet and wire), thermoplastics (sheet and cellular), fabrics, paper, paints, fibres, foodstuffs and miscellaneous materials;

Fig. 4.1 The making of an effective football rattle calls for investigations into (a) materials — to find the most suitable 'flap' or 'leaf', (b) cam forms — to find the one which gives the best 'click pattern'.

(2) be able to investigate a variety of problem situations in a logical and methodical manner:

(3) have a basic skills ability in the correct use of pencil, paintbrush and fibre-tip pen as a means of visual communication;

(4) be able to safely use basic hand tools and craft equipment to acceptable levels of performance;

(5) be able to relate experimental procedures to findings so as to achieve a reasoned conclusion;

(6) be able to verbalise as to why certain decisions are being made (choices in relation to aesthetic, functional and other design factors);

(7) be able, using basic methods of manipulation and assembly, to make simple structural forms;

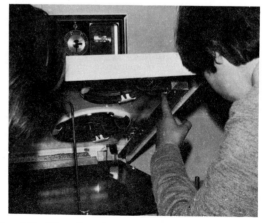

Fig. 4.2 'How does it work?' Items of domestic equipment provide excellent starting points for discussion because they are within the pupil's existing experience.

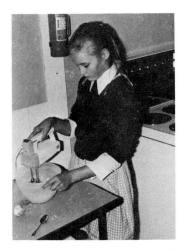

Fig. 4.3 Cooking—a combination of art and technology.

(8) become increasingly aware at appropriate levels of the inter-relationship of science and technology and the creative domestic arts;
(9) be aware of, and gain some working experiences in, the more specialised skills and techniques that pertain to specific materials;

and so on.

Once this random list is produced, certain groupings will begin to suggest themselves. Areas of activity and experience such as those suggested in Fig. 4.4 are likely to provide a context for some of the major objectives of a design-based course. They are outlined as follows.

4.1 Materials

Up to and during the middle years of schooling children will have played in a natural environment and come into contact with materials such as stone, grass, twigs, sand, mud or clay. They may have also used objects made from a variety of media, e.g., paper, card, wood, plastics, egg boxes, empty cans, glass bottles, etc. Desirable as these predominantly 'play' experiences are, they are not particularly related. Likewise, general 'art and craft' lessons in schools provide useful experience in materials but usually only as a 'spin-off' from the main purpose of the particular activity, which may, for example, be making classroom decorations for Christmas celebrations. In either case materials will have been compared subconsciously and their properties hardly appreciated.

To create, in the physical sense, must involve the use of materials. If the pupil is to be successful in this creating he will need to develop a thorough understanding of them. This can only be gained over a period of time and in a structured, rather than arbitrary fashion where experiences are programmed to draw together what might otherwise remain as unconnected pieces of background information.

The pupil therefore needs to:

(1) gain experience of the tactile as well as the visual properties of a wide range of materials which he can control and manipulate;
(2) understand terms such as relative density, durability, toughness, hardness, strength,

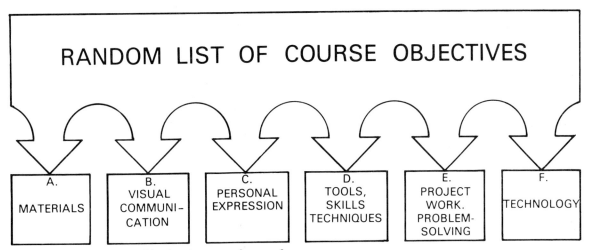

RANDOM LIST OF COURSE OBJECTIVES

| A. MATERIALS | B. VISUAL COMMUNI-CATION | C. PERSONAL EXPRESSION | D. TOOLS, SKILLS TECHNIQUES | E. PROJECT WORK. PROBLEM-SOLVING | F. TECHNOLOGY |

Fig. 4.4 Grouping course objectives in terms of areas of pupil activity.

plasticity, elasticity, insulation, conductivity, and how they apply to specific materials;

(3) within this repertoire become increasingly aware of the ways in which mechanical and other properties affect the methods of manipulation employed and the end use of the product when complete.

As knowledge and experience develop, the pupil will, when producing two- or three-dimensional work:

(1) be able to select the most appropriate materials for the function or qualities desired;
(2) understand and be able to express the reasons for choice;
(3) develop the skills and techniques appropriate to the materials he has chosen and the art or craft work he wishes to produce.

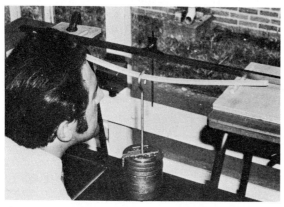

Fig. 4.5 Comparing the relative stiffness of different materials or of different cross sections of the same material. Good experience for teacher too!

Fig. 4.6 Constructing an armature for a sculpture.

4.2 Visual Communication

As the spontaneity of early childhood gives way to the more considered and critical approach of the 10-year-old, the child develops the desire to firstly see 'in the mind's eye' an object to be made or picture to be painted. Mentally held ideas require expression. In most disciplines this expression is verbal, but in the case of the 'thing to be made' pictorial or visual expression is far more effective and valuable as an aid to thinking, as well as expressing a thought or feeling.

The practice of sketching, indeed of keeping a personal sketch book, should be encouraged. In this a child can record first impressions, which may be graphical reactions to stimuli such as poems, music or verbal descriptions, representational or interpretative drawings of objects, 'ideas' for constructions and arrangements, or even doodles. The sketch book serves as a reference source from which items can be selected or elaborated upon at will. Two-dimensional picture making could involve the combination of a number of selected sketches, but many teachers fall into the error of expecting complete, accomplished pictorial pieces of work at the 'drop of the inspirational hat'. Some children, like mature exponents of the visual and musical arts, require varying degrees of time in the preparative activities. They need to experiment, to examine in detail, they need to collect and arrange isolated pieces of composition that evolve perhaps from a verbally indefinable idea, or which represent the reactions to the stimulus of subject or theme. Not until they have gone through these preliminaries are they ready to assemble the parts into a final product. Further allowance must be made for the processes of rejecting, re-organising and redefining. However, despite the disciplines a

Fig. 4.7 Painting—spontaneous personal expression.

teacher might seek to encourage in picture making he must allow for the individual child's spontaneous desire to make and complete a picture, possibly at one sitting. This phenomenon is likely to be confined to the lower regions of the age group being considered; the older pupils are more likely to respond to requirements of preparative disciplines if the end product is likely to profit. It must be reiterated however that any group of pupils in their middle years will display, in image making, as with other aspects of behaviour, a wide variation in levels of maturation and approach.

4.3 Personal Expression

Pupil activity arises as a response to the stimulus offered by the teacher or generated by a learning atmosphere that has been created in order that objectives may be pursued. The question, 'What do I want a child to learn?' determines what is given to the child. The responses of individual pupils to a stimulus are likely to differ, often considerably, in nature and quality. They result from the interplay of factors within the mind of the child (e.g. his temperament, character, etc.) and factors external to him (e.g. the relationships he has with other children and adults, including teachers, and the social and cultural quality of his life at school, in the home and in society at large).

If the objectives of a programme of activities are to be realised in terms of pupil response, a teacher must be aware of these factors and be able to discern, within the individual child or group, their presence and the degree to which they are operating. Employing this knowledge diagnostically, he is then likely to be in a better position to alter or modify experiences and stimuli, create changes in atmosphere, guide pupils and decide when or when not to intervene in order to elicit the required responses and facilitate further learning.

The psychology of creative and mental growth and development has been thoroughly studied by Piaget, Lowenfeld, Kellog and many others. It is not the authors' purpose to deal in depth with what is described elsewhere (see the Bibliography), although certain general aspects of development are outlined in Chapter 9.

Nevertheless when making qualitative assessments of a pupil's work of an expressive nature, several important factors should be noted:

(1) Since normal children pass through fairly well-defined stages of development, identifiable at each level by the images and objects they produce and their patterns of behaviour, it follows that they are perceiving and interpreting the world in a way peculiar to that stage. They are doing so, in reality, in a much simpler way than an adult who views the world as a more complex place. Care should therefore be taken at any time not to employ adult criteria in forming judgements and setting standards with regard to the expressive quality of children's work. Responses are also conditioned by personality and temperamental factors. The characteristic patterns of thinking and expression have been termed 'schemata' (see Chapter 9). The child employs the schemata to state his understanding of the world about him, what he thinks, feels and knows about it. Within a group of pupils of the same chronological age there may be a wide difference in schematic levels and any sequentially structured scheme of work, programmed as it may be for normal development, must be flexible enough to accommodate this phenomenon.

(2) The middle years also witness a transition from the child's preoccupation with self and the world of imagination to an awareness of the reality of things in the environment. This awakening is frequently accompanied by periods of intense and sometimes exclusive interest which focuses on a subject or objects, e.g., horses, football, or looking after pets. Along with reading, talking and playing as the usual means of gathering information and expressing ideas, the child may employ painting, drawing or making things. At these times maturational energies — receptivity, perseverance, perception and emotional involvement — are high. If these special interests are exploited to educational advantage, a child's progress, both in expressive qualities and technical abilities, might develop considerably faster than might otherwise be expected if the interest level were lower. The child will also submit to tedious routines, menial tasks, or attention to details in pursuit of an ultimate objective. The focus of interest is however prone to shift, often in an arbitrary and erratic manner. Former interests can be abandoned in favour of the new. Subject matter may also, by adults' standards, be considered trivial or of little relevance, yet it possesses the power to captivate and stimulate the imagination.

(3) Despite the efforts a teacher may make to prevent his influence being expressed in the work of the pupil, there is always a certain amount of feed-back from himself which, to a degree, hides

the true expression of the pupil's thoughts, ideas or feelings. The child of ten and upwards becomes keenly sensitive either of his peers or his elders in what he expresses or how he expresses it. Reality can be observed and emulated in terms which are borrowed rather than personal. Commercial and social pressures operating through the media of the 'pop' sub-culture are particularly strong, tending to induce a conformity of imagery in visual expression which submerges rather than eradicates personal imagination, the influences of which nevertheless remain strong.

(4) A misconception held by some teachers and many adults generally is that a child's total development is a steady on-going progressive continuum. This belief extends to expressive abilities in visual as well as literary and oral forms. Observations of physical growth alone demonstrate the falsity of this notion. Development follows an erratic course, being punctuated with periods of rapid growth, intense activity, spells of inertia or dormancy, or even regression. There are times when the child appears to have no personal statement to make in visual terms, and indeed no desire to do so. Consuming interests may lie elsewhere or expression be through the media of writing, drama, dance or dress. On the other hand the fact that a child will not, or does not appear to be able to, express himself visually may not so much be due to his lack of desire, but through the lack of encouragement or opportunity to do so in the home or, in some cases, the school. Houseproud or indifferent parents may prohibit, much less encourage, natural and spontaneous expressive activity of a tactile, constructional or graphic nature. A number of teachers still refrain from engaging children in art/craft activities which they erroneously associate with disorder and 'mess'. Absence or minimal experience of visually expressive work is likely to result in arrested development of expressive capabilities which could be possibly associated with emotional/social/behavioural disorders.

As a child grows older his store of knowledge, experiences, ideas, thoughts and qualities of feeling increase. Skills and abilities develop and relationships assume a different importance. The child in the upper-middle years begins to relate and reconcile these things to one another in an effort to understand them and discover and express a personal identity. Visual expression through the arts/crafts offers a medium through which this process can take place and statements about that identity be made.

4.4 Tools and Techniques

The width of experience with tools, techniques and skills met with in the middle years relates to the range of materials being employed, and work being undertaken in the studio/workshop situation. Where this is extensive, 'potted' courses in woodwork, metalwork, painting, plastics, pottery, fabrics and so on may suggest themselves. But this approach carries inherent weaknesses, the most important one being that the idea, design or job becomes subordinate to the technique used. In learning the various uses of a tool, a pupil may become more concerned with mastering techniques for their own sakes than with the purposes they serve. The object of a programmed scheme of work for the middle years of school reverses this emphasis, since the idea, design or work in hand tends to assume greater importance in the mind and creative energies of the pupil in this age range. In the mind of the child the tool or technique is regarded as of value only if it serves to attain certain ends.

Note: The teacher however *must* be adequately trained and experienced in the safe and appropriate use and teaching of tool skills and techniques. Anything short of competency is almost certain to lead to hazardous workshop/studio conditions and situations, and the learning by pupils of incorrect and possibly dangerous methods of tool usage.

Ideally the most appropriate time to introduce the use of a particular tool or give instruction in a technique is when the level of receptivity is highest. This is likely to occur when the pupil needs to employ them to accomplish his objectives, or when he realises they can produce the effect he desires. Practically, however, this approach is likely to encounter teaching difficulties. When a variety of processes are in operation at one time, children are working at different rates on different pieces of work, e.g., printing, working with wood, metal and clay, and the teacher cannot always be available as and when required to provide individual attention. Group instruction/demonstration at appropriate junctures to those pupils whose current work is relevant to either tool or process gives them an awareness of their potential to accomplish particular objectives.

It could be that several classes of children may be shown an instructional film at one showing. Pictorial wallcharts, block diagrams, cassette loops and transparencies can be obtained or made to which pupils may refer for guidance or revision. Generalised instruction can be followed up when required by personal attention where the teacher gives help or guidance suited to the particular personality needs of individual pupils. To successfully help a child in tool handling, the teacher must be fully aware of those factors which enable the child to perform competently or present difficulties. Many are able to copy easily from a teacher's demonstration, whilst others, through lack of neuro-muscular control, motivation or what appears to be an in-built manipulative ability factor, require step-by-step instruction and encouragement. Since a certain familiarity of tools and techniques can be gained through observation, a multi-media situation in the studio/workshop, where a variety of work is in progress, is likely to provide a beneficial experience for children. Whilst it is no complete substitute for direct active personal involvement on a one-to-one basis, 'know-how', as well as ideas, can be caught as well as taught.

The 'potted' course approach would also suggest that *basic* skills in different crafts are very different, whereas for the younger pupil in the middle years many, indeed most, of the skills involved are common to most of the materials involved. Basic skills/techniques in art/craft activities in the middle years could be considered as coming under headings such as:

(1) *measuring and marking out*, using ruler, try-square, scriber, tape measure, etc.;
(2) *cutting*, using scissors, snips, knives, hacksaws, tenon (and other types of saws) and chisels;
(3) *bending and forming* sheet materials, wire, etc.;
(4) *fixing/joining*, using nails, screws, nuts and bolts, hard/soft solder, adhesives, sewing (hand and machine), simple joints, etc.;
(5) *shaping*, using hot wire cutters, surforms and files, carving gouges, knives, spokeshaves, etc.;
(6) *treating* — painting, varnishing, kneading clay, burnishing, planishing.

An appropriately programmed course must be inherently flexible enough to accommodate the individual growth patterns of the child in the middle years. The 'potted' course approach would not allow for these variational differences, but willy-nilly, succeed or fail pupils would be obliged to submit to course requirements. A middle years course should take into account the following:

(1) The ability of children at certain stages of physical development to manipulate specific tools; e.g., a small ten-year-old child might not be able to handle a steel jack plane, whereas a physically larger and stronger one could.
(2) The transitional development of mind and feeling from the preoccupation with self and fantasy to objectivity and reality. Thus a child needs to employ tools and processes requiring advancing degrees of discipline and greater sophistication.
(3) The maturity and attitude of individual pupils towards tools and processes, i.e., an appreciation that a particular tool or technique has a capability of serving a particular function relevant to the requirements of the work in progress and the material being employed; that the tool or technique is limited in its range of application, e.g., that stone, metal and wood can be cut with chisels, but only particular *types* of chisels.

Clearly, with mixed ability/maturity groupings of pupils in the 8-14 range, no rigid generalisations can be made. Comparatively young children are capable of handling heavy craft tools safely and unself-consciously. Others, usually older ones, of employing sophisticated techniques or equipment responsibly and competently, whilst others, with an almost instinctive feeling for tools and materials, require an absolute minimum of guidance. Yet the reverse could apply in each case to pupils within the same chronological group. Participation of girls

Fig. 4.8 Sex-role casting is out of place in contemporary design and education.

Fig. 4.9 Sex-role casting is out of place in contemporary design and education.

and boys alike in common activities refute traditional sex-role typecasting with regard to tools and their handling. With safety factors uppermost in his mind a great deal must be left to the teacher's judgement in matching the individual child and job to materials and tools in order that the pupil may be effectively creative in the physical sense.

A view persists amongst art/craft teachers that prescribed techniques obtain the best results from both tools and materials. Tried and tested tradition attests this claim and teachers may consider it a responsibility, if nothing else, from a safety point of view or for the prevention of damage to expensive tools, to instruct, using these traditional approaches. Certain factors must be considered however. Children cannot be prevented from knowing what the use and potential of tools are. They may have observed, indeed assisted older family members, tradesmen, craftsmen or fellow pupils and teachers using them. Their urge to employ them often ignores considerations of personal physical limitations. Since 'junior' models of suitable quality are not available in a large range of workshop tools, the child naturally goes for the man-sized tool if freely available, and this is likely to result in frustrated effort, clumsy handling and possible danger. But children's aspirations must be respected. To sell them short measure is to undermine the confidence and faith they may have in themselves and their work. Alternative methods could be suggested together with more manageable tools. Furthermore

it should not be considered bad practice to give practical help to a child over constructional difficulties in order that he may gain confidence by the realisation of his objectives. A certain degree of failure and frustration is however implicit in the acquisition of skills, and a child must learn to acquire personal disciplines in practice and submit to those imposed upon the artist/craftsman by the properties or characteristics of the material and tools being used. The relevance of skills levels to job requirement should always be stressed, the degree of accuracy necessary being closely in line with what is needed for a satisfactory construction or operation, not an arbitrary level set by the teacher.

The peculiar perverseness of children is another factor to be considered. Although a child may be fully aware, through demonstration, of the orthodox manner of handling tools and performing processes, he may feel he has a better way of achieving the required results. Obviously the teacher must uphold standards of safety and prevent injury or damage to tools and equipment, but there may be a case for allowing the child to work through to the most efficient method, as indeed Man, in his evolution as a maker and user of tools, has done. Carelessness and indifference towards tools and processes, however, are attitudes that must not be tolerated. Good habits, as well as bad ones, acquired early, persist for a lifetime.

The precept that 'learning is by doing' is one that pertains to the handling of tools. Although demonstration is necessary in 'showing how' it does not engender a personalised feeling for either tool or material. This is acquired through direct experience which is not without its difficulties or failures.

4.5 Project Work, Discovery and Problem-solving
The interdisciplinary role of design studies, as conceived and described in Chapter 1, is such that the problem-solving approach (described in Chapter 2), provides an obvious basic methodology.

4.6 Technology
It is widely recognised that aspects of the curriculum must investigate the society of which the child is a member. By including studies in technology, children are examining something which exerts a powerful effect on the whole fabric

of society. Science and technology have produced an explosion of knowledge, stimulated changes in values and have changed the form of society in which we live.

The education of children beyond the age of 13 is circumscribed to a great extent by examination requirements: also many attitudes have already formed at this age, and currently they have done so in near ignorance of technology. The middle years may be the best age range to introduce technology to balance other influences in these formative years.

The Schools Council Working Paper 18, 'Technology and the Schools', provides the definition of technology as employed in this context: 'Technology is the purposeful use of man's knowledge of materials, sources of energy and material phenomena.' 'Purposeful use' implies that technology in schools must be something more than an academic study. It is the positive and practical application of these things in the service of people. It also involves an understanding of a person's needs as an individual and as part of society. Design-based studies where the science, environmental studies, and craft content are strong obviously come under this heading, but in addition pupils might consider subjects such as technology in the home, technology and transport, technology in society, alternative (or appropriate) technology, the history of technological development and possible future technology, the survival of society (including pollution and conservation or resources), and so on.

Three fundamental aims of school technology thus emerge and can be stated:

(1) That children should have a general understanding and appreciation of, and sympathy for, scientific and technological developments and the ways in which these developments affect society.
(2) That children should become involved in at least some part or parts of the design/technology process.
(3) That children should be helped to increase their personal resources of technological knowledge and skills.

When the random list of major course objectives has been made, each item can be taken and broken down into smaller units after being grouped under one or other of the main areas of experience such as the six which are suggested. Reference to Fig. 4.10 shows, for example, how the first objective – 'That a child at the end of four years will have a working knowledge and experience of wood, clay, metals (thin sheet and wire), thermoplastics, fabrics, paper, paints, fibres and miscellaneous materials' – has been partially treated in this manner for illustrative purposes in terms of desired objectives related to individual materials. Similarly examples have been worked for objectives (4), (8) and (9). It will be noted from Fig. 4.10 that major objectives (4) and (9) are grouped under the main area of tools/skills/techniques.

Inevitably long lists of detailed and more specific course objectives, written in terms of pupil activities and behaviours, will be produced. They may well not all be produced at once but may be added to, subtracted from or amended as staff and/or teacher knowledge and expertise develops, or as contributions are otherwise forthcoming. For example, an in-service teacher training course in plastics or macramé may enable its members to expand and enrich the activities in their school in that particular area. By employing their professional expertise they will be able to translate their (possibly) newly acquired knowledge into appropriate pupil activity, dovetailing it into an overall scheme of work, rather than 'tacking a bit of plastics or macrame on to the "art", the "science" or whatever'.

In the context of design course planning for younger pupils in secondary school situations, the following slightly different 'performance' groups of objectives could form a basis for further teacher discussion. This partial list of general objectives was drawn up following consultation with a group of experienced teachers.

1 Design Processes

The pupil should have a working knowledge through experience of design processes. This includes:

Linear Design
1.1 Problem awareness – the context within which the problem or potential need arises.
1.2 Problem identification – clarification and precise definition of the problem.
1.3 Possible solutions.
1.4 Information search and retrieval. Information search to include the use of library and other sources of information. The pupil should be able to select appropriate information from that which is obtained.

THAT AT THE END OF THE FOUR YEAR COURSE EACH CHILD WILL:

1) Have a working knowledge and experience of wood, metal (thin sheet and wire), thermoplastics, fabrics, paper, paints, fibres, miscellaneous materials.

2) .... 5) ....

3) .... 6) ....

4) Have the ability to safely use basic hand tools and craft equipment to acceptable levels of performance. 7) ....

```
                    MATERIALS              VISUAL COMMUNICATION        PERSONAL EXPRESSIO
```

DETAILED COURSE OBJECTIVES: MATERIALS

Objective 1 : Child to possess a working knowledge of the following materials as defined.

A Clay
  i) To know of the sources and of the different types of clay
  ii) To know about, and be able to extract, the raw material
  iii) To prepare and purify raw material for use
  iv) To be able to maintain material in a workable condition
  v) To be able to reconstitute waste material
  vi) To be conversant with the behaviour of the material in its different states
  vii) To be able to modify the behaviour/and properties of material, (eg by grogging)
  vii) To be conversant with the theory of physical and chemical changes in firing
  ix) To understand/know about primitive and electrical kilns
  x) To understand the theory of glazing, of slipware and other decoration
  xi) To be aware of design factors in making pottery
  xii) To be aware of historical/cultural backgrounds of pottery
  xiii) To know something of commercial pottery-making

B Wood
  i) Possess an elementary knowledge of timber technology
  ii) To know about the main characteristics/qualities of hard/soft timbers
  iii) To have had experience in carving/shaping and constructing in timber in 2 and 3 dimensions
  iv) To have worked in hard, soft and manufactured timbers
  v) To have made a utilitarian article and a piece of 'art' work in wood
  vi) ....
  vii) ....

C Metal
  i) ....
  ii) ....

D Plastics
  i) ....
  etc. etc.

DETAILED COURSE OBJECTIVES: VISUAL COMMUNICATION

DETAILED COURSE OBJECTIVES: PERSONAL EXPRESSION

Fig. 4.10 Developing a course plan.

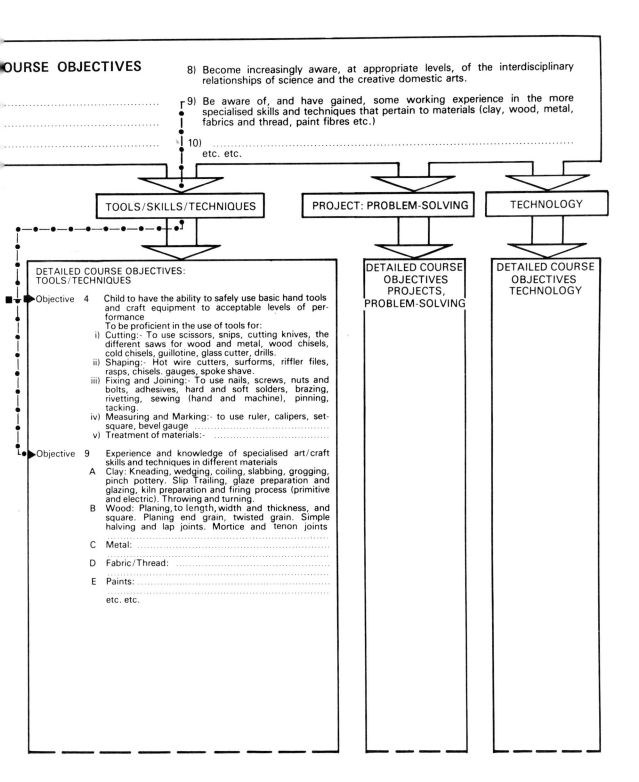

COURSE OBJECTIVES

8) Become increasingly aware, at appropriate levels, of the interdisciplinary relationships of science and the creative domestic arts.

9) Be aware of, and have gained, some working experience in the more specialised skills and techniques that pertain to materials (clay, wood, metal, fabrics and thread, paint fibres etc.)

10) ....

etc. etc.

TOOLS/SKILLS/TECHNIQUES	PROJECT: PROBLEM-SOLVING	TECHNOLOGY

DETAILED COURSE OBJECTIVES: TOOLS/TECHNIQUES

Objective 4   Child to have the ability to safely use basic hand tools and craft equipment to acceptable levels of performance
To be proficient in the use of tools for:

i) Cutting:- To use scissors, snips, cutting knives, the different saws for wood and metal, wood chisels, cold chisels, guillotine, glass cutter, drills.

ii) Shaping:- Hot wire cutters, surforms, riffler files, rasps, chisels. gauges, spoke shave.

iii) Fixing and Joining:- To use nails, screws, nuts and bolts, adhesives, hard and soft solders, brazing, rivetting, sewing (hand and machine), pinning, tacking.

iv) Measuring and Marking:- to use ruler, calipers, set-square, bevel gauge ....

v) Treatment of materials:- ....

Objective 9   Experience and knowledge of specialised art/craft skills and techniques in different materials

A   Clay: Kneading, wedging, coiling, slabbing, grogging, pinch pottery. Slip Trailing, glaze preparation and glazing, kiln preparation and firing process (primitive and electric). Throwing and turning.

B   Wood: Planing, to length, width and thickness, and square. Planing end grain, twisted grain. Simple halving and lap joints. Mortice and tenon joints ....

C   Metal: ....

D   Fabric/Thread: ....

E   Paints: ....

etc. etc.

DETAILED COURSE OBJECTIVES PROJECTS, PROBLEM-SOLVING

DETAILED COURSE OBJECTIVES TECHNOLOGY

1.5 Selection of solution, bearing in mind such constraints as: availability of materials/equipment/technique/time/level of skill/finance.

1.6 (i) Design realisation — see 3 — Design Realisation — Making.

(ii) Preparation of appropriate visual representation — see 2 'Visual Communication'.

1.7 Trial, appraisal and possible revision: consideration to be given to objectives in 5 'Design and Society', in addition to appraisal in terms of immediate effectiveness and effects of the design solution.

Intuitive Design

1.8 The accent on logical thinking should be paralleled by experience of intuitive design — particularly with respect to those aspects of design having strong aesthetic characteristics. The possibility of 'way out' solutions should never be discounted.

2 Visual Communication

At the end of the course, the pupil should be able to:

2.1 Perform language skills to appropriate levels. (Skills include pictorial signs and symbols in addition to adequacy in the use of words — both spoken and written.)

2.2 Demonstrate an understanding of simple proportion.

2.3 To communicate his ideas by freehand sketching and simple two- and three-dimensional modelling.

2.4 (i) Recognise whether a drawing is in isometric or orthographic projection, and, be able to 'read' and

(ii) produce 'freehand' versions of isometric and third-angle orthographic projection.

2.5 Make basic measurements (length of a line, degree of an angle).

2.6 Use simple drawing instruments (e.g., ruler, set-square) to an appropriate degree of accuracy, particularly with reference to (2.4ii) above.

The pupil should have experience of:
exploration of line, form, shape and texture and the uses and effects of colour.

3 Design Realisation

The pupil should be able to:

3.1 Mark out, cut and shape to an appropriate degree of accuracy a range of materials which may include wood, metal, plastics, ceramics and fabrics (this includes joining and forming). (See also Section 4, Materials, item 4.3.)

3.2 Understand the purpose, maintenance and safe and appropriate usage of basic hand tools.

3.3 Use basic hand tools safely, appropriately and employing correct techniques.

3.4 Decide upon the degree of accuracy of construction appropriate to various design situations and have the ability to work to such tolerances, bearing in mind the pupil's age and experience.

3.5 Use basic machinery/equipment with regard to particular materials. (Safety in all aspects of workshop practice must be an essential part of all design based courses.)

3.6 Produce a simple three-dimensional object or component from drawings and/or pictorial instructions.

3.7 Use levers, linkages, gears and pulleys, and should develop an understanding of motion and its purpose. Identify simple technological applications of natural phenomena.

4 Materials

The pupil should be able to:

4.1 List the primary properties of materials (both engineering and aesthetic), e.g., structure, strength, durability, conductivity, texture, colour.

4.2 Make reasoned choices from a range of common materials, e.g., wood, metals, plastics, ceramics, to meet specific design requirements.

4.3 State appropriate methods of shaping and fabrication of materials with respect to the properties of the materials concerned and have an awareness of the use of appropriate materials technologies (see also 'Design Realisation' section 3).

5 Design and Society

At this level Design and Society is not to be taught as a separate section, but will appear where appropriate as an overlay to other defined sections. It is delineated to draw attention to what might otherwise be overlooked.

The pupil should:

5.1 Be able to list and describe briefly ways in which design and technology has affected society and/or society has affected or influenced design and technological activity. For example: the Health Service and medical treatment; housing needs and solutions; transport, roads, applications of power and energy; clothing; domestic and other equipment and tools. In terms of syllabus content passing reference should be made to the interaction between man, energy sources and finite natural resources. For example: the use of coal and oil to provide energy, and the connection with home heating/lighting, transport, expenditure of natural resources, pollution, industry, motorways.

From this introduction he should develop a basic awareness of how the products of design and technological activity and uses of different materials/energy sources affect manufacture and the environment, e.g., the history and development of the motor car and its resultant interaction with society.

5.2 Be introduced to technological innovations such as the internal combustion engine and telephone and how these have affected, and are still affecting society — both for good and ill.

5.3 Have practical experience of the ergonomic factors in design — for example, the ease of use of a design in human terms. Are dials easy to read, the machine easy to use? Are heated areas properly insulated (such as tea-pot and kettle handles)? Does the design of a kitchen/workshop make it safe and easy to work in, and eliminate unnecessary movement? Are lighting levels adequate?

5.4 Be introduced to consumer awareness, primarily through the material/ideas from such organisations as the Design Centre and the Consumer Association, etc. (See also 'Design Processes' section 1.4).

Similarly a parallel list of 'attitude' objectives can be produced.

At this stage in planning, say, a four-year course, constraining factors with respect to individual school situations become decisive: e.g., 'we would like to provide metalcrafts but are limited in facilities and equipment', 'other timetable commitments prevent staff and children in the third year from doing . . .', 'we have no member of staff with knowledge/expertise in science/crafts/technology', 'there is insufficient money available for the purchase of sheet metal in the quantities we want',

and so on. These are common everyday problems even in the most efficiently run establishments, and are often overlooked by educational theorists, but they exercise a considerable influence on what activities may or may not be pursued in a school. Nevertheless they do not alter the fact that imagination, initiative, improvisation and enthusiasm on the part of the teacher can go a long way towards overcoming these restrictions, and that rudimentary activities, often performed with a minimum of simple and unsophisticated equipment or limited facilities, are preferable to none at all. Furthermore, consistent adherence to a programme of activities, however circumscribed it may have to be, can, in the long run, provide a greater depth and breadth of creative experiences than might be the case if the activities were not structured at all, even though the resource availability might be better in the latter case. A thorough, systematically acquired and intelligently devised range of experiences in a comparatively restricted range of materials is also beneficial to the child in fostering what might be termed an 'art/craft intelligence and awareness' coupled with positive attitudes, which at later times, possibly in adulthood, could prove advantageous when encountering design-problem challenges in a variety of media and situations.

With these factors in mind, determining realistically what activities/experiences can be provided within the school, as opposed to those perhaps idealised or desired ones in the list of detailed course objectives, the next stage is to regroup the objectives which it is felt are attainable within the limitations or availability of resources of the school. This should be done appropriately not only in terms of areas of activities, e.g. fabrics, clay/pottery, painting/drawing, etc. or behavioural direction, but also in some order of priority and in what appears a logical sequence. A pupil cannot, for example, throw a pot without previously gaining knowledge and experience of freely manipulating clay and hand-built work, nor make a dress without the ability to cut and shape; he must make simple patterns before complex patterns and he must work through the basic stages before attempting to solve the problems of a complete design. In choosing sequences of activities for pupils, previous knowledge and experience and personality/psychological factors are more critical than chronological age, although this element must not be totally discounted. It must be restated that these factors vary considerably in a year-group of children, but year-grouping is likely to provide the most suitable framework for the programming of activities. However the scheme and its implementation *must* be flexible enough to accommodate individual pupil differences.

There are many factors to be considered in presenting a course that touches on various disciplines (e.g., science and technology, environmental studies, expressive painting and craftwork, etc.). How are these disciplines to be weighted? How are they to be fitted in: can they (and should they) be presented concurrently or sequentially? If it is decided that pupils should work on one restricted field for a period and then move on to a different one, how long should this period be? How can individual pupil work rates, personalities and preferences be effectively reconciled with restrictions on facilities and with the demands of organisation and administration? These are questions that can only be answered in detail with respect to individual school situations.

As has been previously stated, however, the simple linear activities programme is neither desirable nor, in practice, attainable. Chapter 5 offers guidance on how it might be possible to turn a detailed teaching syllabus into a scheme of work, collective and individual which at the same time provides a diagnostic record of the work and progress of each pupil.

Chapter 5   The Detailed Construction of a Design-based Course

5.1   The Need for Structure

Having defined overall course objectives as indicated in Chapter 4, the problem remains of how to realise these objectives by organising a programme of balanced day-to-day activities.

It must be restated that any scheme of work for design-based studies envisaged for the middle years of schooling must avoid the tendency to become a dogmatic, inflexible syllabus. The scheme should support the philosophical and educational aims of this period of schooling and satisfy the concept of design education outlined in previous chapters.

The absence of any structure is likely to result in a situation which is familiar in many primary schools where pupils tend to receive a haphazard, unbalanced and unrelated range of art/craft experiences. A scheme of development, possibly as a programme across a given time-span, is usually associated with subjects such as mathematics and English, but the visual arts are not usually accorded this status. Excellent work is produced in many schools but this may result from a particular 'flare' of a teacher or group of teachers for a subject or a favourable set of circumstances existing in a school at a given time. In such a situation elements of a soundly based course exist, yet a well-conceived developmental programme of activities, designed to be performed throughout the school, is lacking. In many schools pupils are engaging in activities which (a) bear little reference to the art/craft experiences they may have previously had or may have in the future, (b) are irrelevant to thematic or other studies, or indeed to any other curricular areas, and (c) do not take into account their personal abilities, attainments or personalities. As, for example, in language development, foundations of experience are necessary upon which pupils can extend their knowledge, develop skills, and form attitudes.

'Arts and crafts', being incorporated into the concept of design education, carry a new status and broader relevance in the education of the middle years (see Chapter 1). A direct implication for pupils and teachers alike is that the notion of absolute freedom in the choice of activity and of how and when it will be performed, will have to be modified, if not on occasions severely curtailed.

5.2   The Teacher/Co-ordinator

Several features emerge from the concept of design education outlined so far:

(a) A design-based course can be intimately involved with other areas of the curriculum.

(b) It should incorporate into the teaching repertoire specialised skills and knowledge predominantly associated with art, craft, home economics and technology.

(c) It should have a progressive character extending over several years.

(d) Some form of record keeping is necessary (see Chapter 6).

(e) Specialised knowledge will be required to teach the safe and appropriate handling of the more sophisticated tools and equipment likely to be installed in the school, and to organise their deployment to other teachers in the school. Running maintenance of tools will have to be carried out. Blunt and ineffectually functioning tools and equipment constitute a potential danger as well as creating frustration for the user, pupil or adult.

The view may have been evoked that these aspects are beyond the traditional modes of organisation of the primary school, and that efficient control of all these requirements is outside the normal scope of a class teacher's responsibilities. Already much is required of the class teacher in teaching efficiently and effectively other areas of the curriculum. The presently established patterns of secondary school staffing, subject centred as they are, do not offer any suitable alternative.

The DES pamphlet No. 57, *Towards the Middle School*, discusses staffing arrangements. It suggests two co-ordinating roles as being distinguishable in middle schools. The first is 'that of a teacher or the teachers concerned with one or perhaps two year groups', but the second is that of 'consultant or leading teacher in charge of an area of the curriculum, or of subjects within an area'. The authors regard an arrangement of the latter kind as desirable, if not essential, for the efficient operation of a design-based course. Without such a person it is unlikely that the course could be planned initially. Without a focal figure or leader any course is likely to flounder through lack of cohesion and direction, although the general level of co-operation between members of staff may be high.

Paralleling the position of the teacher co-ordinator in the middle or primary school is a similar role to be played in the secondary school by the head of the design department or subject departments involved in this area of the curriculum. Thus wherever reference is made to the 'teacher-co-ordinator' this also refers to the teacher responsible for design studies in the secondary situation.

Within the overall philosophical aims and organisational modes that are emerging for education in the middle years, one of which is team teaching, it is neither likely nor desirable that a teacher-co-ordinator would assume total control of the course. He would not plan or teach it entirely, as the nature of the course involves other subjects and relies heavily on the contribution of other members of staff. It is likely, however, that the teacher-co-ordinator will be responsible for drawing up and detailing the major course activities and will be given oversight of their operation throughout the school.

Pamphlet 57 continues, '. . . teachers will become fitted for overseeing sequential curricula work up to 13'. Nevertheless, a co-ordinating teacher whose semi-specialist role may be of a supervisory and advisory nature must be familiar with the content and teaching methods of subjects in other areas of the curriculum if arts and crafts, through design, are to play meaningful core and supportive roles.

5.3 Factors Affecting the Choice of Course Activities

In planning a detailed course, there are a number of important factors governing the actual choice of activities. These must be taken into account and accommodated within the programme. They include the following:

(1) That the agreed overall, and detailed course objectives be met insofar as the variable factors of staff expertise, facilities and time will allow (see Chapter 7, and Chapter 4 dealing with formulation of objectives).

(2) Activities should, in general, be sequential in character, developing by degrees of sophistication until the ultimate objectives (i.e., those defining hoped-for final levels of performance) are attained.

(3) The programme planned for the period of time directed by the organisational patterns of the school should cater, *as far as possible*, for the levels of ability, attainment and personality of individual pupils. In practice this is not always possible, for despite recent innovations designed to educate children at their personal levels, the chronological-class pattern of the year-group is likely to remain a normal feature. If not educationally expedient, it is administratively convenient and teaching methodology must inevitably adapt itself to accommodate such requirements. Instead of taking a small group of children of mixed ages but with approximately the same level of interest, ability or attainment, teachers are faced with larger mixed ability groupings. Time is also specified. The timetable also fixes the duration of the lesson, although more flexibility is provided if teaching is planned on the principle of the integrated day.

Planning *in the main* must therefore inevitably aim for the 'normal' development of the chronological year-group, but must not be allowed to degenerate into total disregard for individual performance factors. Note must also be taken of the general ability level of a year-group, for as experienced teachers know, this can vary from year to year.

(4) In planning a programme it is important to assess the likely duration of each activity. It is asking the impossible to estimate accurately how long pupils will take to accomplish a set piece of work, as individual time depends on so many factors internal and external to the child. But the teacher co-ordinator must make some attempt to do this with regard to the activities that are to be included in the programme schedule so as to be able to fit these into the

total time available during the course. It is better to err on the side of planning for too much than for too little.

(5) There is a danger that too wide a range of activities may be performed in the studio/workshop at the same time. The number of different operations must relate realistically to the facilities available and the teacher's capacity to supervise and teach properly. If there is an imbalance, pupils are likely to lack the help and guidance they need at a critical stage of operations in the work in hand. They may be distracted or become idle, or they may handle tools and improvise techniques in a potentially dangerous manner, or pay inadequate attention. This may argue a case for more generalised class involvement in a specific activity, or the deliberate elimination of processes that require excessive explanation to a few pupils at a time, but it does not make a case for the traditional step-by-step methods of art and craft teaching, in which the whole class follows the same activity. A workable compromise could be found in small groupings of pupils engaged in common activities, but differing from group to group, perhaps alongside some pupils pursuing individual tasks. Some collective, direct teaching may be found to be a reasonable and efficient way of tackling certain points of instruction.

(6) The activities performed by a year-group must present the range of educational/developmental experiences 'normal' to that stage of chronological growth. These activities need to be dissimilar in form, but not necessarily in content, from those of previous or later years. A pupil may cast plaster into a pre-formed sand mould, and another may carve a plaster block that he has cast. Both are receiving similar experiences in the material, yet in name and final product the results might be considered by pupils to be different. A certain amount of repetition, however, is unavoidable.

(7) The activities comprising the course should strike a good balance in the following ways.

(a) In the amount and diversity of experience in the materials available in school. Suggestions of how to plan to accomplish this are explained in following sections.

(b) In the proportionate allocation of time and activities to central, core and (where possible) supporting roles. Where activities

feature under the latter two it must be assumed that there is a parallel development in other areas of the curriculum and an organisational mode which facilitates the blending of disciplines. Success in inter-disciplinary studies depends, in part, upon the teacher-co-ordinator's ability to sustain a meaningful dialogue with colleagues in other disciplines. He requires their support and co-operation, but they in turn require the same from him.

5.4 Sources of Activities

Frequent use has been made of the term 'activities'. They represent the 'bricks' of the course. In down-to-earth terms they are the actual things the pupils do. Where do they come from? It is not within the scope of this book to provide neat, 'how-to-do-it' material, but some guidance can be afforded.

The sources of practical information are many. At the present time numerous books, magazines and articles are being published. They are being produced as a result of the revival of interest in the arts and crafts and a growing desire amongst ordinary people to employ their creative energies in this way.

The educational press has contributed its share of material geared to the primary and secondary child and of instructional guidance for teachers.

This material extends across the spectrum from traditional 'light' to 'heavy' arts and crafts (see Fig. 2.14), to the craft/science/technology aspect, and art/craft/home economics, art/craft environmental studies, the art/craft/humanities aspects and so on. The Schools Council has already engaged in a number of research projects and publish both reports and teaching material in a number of these aspects; notably the 8-13 Art/Craft Education Project, Design and Craft Education (concerned with the 13-16 age range but not without relevance to the middle years). More towards science and technology are the Nuffield Combined Science (11-13), Science (5-13) and Project Technology (11-18) projects.

Attendance at in-service courses held throughout the country and organised by professional bodies, academic institutions, and teachers' centres are likely to provide sources of information, instruction and exchange of ideas. Courses fall roughly under two headings: those concerned with personal development to improve skills and abilities in all creative/technological aspects of design, and those with professional training designed to increase the teacher's capacity to organise and run design-based courses/activities using appropriate apparatus, modes of organisation, teaching material and methodology.

The concerned teacher, anxious to provide a coherent, design-based course, must 'go searching'. His rewards are, however, likely to be profitable in terms of developing his own awareness and expertise as well as contributing to a rich and stimulating variety of activities for pupils. Whilst ideas may be taken from a variety of sources direct, 'cribbing' and wholesale application of such ideas must at all cost be avoided. Any externally 'found' topics must be reviewed in strict relation to course objectives before their implementation as studio/classroom/workshop activities. Given the basic

technical information, for example, on how to make a mosaic, it can be adopted and adapted, if necessary to accomplish the specific objectives of the particular activity, and then taken into the on-going course to serve the educational needs of the pupils.

5.5 Activities and Objectives: An Overview of the Course

There is a simple visual device which the teacher-co-ordinator and his colleagues will find most useful. It provides a convenient 'at-a-glance' over-view of the course as a whole or across a given period of time. It presents, in the form of a simple chart or graph, the relationship between the projected activities and the course objectives they contain. It is illustrated and explained as follows.

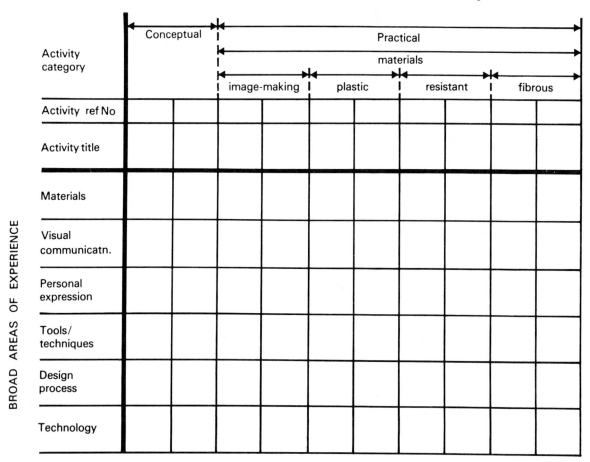

Fig. 5.1 Axes of overview chart for central-role activities.

(1) Central-role Activities

As stated in Chapter 1, design-based activities may be resolved into three related roles: central, supporting and core. Taking the central role first (the creative/manipulative activities involved in art and craft, experienced and enjoyed for their own sake), we can roughly group and categorise the projected activities under the headings of

(a) conceptual, where the term expresses the *character* of the activities, e.g., a theme of 'monsters and midgets' where pupils explore an idea through the media of art and crafts;
(b) practical, which are generally capable of being interpreted under the sub-headings of
   (i) image-making,
   (ii) techniques using materials that are plastic, resistant, or fibrous.

Activities throughout the course may be categorised in this manner and form an on-going programme through its duration, i.e., developmental work will be expected to continue in these categories throughout the course.

The projected activities so grouped could be set off along the horizontal axis of a grid (see Fig. 5.1). We have also seen how the course objectives might be resolved into six main areas of activity and experience (see Fig. 4.10). These can be set off along the vertical axis of the grid.

For the purposes of illustration and explanation a hypothetical case may be taken of the projected central-role activities of a third-year group of pupils aged 10 + to 11 + (see Fig. 5.2).

Grouped along the horizontal axis under their category headings are the titles of the projected central-role activities for the school year. Their titles are accompanied by a reference/coding number (an example of which is shown on p. 57).

An analysis can be made of every major proposed central-role activity for the session. Each one contains to greater or lesser degree, experience(s) which lie within the main areas previously defined. It may well be that the element of a specific area of experience is minimal, or obscure, but the element is always present. Alternatively it may be decidedly strong, perhaps to the extent of being the main reason for including the particular activity in the programme, e.g., Activity C4 'Clay: Forms from Moulds' may be included to instruct pupils of that age, who have already acquired experience earlier in the course, in the technique of producing pots in this (traditional) manner. The possible desire of the

pupils to select a mould, or even make one, and perhaps decorate the form produced (under personal expression) may be subordinate to the technique/skill element in the activity.

The subdivisions on the axis of the grid provide spaces in which the main objectives, in terms of the broad areas of experience, can be briefly stated. The complete chart becomes a total statement of what, in practical terms, is to be 'done' in the term, year, or indeed the course, and why it is being done, i.e., how it will contribute to achievement of the main course objectives.

Examination of the chart may reveal to the designer of the course strands of weaknesses in experience running through a set of activities; for example the scope given for design problem-solving in central-role activities may be limited in a particular session. Does the scope need to be broadened? If so, it suggests the introduction of activities in the following session to rectify this deficiency. Through this method of analysing the content of activities the pattern of experiences can be controlled to achieve major course objectives. It also provides a device for record keeping (see Chapter 6). The example illustrated in Fig. 5.2 proposes an allocation of one activity of a conceptual nature, three to work in plastic materials, two to resistant, four to fibrous materials and two devoted to image-making. This proportion is *not* advocated as a model, the examples being given only to clarify the method of presentation of information. The number of activities allocated to a specific category is determined by the overall pattern and balance that is sought, or feasible, within the context of a particular school.

(2) Supporting and Core-role Activities

The principle of the axes and grid can also be employed to provide an overview of activities featuring in core and supporting roles during a session.* The horizontal axis (Fig. 5.3) maintains its divisions as activities comprising the supporting-role component of the designed-based course and the vertical axis, representing the core role (Fig. 5.4), is sub-divided to list the other curricular subjects of the school.

*Supporting role: where two- or three-dimensional work complements and supplements pupil activities initiated in other disciplines.
Core role: where experience provided in other curricular areas is initiated by design-based work.

YEAR GROUP: III   AGE: 10+/11+   SESSION: 1975-76

SESSIONAL ACTIVITIES/OBJECTIVES OVERVIEW
CENTRAL ROLE

Activity category	Conceptual	Practical										
		Image-making		Plastic materials			Resistant materials		Fibrous materials			
Activity ref	Pr.2.	A.6.	A.8.	C.4.	C.6.	Pl.2.	P.2.	W.3.	T.2.	F.4.	F.5.	F.6.
Activity Title	Studies in Texture	2-D mural 'City at night'	2D pictures 'Faces'	Clay: Forms from moulds	Clay: Cylindrical Forms	Plaster Block sculpture	Plastics Sheet manipulation	Wood: Abstract 3-D Forms	Threads: Decorative weaving	Fabric Simple dress making	Fabrics: Fabric Collage	Fabrics: Batik
MATERIALS	Wide range as possible through which concept will be developed.											
VISUAL COMMUNICATION	Textural effect and quality through agency of light and shade.											
TECHNIQUES SKILLS	Cutting into. Incising. Surface Treatment. drawing, painting, modelling, moulding.											
PERSONAL EXPRESSION	Select and produce textural effects appropriate to situation and object.											
DESIGN PROCESS	Research into study of natural and man-made textures.											
TECHNOLOGY	The production and study of man-made textures in the environment and objects.											

BROAD AREAS OF EXPERIENCE

Fig. 5.2 Example of overview chart—central role—pupils aged 10-11 years.

54

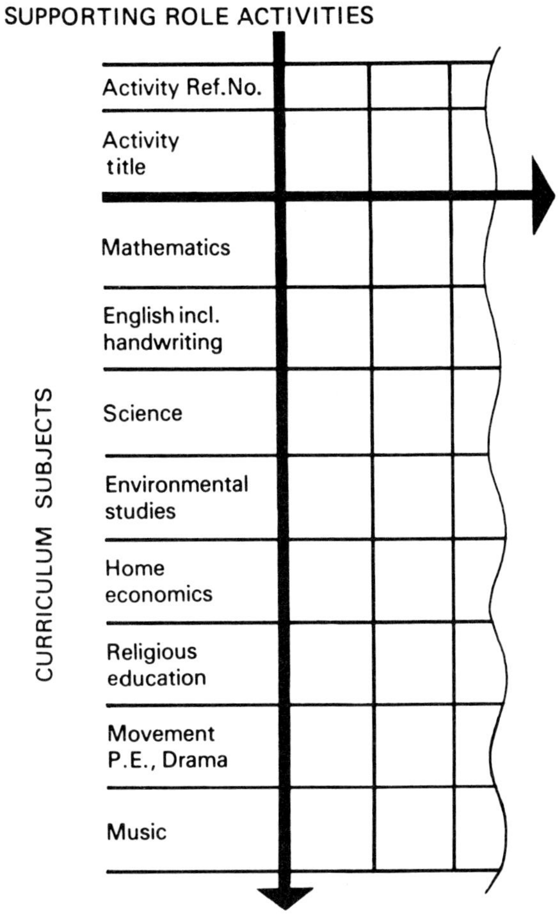

SUPPORTING ROLE ACTIVITIES

Activity Ref.No.			
Activity title			
Mathematics			
English incl. handwriting			
Science			
Environmental studies			
Home economics			
Religious education			
Movement P.E., Drama			
Music			

CURRICULUM SUBJECTS

Fig. 5.3   Supporting role activities chart.

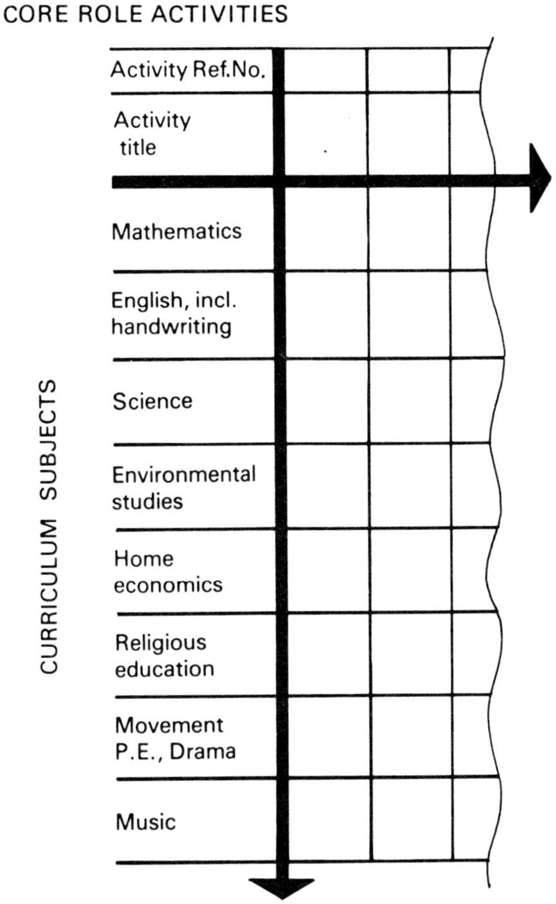

CORE ROLE ACTIVITIES

Activity Ref.No.			
Activity title			
Mathematics			
English, incl. handwriting			
Science			
Environmental studies			
Home economics			
Religious education			
Movement P.E., Drama			
Music			

CURRICULUM SUBJECTS

Fig. 5.4   Core role activities chart.

Figure 5.5 continues the hypothetical case quoted above of a third-year, 10+ to 11+ age-group programme of design activities, but this time drawn up for those providing a supporting role. The spaces on the grid are blanked off where the activities are supporting work in other subjects.

The purpose of this chart is to:

(a) give an overall indication of the degree to which design activities are extending into other areas of the curriculum during the session,

(b) list the subjects that a specific activity is supporting.

The integrative character of many aspects of studies in the middle years implies that design-based activities may support more than one subject in a particular project. Taking the example of activity JP2, 'The Rainmaker', this project could

have had its initial stimulus in dance/drama/movement yet could extend to religious education — a study of man's relationships to deities expressed through rituals and ceremonies, music, primitive rhythm, etc. and English, in the form of creative writing, notes and essays, etc. In the making of costumes, adornments, ritual objects, primitive musical instruments and in the production of drawings, diagrams, paintings and models, the 'design' aspect of the curriculum are being fully exploited to realise their supportive potential in other areas. In other instances the supporting activity may be limited to only one or two subjects.

The claim that design-based studies can be roughly classified into three inter-related roles (see p. 2) can also apply to other curricular subjects; they too can play a central, core and/or supportive role.

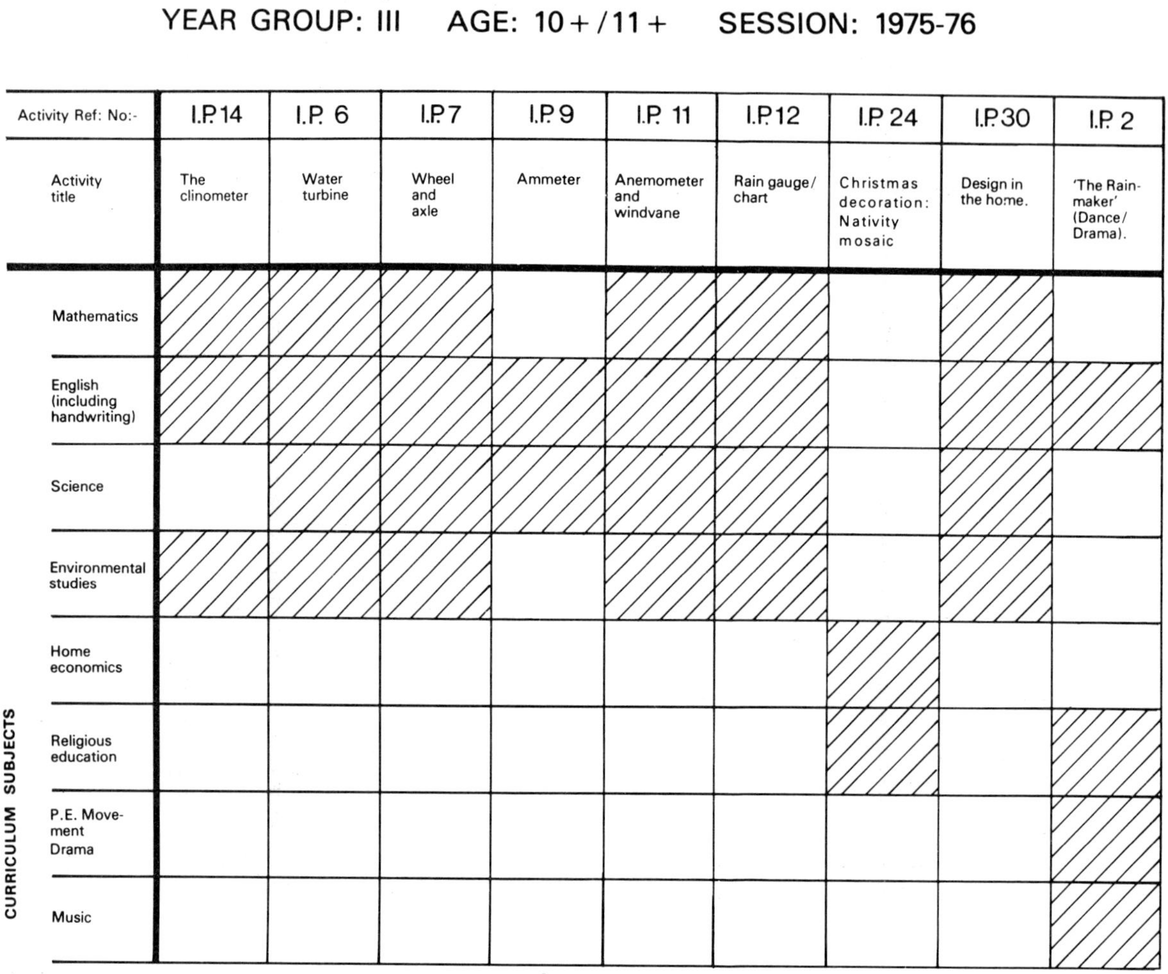

Activity Ref: No:-	I.P.14	I.P.6	I.P.7	I.P.9	I.P.11	I.P.12	I.P.24	I.P.30	I.P.2
Activity title	The clinometer	Water turbine	Wheel and axle	Ammeter	Anemometer and windvane	Rain gauge/chart	Christmas decoration: Nativity mosaic	Design in the home.	'The Rain-maker' (Dance/Drama).
Mathematics	▨	▨	▨		▨	▨		▨	
English (including handwriting)	▨	▨	▨	▨	▨	▨		▨	▨
Science		▨	▨	▨	▨	▨		▨	
Environmental studies	▨	▨	▨		▨	▨		▨	
Home economics							▨		
Religious education							▨		▨
P.E. Movement Drama									▨
Music									▨

(Left axis label: CURRICULUM SUBJECTS)

Fig. 5.5   Example of overview chart—supporting role—pupils aged 10-11 years.

Figure 5.6 is of a curriculum subjects-core-role activities chart for the same hypothetical third-year programme. Although a single activity/theme, 'Kilns', features in this role, being a subject intimately involved with pottery and claywork, it can stimulate studies in history and science.

The extent to which supportive and core-role activities feature in a schedule of a design-based study is, to a large extent, determined by the content of parallel courses in other areas of the curriculum. Mutual exchanges between semi-specialists and general teachers should aim to create a balanced distribution of design-based activity in other subjects if the concept of inter-disciplinary activity is accepted as a policy to be pursued in the middle years of education.

Teacher Guidance

With the wide range of organisational methods likely to be operated in teaching pupils in the middle years, a number of teachers in a school may be employed in design-based activities. Individual teachers may possess expertise in the several facets of design education but at a variety of levels. Some may have had no previous experience. The adviser or teacher-co-ordinator of design-based studies is likely, at most times, to be working in close liaison with many members of staff. These will include those who are specialist or semi-specialist, trained in other areas of the curriculum, and possibly those who have a high degree of knowledge and expertise in a single or limited range of art/craft, technological or expressive activities.

Activity Ref. No.-	C.8.		
Activity title	Kilns		

CURRICULUM SUBJECTS				
Mathematics	/////		
English (including handwriting)	/////		
Science	/////		
Environmental studies	/////		
Home economics			
Religious education			
P.E. Movement Drama			
Music			

Fig. 5.6   Example of overview chart − core role − pupils aged 10-11 years.

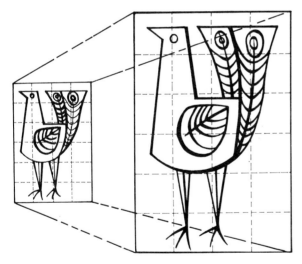

Fig. 5.7   Enlarging by squaring. The use of a grid makes accurate enlarging quite easy.

Whatever their background, staff engaged in design-based activities will benefit from positive, practical guidance to which they may refer and which will supplement the guidance offered by the teacher-co-ordinator. 'Activity cards' provide such a source of guidance. They not only give the technical information relevant to the particular activity but may include specific points of organisational value peculiar to the particular school situation. Examples of such are:

(a) a time usage plan;
(b) pupil/group organisation;
(c) materials and tools indicator.

Additionally, reference may be made to other sources of detailed information or book lists.

Teachers' Activity Cards

An example of a teachers' activity card is set out below:

Activity Card. Ref. No: AP/1

Enlarging by squaring
  Role of activity: Central
  Age suitability: 10 years and upwards.
  Activity time: 4-6 hours
  Aim: To enlarge a small picture, maintaining the same proportions by the process of sub-division and enlargement (known as 'squaring off').
  Materials: Drawing materials
        Hog hair brushes
        Powder and tempera paints
        Scissors
        White cartridge paper

Procedure
(1) Establish group(s) of size, even-numbered between six and twenty.
(2) Each pupil is given, or makes, a viewer having aperture 75 mm × 50 mm (see Fig. 5.8).

Fig. 5.8   Using a 'viewer' to help select a part of the picture.

57

(3) With viewer pupils scan magazines, newspapers, etc., to find part of picture which they visualise would be attractive when enlarged. Impose a time limit for this operation.

(4) Pool findings, discuss them, and groups select one for enlarging.

(5) Draw a grid on the selected sample (as shown in Fig. 5.9), dividing it into the number of pupils engaged in the project.

(6) Number the parts in order (as shown in Fig. 5.9).

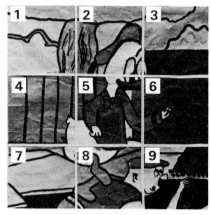

Fig. 5.9 A numbered grid superimposed on the selected part of the picture.

(7) Take same number of large pieces of paper of unit size and number on opposite side to the surface on which picture is to be made.

(8) Samples of picture and matching sheets of paper are distributed to pupils. Keep record of names and numbers to co-ordinate and control project.

(9) Pupils reproduce their picture part on to large sheet, taking care to check the lines on their drawings against adjacent units.

(10) When drawings are complete and checked for matching up, pupils paint their units. Care to be taken that colours match in hue, tone, and intensity.

(11) When all units are painted they are set up for viewing. Adjustments made where necessary.

(12) When satisfactory results are obtained, all units are combined by attaching on reverse side with adhesive tape.

The above illustrates the essential nature of the information required on an activity card, but further elaboration could be made. For example the objectives (relating to major course objectives) could be included as follows:

(1) That pupils be conversant with the technique of enlargement by the method of 'squaring off'.

(2) That pupils develop techniques of free-hand drawing working from an original picture.

(3) That pupils gain further experience in painting comparatively large areas.

(4) That pupils gain further experience of co-operating within a group.

(5) That opportunity be given for pupils to look closely and critically at contemporary illustrations.

(6) That the idea be developed of giving a subject a broad treatment and that visualisation of large-scale two-dimensional objects be improved.

During the course of the activity teachers may notice points of growth, extension and adaptation. Areas of difficulty or points conducive to success may be observed. These are of value, and in consultation with the course leader they can be noted on the activity card, further enhancing its usefulness. Possible examples of these notes with reference to the quoted activity are:

(1) Ensure correct line continuity across adjacent unit.

(2) Fast worker/abler pupil could be given two units to complete or encouraged to help slower/less able child.

(3) Insist that pupils put their names on their work. Pictures may have a high degree of similarity and pupils may not readily recognise their unit.

(4) Extension: Developing from matt and uniform treatment of subject encourage subtleties of texture, tone and colour. Textural effects may be enhanced by employing a variety of materials.

The cards are not to be treated as laying down fixed rules. Freedom is essential in the manner in which the teacher chooses to organise the activity and in the way pupils interpret it. A flexible attitude, using the card as a guide, allows scope for creative originality for teacher and pupil alike. It is also unlikely that the circumstances under which the activity is repeated will ever be identical because of the many variables involved in school situations.

Chapter 6 The Recording and Evaluation of Pupils' Performance

The keeping of records is generally regarded as a professional responsibility. Its practice with regard to art or craft in primary schools normally receives scant attention and frequently extends to little more than a note in the class teacher's record book of the activities performed and a generalised statement such as 'Good — can draw well' on a pupil's school report. This treatment is clearly inadequate if a sound design-based course is to be run in a school and pupils are to profit by it.

Record-keeping in schools basically serves two purposes:

(1) To indicate in some way the studies and activities in which pupils have been involved.
(2) To measure pupils' attainment levels against some standard or line of progress. This would include behavioural changes.

With regard to design education, record-keeping should:

(A) (1) List activities which have been performed, are being performed, or are proposed. Ideally this record should be made for individual pupil's progress, but, if necessary, it could be kept for pupil grouping up to class size.
(2) Indicate the degree to which course objectives are being realised.

(B) Provide an on-going assessment of a pupil's coursework in terms of:

(1) Improvements in levels of performance compared with the course objectives embodied in the activity.
(2) Changes in pupils' attitudes, individually or collectively, compared with course objectives relating to behavioural qualities. The method of assessment employed should be as objective as possible.

There is a close relationship between A and B, the success or otherwise of one being reflected in the other. However, teachers must accept that if pupils achieve neither the standards of work sought after nor the intellectual and emotional involvement which is looked for it may be the result of the inappropriateness or inadequacy of the studies or activities in which they are engaged.

Whatever means of recording are devised they must be sound in principle, and, if non-specialist teachers are to be expected to employ them, uncomplicated and relatively easy to apply. The teacher-co-ordinator of design studies might be expected, however, to make use of the records for a more detailed review of progress in order to programme future activities. The following devices offer practical ways of objective record keeping for (A) and (B).

6.1 Record-keeping with respect to Course Activities—Pupil Coverage of Course

The recording of pupils' accomplishments in terms of activities done throughout a programmed period is relatively straightforward. For this the 'overview' charts described in Chapter 5 (Figs. 5.2, 5.5, and 5.6) serve as a basis. A pupil may be expected to engage throughout a given sessional period (term, half year or year depending upon the time scale upon which the course is based) in some, if not all, of the central, core, and supporting-role activities programmed for the period. These activities can be listed and the pupil's coverage of them recorded by merely ticking in the appropriate box. For illustrative purposes we may again take the case of a child in the hypothetical third-year taking the course programme quoted in Chapter 5 (Fig. 5.1).

If an individual card system cannot be operated to record pupils' progress, possibly because of the time it might consume, an alternative is to replace a single pupil's name by a list of those members of a group (as shown in Fig. 6.2, where the hypothetical

PUPIL'S COURSE COVERAGE RECORD

Name:...................　　Age: 10+/11+　　Year: 111　　Session: 1975-76

Role		Pr.2.	A.6.	A.8.	C.4.	C.6.	PI.2.	P.2.	W.3.	T.2.	F.4.	F.5.	F.6.
CENTRAL ROLE	Activity Reference Number	Pr.2.	A.6.	A.8.	C.4.	C.6.	PI.2.	P.2.	W.3.	T.2.	F.4.	F.5.	F.6.
	Activity Title	Studies in Texture	2-D mural 'City at Night'	2-D picture 'Faces'	Clay: Forms from Moulds	Clay: Cylindrical Forms	Plaster: Block Sculpture	Plastics: Sheet Manipulation	Wood: Abstract 3-D forms	Threads: Decorative Weaving	Fabric. Simple dressmaking	Fabric. Fabric collage	Fabric. Batik
	Accomplishment	✓	✓	✓		✓		✓		✓			
SUPPORTING ROLE	Activity Reference Number	I.P.14.	I.P.6.	I.P.7.	I.P.9.	I.P.11.	I.P.12	I.P.24	I.P.30	I.P.2			
	Activity Title	The Clinometer	Water Turbine	Wheel and Axle	Ammeter	Anemometer and Windvane	Rain Gauge	Christmas decoration Mosaic	Design in the home	The Rainmaker Dance/Drama			
	Accomplishment	✓		✓				✓		✓			
CORE ROLE	Activity Reference Number	C.8.											
	Activity Title	Kilns											
	Accomplishment	✓											

Fig. 6.1　Individual pupil course coverage record.

PUPILS COURSE COVERAGE RECORD

GROUP: III year   AGE: 10+/11+   SESSION: 1975-76.

	Central Role												Supporting Role									Core Role
Activity Ref: No:-	A.2	A.6	A.8	C.4	C.6	Pl.2	P.2	W.3	T.2	F.4	F.5	F.6	I.P.14	I.P.6	I.P.7	I.P.9	I.P.11	I.P.12	I.P.24	I.P.30	I.P.2	C.8
ACTIVITY TITLE	Studies in Texture	2-D mural 'City at night'	2-D pictures 'Faces'	Clay: 'Forms from moulds'	Clay: Cylindrical forms	Plaster: Block sculpture	Plastics: Sheet manipulation	Wood: Abstract 3-D forms	Threads: Decorative Weaving	Fabric: Simple dress making	Fabric: Fabric collage	Fabric: Batik	The Clinometer	Water turbine	Wheel and Axle	Ammeter	Anemometer/windvane	Rain Gauge	Christmas decoration—mosaic	Design in the home	The Rainmaker Dance—Drama	Kilns
Adrian Alcock	✓		✓			✓									✓							✓
Thomas Andrews	✓			✓			✓						✓									
Christopher Burns			✓		✓									✓								
Nigel Babcock			✓					✓							✓							✓

Fig. 6.2   Group course coverage record.

year is again taken for illustration). This type of record can be centrally displayed so that pupils can record their individual accomplishments in terms of work done. An overall view of group progress is also afforded at a glance.

Analysis of these records gives the following information:

(1) It reveals just how many activities individual pupils have engaged in over the session — and indeed the course up to a given point,

(2) By inference, it shows individual strengths or weaknesses as indicated by the activities undertaken. The teaching staff are therefore in a position to note deficiencies and rectify them by remedial activities in a subsequent session.

Note that the engagement of a pupil in an activity does not necessarily imply that he completely satisfies the objectives embodied in the activity.

As previously stressed, personality and experience influence the quality of performance, and a series of treatments, perhaps involving a number of related activities of a remedial character, may be required before the pupil attains a satisfactory level. Pressure should never be exerted upon a pupil to cover the whole of a scheduled programme of activities if this is likely to result in inadequate depth of study. The pupil is likely to gain more in terms of real satisfaction and personal development through a few activities successfully accomplished than many poorly or negligently performed.

6.2   Record-keeping with respect to Course Activities—Realisation of Course Objectives

Figure 6.2 illustrates how the activities scheduled for a given period of study may be categorised and the detailed objectives stated in terms of the (previously defined) broad areas of experience. The analysis of course content can be carried further and presented in visual terms.

Theoretically the course content can be analysed on the basis of any one of the identified areas of experience and its relationship to the others. For example, the basis chosen can be what the course activities provide in the extent, degree and diversity of skills and techniques in relationship to the materials available to the pupil, and the scope given for personal expression. Or it can be the extent to which course objectives relating to the design process are accomplished through experience in personal expression or technology.

A suggested device providing such analysis may be exemplified by taking 'materials' as the basis. In a sense, materials experience can provide a practical, readily understood foundation upon which the course can be built, as materials represent something 'concrete' and easily appreciated in physical terms, whereas an abstract concept such as 'personal expression' is less tangible.

Materials are the media or vehicle through which the aims and objectives of design education can be manifest in visual terms; through materials they are realised. A list of materials provided for the design area of a school's activities may consist of wood, metal, plastics, clay, paints/inks, fabrics, threads (including string), marking materials (pens, pencils, fibre tips, pastels, chalks, etc.), paper, card and plaster. Such a list would undoubtedly differ from one school to another and could include less commonly employed materials such as natural and man-made stone, heavy fibres (rope), and film.

A major course objective may be 'To provide pupils with a broad range of experiences in as wide a variety of materials as possible', or conversely 'To provide pupils with an intensive but limited range of experiences in a restricted number of materials'. Whatever the merits of otherwise of either

	Materials awareness	Visual communication	Personal expression	Techniques, skills	Projects/ design process	Technology
WOOD	1	2	3	4	5	6
METAL	7	8	9	10	11	12
PLASTICS	13	14	15	16	17	18
CLAY	19	20	21	22	23	24
PAINTS/INKS	25	26	27	28	29	30
FABRICS	31	32	33	34	35	36
THREADS	37	38	39	40	41	42
PAPER/CARD	43	44	45	46	47	48
MARKING MATERIALS	49	50	51	52	53	54
PLASTER	55	56	57	58	59	60

Fig. 6.3 A materials experience grid.

objective, rightly or wrongly the course will be designed to achieve it. Assuming it to be the former in our hypothetical school, the course would be constructed to provide a broad but balanced range of experiences constituted under the six main areas employing some ten different materials. The course, in this case, is able to draw upon some sixty classes of experiences, which will be embodied in the activities that comprise the course. These classifications of experience may be expressed diagrammatically in the form of a 'Materials/experience grid (see Fig. 6.3) where the materials available in the school and the six main areas of experience form the vertical and horizontal axes respectively.

The digits shown on the grid (1, 2, 3, 4) do not indicate or imply any order of priority either of importance or sequence; they are merely characters denoting the specific classes of experience. For example at 19 are those relating to the properties and behaviour of clay, at 55 the corresponding aspects for plaster and at 31 those for fabrics, while 4 denotes those experiences relating to the techniques and skills associated with wood and 16 those for plastics.

A particular craft activity may involve using wood and no other materials. As has been noted (p. 54), each activity involves at least one element of experience under the six main areas defined. Nevertheless certain specific experiences, for example the techniques and skills associated with handling wood, in a particular activity, may be prominent. It may constitute the main reason for the inclusion of the activity in the programme. With wood, therefore, the pupil may be receiving some, or perhaps all the classes of experiences 1-6. Another activity may feature the exclusive use of plaster, in which case experiences range between 55 and 60 inclusive.

Exactly which experiences are offered by the activity depends essentially upon its nature and content. The making of a thumb pot can be taken as a very simple example. A child doing this learns something of the properties and behaviour of clay, e.g., it cracks if it gets too dry whilst one is working it, it can be easily shaped and so on. These experiences and the knowledge gained through them can be recorded as coming within the compass of classification 19 on the grid, i.e., materials awareness of clay. The child might desire a big, decorated pot, or a small thin-walled undecorated one, or any other product of his choice and/or imagination (Fig. 6.4). To achieve the peculiar

Fig. 6.4 Materials experience can be provided in a wide variety of forms.

Fig. 6.5 The visual aspect of problem-solving is of great importance. This pupil uses resource material to help her to decide on the shape of a proposed pot.

form of the thumb-pot he must have learnt the techniques of shaping it in the hands. This could be recorded as classification 22 on the grid as techniques and skills associated with clay. The element of design-problem-solving in this activity can, if the teacher wishes, be reduced to a minimum, but nevertheless it is always present to some degree. Finished form and decoration may evolve during the construction of the pot, obviating any real necessity for visual communication in the form of drawings. On the other hand this experience could be incorporated as part of the project, i.e., 'What do I want my pot to look like' (Fig. 6.5). The design-problem-solving aspect could form an assignment, for example, in which the pupil chooses to design and construct some utilitarian or decorative structure with the thumb-pot as its basic unit.

With reference to the Materials/experience grid,

the making of a thumb-pot can therefore be analysed as containing the following classes of experiences:

materials awareness   19
personal expression   21
techniques/skills   22

with possible extensions including 20, visual communication, and 23, Design Process.

Activities vary in their complexity and sophistication and may involve the use of two or more materials. For instance, the construction of a marionette can be resolved into several parts.

Fig. 6.6 The production of measured working drawings calls for a number of related skills and in this case for a knowledge of human dimensions too.

(1) Drafting ideas which might involve sketching/ technical drawing and employ the use of picture-making materials (pencils, fibre tips, crayons), paints, and papers (Fig. 6.6). This operation would involve experience in materials, visual communication, personal expression, skills and techniques, but the project itself would be essentially of a design-problem-solving nature. An analysis might be as follows: (again refering to the Materials/experience grid)

Paper   43
Marking materials   49-52
Paints   25-28

(2) Forming/shaping wooden blocks. Pupils may tackle this task directly, and this would involve classes of experiences 1-4 and possibly 5. They may however need to develop a deeper tactile/intellectual understanding of the particular three-dimensional form which they may be

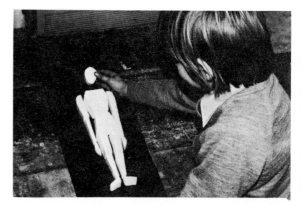

Fig. 6.7 Making 'mock-ups' aids three-dimensional perception. Here expanded polystyrene (polyphenylethene) provides a ready media for such activity.

able to perceive but not readily create. This developmental experience could be supplied by making mock-ups in expanded polystyrene (polyphenylethene) and therefore the project analysis could include experiences 13-17 (Fig. 6.7).

(3) In making, painting and decorating the papier-mâché head, class of experiences 43, 44 (the head having been drawn), 45-47 could be included. These could be extended to 37-40 if threads were to be employed for hair, beard, etc.

(4) Dress and costume. This would include experiences 31-35, the sketch/picture and pattern of the dress having been drawn as well.

The grid and its numerals is therefore shown to be the vehicle for recording those particular classes of experiences inherent in any such design-based activity. They can be employed to extend a materials-based analysis of the programme even further. To do this might be beyond the interest or concern of the ordinary class teacher involved in design studies and activities but it should be of concern to the specialist or semi-specialist teachers engaged in this field. One of the ways in which this analysis may be developed might be to present it visually on a linear strip, one for each activity, and graduated in divisions to the total number of experiences which the school is able to provide (see Fig. 6.8).

Spaces on the strip are blanked off to correspond to the digits signifying the specific experiences involved in a particular activity. Referring to the example of the clay thumb-pot, we have seen from the analysis that it involves classes of experiences 19, 21, 22, with scope for extensions in classes 20 and 23. Classes 19, 21, 22 can be indicated on the strip by solid black, and 20 and 23 by cross-hatching, with the result shown in Fig. 6.9.

The strip for a more complex activity, e.g., the marionette, would be as shown in Fig. 6.10 (taking the data from the analysis that has been made above).

It must be emphasised that not all design activities are necessarily materials based; indeed there may be activities where constructional materials are not directly involved. An activity, for example, 'Looking at pictures by artists' or 'The viewing of buildings, or articles', may fulfil specific objectives through observing, discussing or note taking. If such activities are included in a programme, they cannot therefore be realistically submitted to a materials-based analysis (although

they may perhaps be covered by an analysis based in one or other of the other five areas). Cognisance would of course be taken of the presence and influence of these activities within the programme.

The extent and nature of the experiences contained within any materials- or design-based activity or project, be it thumb-pot, marionette or whatever, can be readily observed if the significance of the numbers be known. A possible aid to this recognition is to group the specific materials or areas of experience under headings, possibly accompanied by a colour coding reference key (as shown in Fig. 6.11).

By placing together the analysis of activities selected from the course programme the range of experiences offered to pupils becomes visually apparent. Although only a thumb-pot and marionettes have been included for the purpose of illustration (Fig. 6.13) actual charts could be

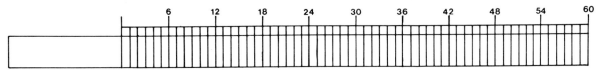

Fig. 6.8   A calibrated activity analysis strip chart.

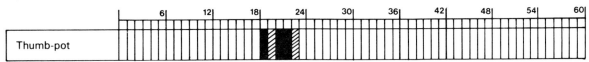

Fig. 6.9   A linear analysis chart for a thumb pot.

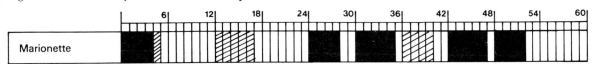

Fig. 6.10   A linear analysis chart for a marionette.

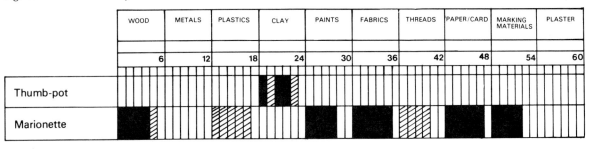

Key:- ■ — Specific experiences involved in the activity
       ▨ — Scope for extension in these experiences

Fig. 6.11   A combined linear analysis chart with materials key.

65

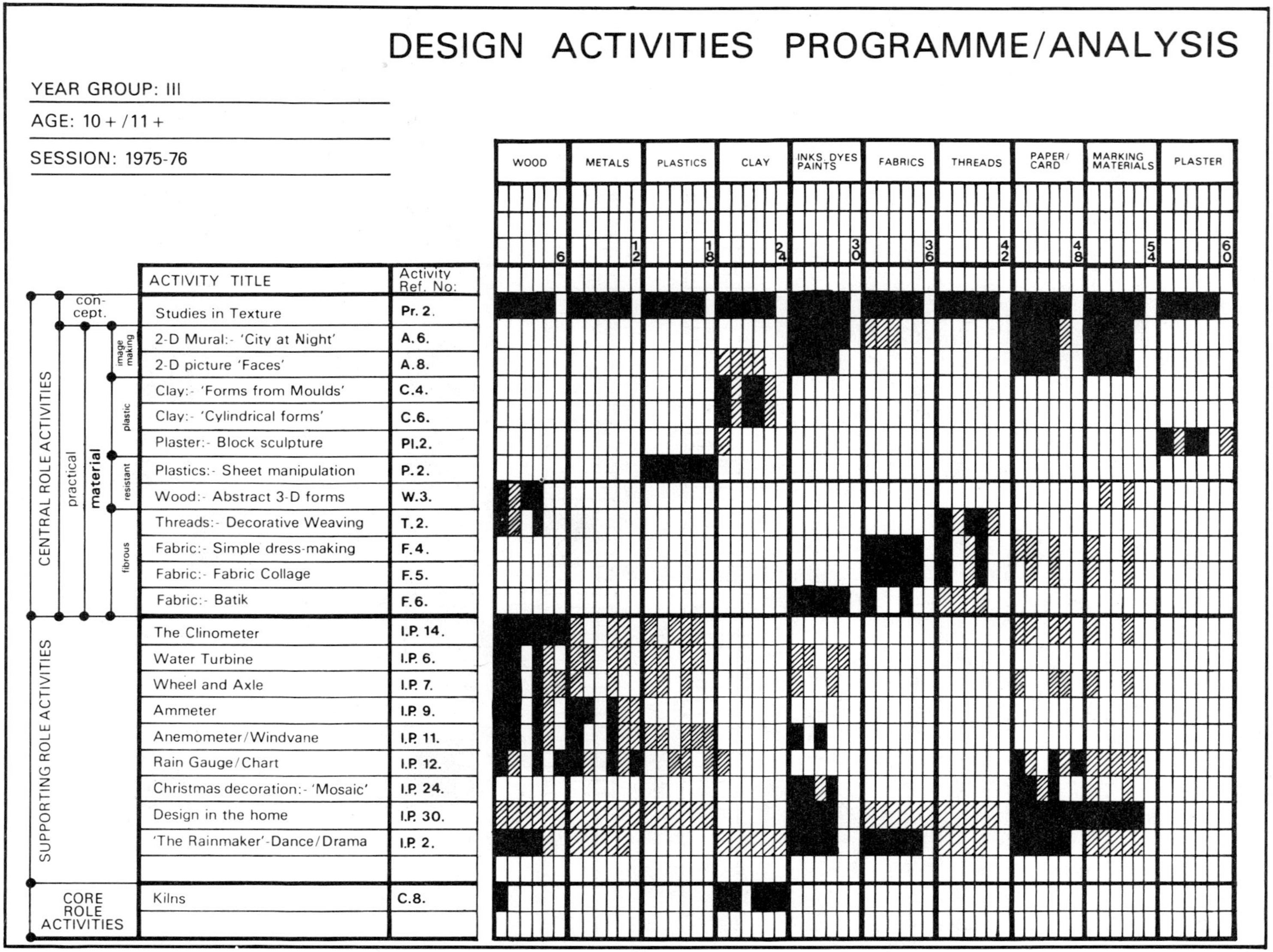

Fig. 6.12 A design activities chart.

extended to an indefinite number of activities.

Figure 6.12 illustrates the use of this device for analysis as applied to the hypothetical case considered in the previous chapter (a third-year group of pupils in an 8-12 years middle school).

6.3 Record-keeping with respect to Pupils' Performance

The field of design education is notorious for the dissent and diversity of opinion which is aroused concerning the criteria against which standards are measured. Whilst most teachers engaged in late primary and secondary education accept that testing and examination form an essential part of the educational programme, many consider as unnecessary the testing or evaluation of pupils' abilities in design-based studies in the middle years.

Two possible reasons for the adoption of this attitude are:

(1) That designed-based studies do not call for evaluation in anything other than the most general terms because of their assumed unimportance relative to the so-called 'academic' studies.

(2) That progress and performance in design-based studies cannot be evaluated in any except the most subjective terms and that to attempt to introduce any real measure of objectivity into such assessment is simply not possible.

The authors accept the validity of neither of these opinions.

The use of progress records greatly assists in the monitoring of a pupil's progress throughout a course of design-based studies. It is straightforward merely to note that he has carried out the activities of the programme, as previously described on pp. 59-60, but a realistic assessment of the qualitative aspects of pupil performance is a much more complex task. Before looking at or considering the possibility of producing any scheme of assessment of a pupil's performance in design-based activities, it is useful firstly to clarify what we mean by the term 'assessment', and then to decide upon the particular use which is to be made of it.

An assessment is an estimate or evaluation of some 'thing'. The 'thing' may take many forms — an atttitude, some work done, an application, etc. — or more particularly, it may be the change in any of these as a result of undertaking a course of study or activity. The type of assessment required here is not a continuous examination or test, consisting of a set of problems geared to a syllabus which is to be examined, nor does it consist of 'sampling' of a syllabus, as in a traditional examination. Traditional examinations try to do one or both of two things:

(1) To note whether candidates reach a predetermined standard based upon the learning which is supposed to have taken place, and

(2) grade candidates in rank order, the standard by which each is judged being fairly heavily dependent upon the personal (and therefore often subjective), experience-based attitudes of the examiner.

The following points are *not* really important in any form of evaluation of performance in design-based work during the middle years of schooling:

(1) the amount of factual knowledge he can communicate in a given period of time (even supposing that this were possible in this area of studies/activities);

(2) that pupils be measured against a set standard upon which learning is supposed to have taken place or skills acquired;

(3) that the pupil be set in rank order against others inside or outside the school or group.

Essentially three things *are* required from an assessment of pupil's performance in design-based studies:

(1) that his progress should be measured in some way against his own previous performance;

(2) his performances be compared and measured against looked-for improvements in the context of tangible course objectives;

(3) looked-for changes in attitude as a result of participation in course activities be evaluated.

Having established this, facets of performances must be listed which assess:

(1) tangible results, i.e., results obtained in terms of hardware produced or achievements attained;

(2) intangible factors of changes in attitudes, personal development, effort and so on.

With regard to a design-based course, these factors are embodied in the course objectives (the drawing up and defining of which has been described in Chapter 5). They provide a context for

67

and criteria upon which a scheme of assessment can be based. In summary, assessment should be an evaluation of the pupil's total response to the content of the course, and the content of the course is largely determined by objectives. Thus a relationship between pupil response and course objectives becomes the foundation of a scheme of assessment.

We have seen how the main areas of activity and experience, described in Chapter 4 (p. 37) provides the vehicle for tangible course objectives (see Fig. 5.2). They can also be employed as the basis upon which to develop a scheme of recording and analysis. Further, they can be used as a basis upon which a system of pupil assessment can be built.

Firstly, each main aspect or area of experience must be resolved into constituent parts, making a generalised statement of the purposes of the experiences in terms of what it is desired that the pupils learn. As an example, with regard to 'materials' the following detailed desired objectives might be envisaged: that pupils at the end of the course should:

(1) possess an elementary knowledge of the properties of materials in general and of the specific properties of common materials in particular;
(2) possess a vocabulary relating to materials;
(3) be able to assess the suitability of materials for function in simple design situations.

Other areas could likewise be resolved into constituent objectives for the pupil such as:

Visual Communication
(1) To possess a rudimentary knowledge of some of the techniques of visual communication, e.g., signs, cyphers, use of colour, shape, form and line.
(2) To be able to select the appropriate method of visual communication for a specific situation.
(3) To be able to interpret using various techniques of visual communication.

Personal Expression
(1) To try to develop powers of imagination.
(2) To perceive an expressive potential in materials, objects, forms, two-dimensional shapes.
(3) To possess an interpretative ability. To communicate personal internalised images, thoughts and feelings through design experience.

Techniques and Skills
Realisation of objectives is achieved through the combined interaction of materials, tools and techniques (see Fig. 6.13).

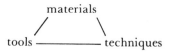

Fig. 6.13 The interaction of materials, tools and techniques.

Objectives might be:
(1) to possess a knowledge of tools with regard to the operations they can perform and the materials on which they can be employed;
(2) in working materials to know what techniques and treatments to apply to realise objectives;
(3) to perform techniques to acceptable standards of skill.

Design-Problem-solving Project Work
(1) To be able to identify a problem through investigation and analysis of factors involved.
(2) To conceive possible lines of approach.
(3) To logically select a chosen solution.
(4) To realise the solution in concrete form or express a solution as a developed strategy produced or proposed.
(5) To evaluate the solution.

Technology
(1) To develop an appreciation of man's dependence on scientific laws through involvement in experimental approaches.
(2) To be able to utilise scientific laws and phenomena in solving design problems.
(3) To develop an awareness of the uses, abuses and hazards of technology and its effect upon the environment, finite natural resources, human beings as individuals and society at large.

As pupils proceed through the course they will, it is hoped, work progressively towards overall course objectives by attaining those objectives embodied in the activities. The level of achievement aimed for by the pupil and provided for by the activity should be consistently high. Pupils' confidence must be boosted by success, stimulated by challenge and built up by effort. But performances vary enormously and in making an assessment the teacher will require a ready 'tool' in the form of a scale of achievement designed to measure relative performance by defining specific levels in each broad area of experience. Such levels may or may not be attained, depending on how pupils respond to work in that area.

Levels of performance are nothing new in rating pupils' achievements but traditionally they span from vague, single-word statements such as 'excellent' or 'poor', with 'average' as a mean. These judgements are not only open to arbitrary interpretation by teachers and amongst staff where differences in personal values and professional attitudes may exist, but they lack any specific definition of performance levels to which reference can be made.

Taking a five-point scale it is suggested that each broad area experience contained within an activity may provide five levels of achievement. For example in visual communication the levels could be defined thus:

(5) Has a wide knowledge and a good command of techniques. Is able to select appropriately and communicate effectively.

(4) Fairly broad knowledge of communication techniques and ability to use them in a wide range of situations. Imaginative approach with some aptitude in communicating.

(3) Working knowledge of techniques. Competent in use of techniques but needs guidance in some areas.

(2) Limited knowledge of techniques. Does not respond well to guidance. Conceptual and interpretative difficulties.

(1) Minimal and fragmentary knowledge of techniques. Work disorganised and lacking in conceptual ability. Continually resorting to guidance.

The following, in rank order, may be defined as levels of achievement for design-problem-solving in its entirety:

(5) Ability to identify a problem competently and produce a design brief. Accomplishment in techniques of research and investigation. Ability to suggest imaginative and carefully reasoned probable solutions. Ability logically to consider alternatives, and to select from them. Imaginative and appropriate choice of materials. Sound production techniques. Imaginative evaluation of solution.

(4) Ability to identify a problem and produce a brief. Ability to suggest several carefully reasoned lines of solution without prompting. Careful consideration of alternative solutions. Thoughtful selection of materials and approach to production. Careful production techniques. Sound, logical approach to evaluation.

(3) Ability to identify a problem fairly well and prepare a reasonable brief in which some guidance has been given. Reasonable solutions offered with minimal guidance. Guidance also required to arrive at a solution. Satisfactory selection of materials and basically sound production techniques but sequence of operations not clear. Well-reasoned evaluation but with difficulty in sustaining some points.

(2) Difficulty in identifying a problem and producing an adequate brief. Limited and derived solutions offered after prompting. Considerable guidance required in making a choice of solution. Needs guidance in selection of materials and production ideas; methods and techniques are adequate. Difficulty in verbally expressing a reasoned evaluation though somewhat better expressed in writing.

(1) Considerable difficulty in identifying the real nature of a problem, and producing a design brief. Very limited, mainly derived, solutions offered after considerable prompting. Haphazard choice of solutions unsupported by any substantiation. Inappropriate and arbitrary use of materials with impracticable and inadequate production. Confused evaluation.

The other main areas of experience could be similarly treated.

Obviously the terms in which the levels of achievement are defined depend to a considerable degree upon that which may be reasonably expected from mixed ability pupils in a given year age group. Pupil performance is also susceptible to influences both on the individual pupil and of a more general nature, as we have noted. A rapid turnover of staff may affect the scope of teacher expertise available to the course and therefore influence what can be accomplished by individual pupils, and the course itself, through the stated objectives and programme of activities, would need to be modified to accommodate changes in circumstances.

A course-work marking grid can be employed on which to record individual pupil performance levels for a given period. The hypothetical case employed to illustrate a pupil's course coverage record across a third-year programme (see Fig. 6.1) can be employed again to illustrate the same child's achievement record for the same period (see Fig. 6.14).

PUPIL ACHIEVEMENT RECORD

NAME: .... AGE: 10+ / 11+   YEAR: III   SESSION: 1975-76

Skill \ Activity	Studies in Texture (A.2.)	2-D Mural: 'City at Night' (A.6.)	2-D picture 'Faces' (A.8.)	Clay: 'Forms from Moulds' (C.4.)	Clay: Cylindrical forms (C.6.)	Plaster: Block sculpture (Pl.2.)	Plastics: Sheet manipulation (P.2.)	Wood: Abstract 3-D forms (W.3.)	Threads: Decorative weaving (T.2.)	Fabric:- Simple dress-making (F.4.)	Fabric:- Fabric Collage (F.5.)	Fabric:- Batik (F.6.)	The Clinometer (I.P.14.)	Water Turbine (I.P.6.)	Wheel and Axle (I.P.7.)	Ammeter (I.P.9.)	Anemometer/Windvane (I.P.11.)	Rain Gauge/Chart (I.P.12.)	Christmas decoration: Mosaic (I.P.24.)	'Design in the home' (I.P.30.)	'The Rainmaker' Dance/Drama (I.P.2.)	Kilns (C.8.)	Average Level (max. av. level)
MATERIALS	4	4	4	3	2		3						3	3					4	4		3	3·3 / 5
VISUAL COMMUNICATION	3	3	4	3	3		3						3	3						4		3	3·2 / 5
PERSONAL EXPRESSION	4	3	4	4	3		4													4			3·7 / 5
TECHNIQUES/ SKILLS	3	3	3	3	2		3						2	2					3	3		3	2·6 / 5
DESIGN PROCESS	3			4			4						3	3						4		4	3·5 / 5
TECHNOLOGY		3			2								3	2								3	2·4 / 5

GENERAL REMARKS	TOTAL AVERAGE PERFORMANCE	18·7

Fig. 6.14 A pupil achievement record chart.

Analysis of the card (Fig. 6.14) suggests that the pupil, Julie Francis, has made a slightly above average general level of achievement in the year as represented by a total average figure of 18.7 out of a possible maximum of 30. Her strengths appear to be in the personal expressive and visually communicative aspects of the course. Clarity and imagination of thought are indicated as being of a reasonably high level but weaknesses tend to lie in the manipulative aspects of the work and the technological aspects of design studies. The information conveyed by the card could then be employed to help decide the emphasis or direction that future studies might take.

As a pupil progresses through the course his collection of achievement record cards will grow to present a clear picture of his overall and specific progress. A personal record may be elaborated by extending to pupils themselves the opportunity of recording their own progress in qualitative terms. It is unlikely that they will be able to do this unless they have been encouraged to criticise and assess their own performance, but this facility can be gradually developed as they gain experience in design problem-solving (see Chapter 2). This, as has been indicated, can be introduced in the early middle years of schooling. Results have demonstrated that children can be uncannily accurate and honest about themselves.

The keeping of a progress folder might be encouraged in which pupils would enter their personal and representative selection of two-dimensional work along with details of two- and three-dimensional work. Although an expensive activity, requiring some degree of skill to produce reasonable results, pupils are well able to photograph their own work during the later middle years. Pictures and/or details can accompany a report/evaluation compiled mutually by themselves and their teachers. This encourages pupils to take a greater interest in their developing abilities, draws them towards a closer identification with their own work, and creates a mutual respect between them and their teachers.

Chapter 7   Resources for Design Education

Whatever the stated objectives of a course, they are inevitably constrained to some degree by the availability of suitable staff, appropriate facilities, and time.

7.1   Teaching Staff

Whether interdisciplinary facets of design-based courses succeed or fail depends largely, in the long term, on how willing teachers are to:

(1) work together. Teachers by tradition are individualists, and until recently the working group has usually been one teacher with one class. Whilst such an arrangement still provides for many activities, as inter-disciplinary courses develop, it becomes more effective for teachers to work together in small teams;

(2) accept a role other than that of leader. Depending on circumstances team leadership may change. This is primarily due to calls for expertise in various areas of the creative field. Sometimes, especially in secondary schools, the artist leads; at other times the craft-trained teacher and at others perhaps the science- or history-trained colleague, or even the form teacher who has a particular interest or ability;

(3) work outside existing personal training and experience. No matter how widey trained or experienced a teacher is, on occasions he may be asked a question he cannot answer, or may have to work or guide his pupils in an area of study where he himself is equally 'in the dark'. There are many teachers who would refuse such a challenge on the grounds that either:

  (a) they do not feel competent and are therefore diffident,
  (b) they 'must' know more than their pupils, or
  (c) they are not prepared to admit to a class

that they do not know the answer, and so on.

Provided there is a good staff-pupil relationship where each respects the other and where pupils in general have confidence in their teacher, the teacher may frankly admit to lack of knowledge or expertise and suggest a joint 'finding-out'. This does not bring about loss of respect but helps the child to appreciate the teacher's role as guide and fellow student, rather than as an all-knowing demagogue. As stated elsewhere, however, the teacher never uses or allows pupils to use potentially dangerous equipment, materials or techniques unless he is thoroughly versed in their use and application (see Chapter 12);

(4) accept an apparent 'cut-back' in specific subject time. Traditionally separately taught subjects, especially in a secondary school regime, have been allocated a fixed share of the timetable and many fruitless staffroom squabbles have broken out over poached subject time. Providing that the overall time allocated to individual subjects is not reduced and their work is more closely linked, teachers must accept a less rigid division of time allocated to their particular areas of study within the discipline. This is one of the penalties for joining this 'educational common market'.

7.2   Provision and Organisation of Facilities

The ability to organise and use facilities, work space and equipment effectively in the time available is a technique most teachers would claim to possess; in fact many are not sufficiently objective in this area of decision making.

A clear statement of what workspace and facilities are required needs to be compared with what is available to ensure that the two match. In addition to the requirements dictated by course objectives, the overall teaching methodology to be used will also have a bearing on facility requirements over and above the general needs of any such course or activity. Whatever the teacher may consider necessary, in the final analysis it is that which is available to him which will have to be utilised as best he can.

But what facilities, work space, equipment and tools *are* required to make it physically possible to run a successful design-based course? Almost invariably the teacher would prefer more extensive facilities and workspace than the LEA can provide, but this obvious truism apart, it must be appreciated that facilities and so on can only be considered 'appropriate' or not when related to the age range, type and size of school and to its internal organisational pattern.

There will be sophisticated art and craft equipment in a secondary school which could not be justified in a middle school, particularly if it were designed for 8-12-year-olds. In fact when providing purpose-built accommodation in middle schools it would be a considerable error of judgement to put in too much by way of specialised facilities and equipment. The middle years should be concerned with exploring possibilities, not with using — and often misusing or under-using — machinery and equipment which could be more usefully placed at the disposal of older, more experienced pupils.

Bearing in mind the philosophical and organisational factors discussed elsewhere a number of rational starting points exist from which to project basic requirements. The following are some of the alternatives.

Alternative A
Where the development of a close relationship between art/craft work and science-based studies is felt to be an over-riding need, then specialist accommodation should be provided, allowing for free movement between science and design areas. A possible juxtaposition of these two disciplinary areas is indicated in Fig. 7.1

Some combined design/science rooms are presently being developed in 8-12-year middle schools. Such a semi-open plan approach allows for free interchange between areas and is particularly appropriate for use by the form teacher and specialist trained teacher working together as a team.

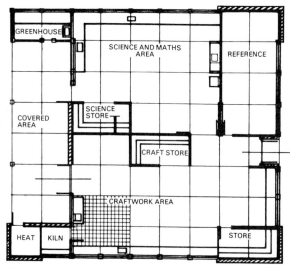

Fig. 7.1 Plan of a Warwickshire Middle School craft/science conversion unit. Courtesy of Warwickshire County Council.

Providing that the timetabling commitment of these facilities is not overloaded, such an arrangement makes it possible to utilise to the full the additional workspace and facilities to be gained by using both areas jointly.

Alternative B
Many 8-12-year middle schools and primary schools (with whose upper age range we are concerned) are provided with art/craft facilities in converted classrooms. While obviously interdisciplinary work is made geographically that much more difficult, the major constraint usually associated with such conversions is that of inadequate space, both for working and storage. Because of the structure and possible physical limitations in such accommodation, the safe but useful positioning of equipment such as a kiln, with associated non-flammable flooring, occasionally presents problems.

Alternative C
In large middle schools, where the whole school has been purpose built, the curricular relationship of design to other areas of the school's educational programme can be reflected in its physical disposition in relation to other special subject rooms and classroom accommodation (as in Fig. 7.2).

Not only will there be specialist workshop/studio accommodation but also a small reference and study area close at hand. Additional to the main

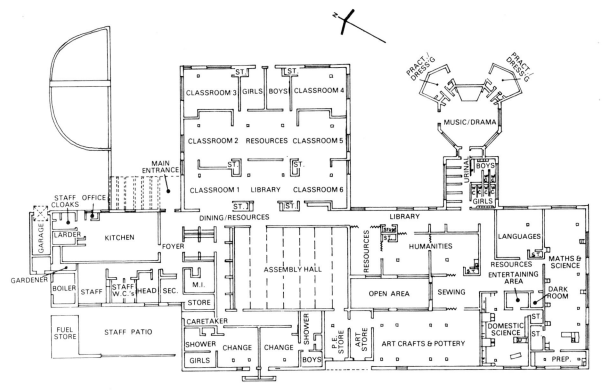

Fig. 7.2 Plan of a middle school showing the physical relationship of craft/design facilities with those of other disciplines and teaching bases. Courtesy of Isle of Wight County Council.

art/craft facilities, if the school is built around year groups then there may also be 'practical areas' specifically associated with each year block (e.g., four classrooms plus practical area for each year of a four-form entry middle school). This practical area could be a covered central area linking the classrooms and would be available not only for 'messy' or large-scale physically creative work, but also for drama and other indoor activities calling primarily for an open space in which they may function.

Alternative D

In some middle schools designed for 9-13 or 10-14-year-olds, as in most secondary schools, more specialised art/craft facilities are likely to be found. In addition to the 'general purpose' studio, individual or interconnected rooms will be provided for work predominantly in wood, two-dimensional work, metal, clay, plastics, fabrics and food. Yet

again there may be fewer but larger rooms each providing a number of semi-specialised 'bays' or work areas. Such a provision certainly promotes the possibilities for an extensive design-based course, but even so, should not be allowed to dictate the direction in which the curriculum is developed. Facilities must always serve the child's educational needs and not in any way be its master.

7.3   General Working Conditions and Facilities

Classroom-based three-dimensional work is inevitably limited in scope through lack of facilities — a wet 'messy' work area is difficult to cater for in a form room, as is the provision of benching for heavy work and sufficient storage space. Nevertheless whether in a form room or general classroom provided with worktables and a sink, a great deal of useful work is possible with both 8- or 14-year-olds, as all experienced primary school teachers know.

The provision of simple removable framed

hardboard table tops or desk top covers preserves furniture whilst allowing greater freedom of activity without undue reluctance on the teacher's part to permit the use of simple cutting tools, knives, portable vices and so on.

In this chapter, however, consideration of the facilities of a design-activities studio is of over-riding importance. An exhaustive list of tools, etc., is not suggested, as detailed requirements (as stated elsewhere) will depend on detailed course content and on the age and ability range of the pupils using the facilities.

In the economic climate of the present and immediate future, allowances of floor area and individual workspace are likely to fall considerably short of what many teachers would consider ideal, and for this reason multi-purpose studios must always be equipped in a flexible manner, so that equipment thought necessary for one type of activity does not inhibit another.

Fixed (wall) benching is usually fairly substantial in construction but should be topped with a variety of working surfaces, including stainless steel (for work involving direct heating), heavy linoleum and laminated plastics, in addition to the traditional but nowadays very expensive hardwood. The provision not only of standard cupboarding but also moulded plastics work, storage and tool containers which are easy to carry, quiet to use and hard-wearing, has much to commend it. Metalworking vices or similar heavy-duty equipment can be fitted to these wall benches, thus leaving the tops of the portable work benches clear of obstruction.

Heavy dual purpose wood or metal benches of traditional design are usually inappropriate for this age range, for they are simply far too heavy for

Fig. 7.3 Multi-purpose benches offer flexibility in workshop arrangement. Photograph Courtesy of Lervad Co.

pupils or female staff to move when additional floorspace is required. Lighter but still rigid multi-purpose benches fitted with woodworker type vices, possibly based on the well-known Danish system, are generally preferable. If working height is not adjustable, then portable benches of differing height should be provided to cover the very wide range of pupil heights in the middle years of schooling. Additional light benching can be assembled from slotted metal angle or square tube. Such benches have the advantage of being easy to dismantle when occasionally a large clear floor space is required.

Guidance on the provision of appropriate flooring surfaces is provided in DES Literature, notably those concerning school building and safety.

Non-slip flooring is essential, and even with this great care is called for when wood dust and shavings are about as these can induce slipping.

Claywork by its nature calls for a specific 'wet' area and should be away from work with traditional tools and all electrically powered equipment. This should, wherever possible, be standardised at 110 volts. (See BS 4163 (1975), *Health and Safety in Workshops of Schools and Colleges*, and appropriate DES literature such as that concerned with safety in the schools.)

Whilst claywork without the use of a kiln is very limited in scope, potters' wheels are needed only for older pupils. Kilns, enamelling furnaces or, for older pupils, brazing hearths should be sited away from passage areas in workshops or studios and should be fenced or guarded to prevent pupils falling against them. Such fences, where gated, should be constructed so that whilst effective in use they are easy to open and close. If not, there is a tendency, human nature being what it is, to leave them permanently open.

The provision of an electrically powered bench drill is suspect in some quarters on the grounds of potential danger. However, as most children now have access to portable power tools and appliances at home, it may be that some instruction under *very close supervision* in the safe use of a powered drill is appropriate and indeed necessary for the older pupils in this age range. Keyed switching is, of course, essential in any such electrical installation.

A domestic electric cooker has a versatility far beyond that of cooking simple sponge cakes and boiling potatoes. In addition to its use in the manipulation of thermoplastic sheet and so on it can be used to teach a good deal of truly domestic science, electricity, heat, insulation, materials and so on.

Specific pieces of equipment in the middle school studio or workshop should, in general, be introduced only if they can be shown to be versatile and flexible in application, as there is a tendency for the equipment of a workshop to dictate the type of work carried on in it merely because it is there.

It is of the greatest importance that powered equipment should, wherever possible, be appropriately guarded and positioned so as to be away from circulation areas.

In workshops or studios where heating of materials takes place (such as with ceramics, metals and plastics, etc.), a 'hot' area should be marked out where materials being cooled in air can be placed safely out of the way of other pupils.

Hand tools in wide variety find a place in the design studio. One of the major problems associated with them is that of storage so that they are easily accessible. Purpose-built trolleys built from slotted angle and plywood, etc., can provide suitable storage yet can be wheeled out of the way when not required.

Storage, not only of tools but of materials, general supplies and work in progress, as well as finished work, can provide a headache, for however much storage room is provided by the authority it never seems to be quite adequate. Particular attention is drawn to the need for the provision of storage facilities suitable for flammable materials (paints, solvents, catalysts used for polyester resin work, etc.). In this and all other matters teachers' attention should be drawn to the recommendations

Fig. 7.4 A resource/reference area, however limited in size, provides useful back up facilities for design-based work.

of BS 4163, which should be followed explicitly. Regular maintenance of tools and equipment is called for and in certain cases this is accepted as an LEA responsibility rather than the teacher's personal one.

A particular requirement, too often overlooked, is the provision adjacent to the studio of a quiet reference study area. This facility can be a major physical bridge between the practical work of the studios or workshops and other disciplines of a more academic nature.

7.4 Time

Timetabling can be critical, particularly when projects of a practical nature are involved. In secondary schools, short periods are traditionally allocated for individual subjects, but increasingly head teachers are bringing in block timetabling, usually across years or parts of them.

Middle schools, based on the primary system, tend to be more flexible in their approach to time-tabling. Here it is possible to use the form teacher in an assistant capacity, when classes are in specialist accommodation, craft or science rooms or areas. At the lower end of the age range it is likely in any case that much art/craft and science work will be carried out in the form room with consequent limitations. Nevertheless, teachers with specialist training should influence such work indirectly through the preparation of complete schemes of work covering the whole school period in collaboration with class and other teachers who will be involved with their implementation. In this way overall planning and continuity of pupil progress may be ensured. In practice the planning of creative activities has frequently been left entirely to the choice of the non-specialist form teacher alone. This has often resulted in disjointed and inconsequential courses lacking in overall philosophy and cohesion.

Referring back to what has already been detailed under course objective headings, when grouped together it is reasonable to suggest that four major aspects of any design-based course can be delineated:

(1) The design process, where an increasing proportion of the decisions will be taken by the maturing pupil with an awareness of the implications of the relationships between design and the environment.

(2) A basic knowledge of materials, both functional and aesthetic, which will enable the pupil to appreciate and correctly apply materials to the solution of design problems.

(3) The ability to manipulate a variety of materials at appropriate levels of difficulty and technological complexity to produce artifacts or satisfy design criteria and to evaluate the solutions so produced.

(4) Visual awareness providing for self expression, and communication which links (1)-(3) together and further stresses the social implications of design.

Given these four components then the teacher's effort should be bent towards an on-going balance between them throughout the course. Priorities will vary from session to session, from week to week, but if the pupil is to appreciate the relationships which are implicit in the study as a whole, then some sort of balance between the 'bankers' must be provided and maintained.

In middle schools, based upon the primary approach where timetabling is inherently flexible, the problem is relatively straightforward and the teacher or teachers concerned allocate time as they feel appropriate.

Given the more rigid secondary regime, where timetabling is much more fragmented and specific, the following suggestions are put forward for consideration. As with all 'Aunt Sally' suggestions, it is possible to throw administrative and theoretical 'bricks' at the model, but in doing so it is hoped that the thrower will, by implication and involvement, become increasingly aware of the problems and their possible solutions.

Model Unit Timetable based on Block Timetabling (in a secondary school)

This involves simultaneously timetabling two or more teaching groups from the same year with two or more teachers covering the disciplines involved.

Any individual timetable is dependent on the resources and constraints associated with a particular school. For illustrative purposes, however, realistic assumptions have been made as follows:

(1) Two blocks of two teaching periods are available each week. This gives a total of eight teaching periods within a fortnightly cycle. This is the minimum provision and many schools provide twice as much time.

(2) Each teaching group will study
  (a) Design. One period.
  (b) Visual awareness and communication. Two periods (one double period).
  (c) Materials. Two periods (one double period).
  (d) Design realisation. Three periods (one double, one single).

(3) There will be at least one teacher per group. Design and visual communication are taught by an art trained teacher, design realisation is taught by a craft trained teacher and materials can be taught by either an art or a craft trained teacher. The time allocated to each aspect of the course can be adjusted to suit on-going requirements.

A possible cycle for the two groups is illustrated in Fig. 7.5. This yields a timetable for each teacher on a weekly basis as shown in Fig. 7.6.

This teaching cycle suggests the following advantages:

(1) Flexibility. Each pair of teaching groups and associated teachers is independent of other teaching groups. This allows a teacher to be moved from one pair of teaching groups to another. In a secondary school this is of considerable value.

This means that specialist trained craft teachers can, if necessary, be circulated round a number of groups over a period of time without upsetting the remainder of the on-going work. 'Craft' teacher in this context includes teachers of home economics.

(2) The minimum number of teachers supervise each group of pupils. This tends towards stability through continuity of contact.

Within the basic half-cycle (one week consisting of two double periods), a certain amount of variation is possible to allow for possible restrictions of work space and facilities.

This arrangement displays (a) Only one group is using the facilities for design, materials and visual communication at any one time, (b) subject specialists can be spread across more than two groups. As the number of groups increases, so does the flexibility, but the timetable is still based on two half-cycles, which themselves are not rigid.

The foregoing worked example shows only one way in which logic can be applied to the inherently

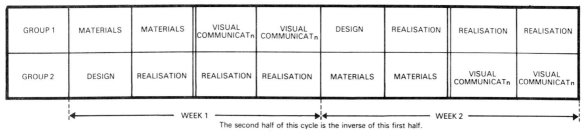

| GROUP 1 | MATERIALS | MATERIALS | VISUAL COMMUNICATn | VISUAL COMMUNICATn | DESIGN | REALISATION | REALISATION | REALISATION |
| GROUP 2 | DESIGN | REALISATION | REALISATION | REALISATION | MATERIALS | MATERIALS | VISUAL COMMUNICATn | VISUAL COMMUNICATn |

|◄──────────────── WEEK 1 ────────────────►|◄──────────── WEEK 2 ────────────►|

The second half of this cycle is the inverse of this first half.

Fig. 7.5 A timetable chart for two parallel teaching groups.

'ART' TEACHER	DESIGN	MATERIALS	VISUAL AWARENESS/ COMMUNICATION	VISUAL AWARENESS/ COMMUNICATION
'CRAFT' TEACHER	MATERIALS	REALISATION	REALISATION	REALISATION

Fig. 7.6 Teacher commitment timetable chart.

TEACHING GROUPS	1	MATERIALS	MATERIALS	VISUAL AWARENESS/ COMMUNICATION	VISUAL AWARENESS/ COMMUNICATION
	2	DESIGN	REALISATION	REALISATION	REALISATION
	3	VISUAL AWARENESS/ COMMUNICATION	VISUAL AWARENESS/ COMMUNICATION	MATERIALS	MATERIALS
	4	REALISATION	REALISATION	REALISATION	DESIGN

Fig. 7.7 A possible variation in the basic timetable sequence.

difficult problems of timetabling. This system is capable of elaboration, but at the same time is eminently workable in a variety of situations. It must however be stressed that many alternative methods of deploying staff and facilities are possible.

Chapter 8   Display Techniques

8.1   Why Display?

Display plays an important role in education. It is not only to be understood in conventional terms of 'flowers in a vase, pictures on the wall and the end of the year Open Day exhibition', but must extend to include the presentation of all aspects of life and work of the school, from the layout and quality of pupils' handwriting to the colour of the classroom walls. A school is judged, amongst other things, by the performance of its pupils and the spirit in which they play games, sing songs, or perform drama. It is, however, with the former aspects that this chapter is mainly concerned, but recognition must be taken of its close association with the broader concept.

Display in schools performs a number of functions:

(1) It internalises external experience and phenomena. To learn about the world, people and things, it is necessary to bring them into the classroom, laboratory and workshop in the form of reference material which can be consulted, looked at, examined and manipulated. Whilst books constitute the main source of reference, they can be supplemented by a wide variety of pictorial and object matter. To create a climate for learning, material that is relevant to studies or activities needs to be close at hand, easily observed, or readily consulted. It must be presented in a lively manner that informs and stimulates interest, enquiry and involvement.

(2) It facilitates the making of statements. These are basically of two categories, namely:
(a) those that inform, made verbally or otherwise by teachers, teaching material or teaching media (TV, film, radio, etc.);
(b) those that are made by pupils which confirm fact and knowledge and establish relationships but which also express ideas, thoughts and feelings and evoke responses. Such statements form an essential component of the learning process.

Whilst display techniques considered in this chapter refer mainly to those statements which are permanent and visual, the performing arts, for example, are statements of a temporary character which may be visual but which may also have a tactile or auditory basis. They have their particular forms of display techniques to which more specialised literature is devoted (see the Bibliography).

(3) It promotes corporate awareness and individual identity. A school is a community of persons who live as well as work together. The individual as a social unit within the institution has responsibilities towards it but at the same time is entitled to certain rights. Through display a pupil can be made aware that his personal contribution is valid and important to the attainment of group objectives, the overall effect and the breadth and variety of experience. Other people can, in fact, learn through and by him. But what he states, whether it be through poetry, painting, calculation or on the games field, must be represented and *tangibly* shown to be of value, if the offering be the child's personal best. Display in schools can help promote this respect and must concern itself primarily with the development of individual members, not the presentation of what might arbitrarily, by adult standards, be considered to 'look or sound good'.

(4) Setting standards. People, and particularly children, are profoundly influenced by their surroundings. Beauty, order, care and a lively interest in visual surroundings, including display, are likely to evoke sympathetic responses from observers, although some teaching may be necessary in order for them to fully appreciate what they see around them. Children are quick to recognise double standards. Quality of presentation cannot be insisted upon if desirable archetypes do not exist or if the ones that do are inferior. It can be argued that standards set by schools which relate to

78

the visual quality of surroundings, of behaviour and respect for another's work are at odds with the prevalent attitudes in society, which do not appear to rate these values highly. This places children in a position of conflict and possible frustration or confusion. The manifestations of pollution, vulgarity, contempt and indifference towards the visual environment are abhorrent and through display schools must reaffirm beliefs in aesthetic values that enhance the quality of life.

(5) It enables a school to project an image of itself. Whilst appearances can be deceptive, a school nevertheless has a duty to inform the wider public, not least the parents who send their children to it, of the values to which it ascribes, and the activities in which it is involved. The visible expression of these features make a significant contribution in creating favourable impressions, establishing good relationships between school and community and possibly enlisting support for its work.

(6) Display is a continuous working example of visual communication. Through it pupils can be introduced to many of the points outlined in Chapters 9 and 10. As far as possible pupils should be involved in display and specifically taught its techniques when time and opportunity allow.

8.2 What to Display

What is displayed in schools is obviously determined by:

(1) curriculum content;
(2) teaching methods;
(3) the extent of available resource material, how much can be produced or obtained;
(4) the availability of space and facilities;
(5) the time and expertise that members of staff can devote. The teacher-co-ordinator responsible for design studies has an important role to play in this respect.

The material that might be displayed is practically limitless, though obviously size and quantity exercise some control.

In general display material will be required to achieve the following.

(1) Stimulate interest and initiate studies or activities, acting as an 'input' of data and information. Such displays might feature when a fresh theme or topic is being introduced, a new term or, more especially, a new session commences.

The level of pupil receptivity is particularly high at these times. This type of display may be of a short duration once having served its purpose, although material from it could be selected and employed in subsequent arrangements that relate to the theme. A school might find it helpful to build up its own catalogued source of reference material, especially for the recurrent subject matter of its curriculum.

(2) Form an on-going commentary as studies progress. There is likely to be an in-flow of material to a theme over a period of time, taking the form of reference material, e.g., books, objects, pictures, charts, etc., and the work of pupils themselves. Inevitably selection has to be made. As stated, as far as pupils' work is concerned the temptation to select 'the best' must be avoided as must also the urge to 'congest' the display with too many examples, particularly if the exhibits have a close similarity. This problem can be resolved by making frequent changes but presenting few items. Variety and frequent change stimulate children's interest.

(3) Make a terminal review. Once projects, the theme, the term's or the session's studies are complete, there is the need to make a final visual statement of progress. This can take the form of an exhibition. It is an occasion when pupils' work, accompanied by selected material that has been employed in studies, *can be displayed to its best possible advantage* (which is the basic aim of all display), by pulling out all the stops of display technique. It is furthermore an opportunity for pupils to reinforce their learning by critical assessment of what has been done and to take warranted satisfaction. Too often studies/activities are left to 'fizzle out' and pupils cheated of 'moments of glory' which are imperative to the climax of effort, the building of confidence and personal confirmation of progress.

(4) Be seen for its intrinsic worth. As a form of decoration objects are displayed in homes, public and private places of assembly for no other reason than that they hold some value of themselves to enhance the visual appearance of the surroundings in which they are placed and create 'atmosphere'. Schools must be no exception and should contain well placed and presented examples such as original pictures or prints, pieces of pottery, sculpture, floral and plant arrangements, wall hangings, antiques, etc. Museums, art galleries and other bodies have loan services. General-interest displays that relate to particular subjects — study areas — e.g., music, studio/workshop/library, laboratory, help

establish the atmosphere of those locations and engage the passing interest of pupils.

8.3 Techniques of Display

Display is an art. It depends a good deal on personal preferences and a certain amount of flare on the part of the person erecting it. Teachers are not trained specialists in this activity, although they can profitably observe and consider the techniques employed by experts in shops and other forms of commercial concern. The objectives are basically the same; to show something to its best advantage, to arrest the attention and stimulate further interest. Although pictures and objects, etc., may be of a mediocre visual appeal, they can be enhanced by good display techniques, whilst those of excellent qualities can be made more so. Conversely poorly displayed items can lose their visual worth.

8.4 Space and Colour

The situation regarding the availability of space for display in British schools is a varied one. More provision in the form of pin-board cladding of walls is being made in recent designs but this advantage is not universally capitalised on. Some older schools in derelict, industrial and visually uninspiring surroundings have performed minor miracles through improvisation and a considered approach to display.

If display is to be taken seriously in a school, a well-conceived policy is required to review the amount of space for two- and three-dimensional exhibits and see how, if necessary, it can be supplemented (see below). Likely places are corridors, stairwells and recesses under the stairs, alcoves, entrance halls, and most importantly, classrooms. Windows are sometimes used for art and science exhibits which require the incidence of strong natural light. Wall expanses, usually above head height, can carry large, two-dimensional exhibits such as murals, friezes and paintings. Certain areas, such as cloakrooms, that carry the bustle of school traffic may be unsuitable for some or even all types of display, but the walls can be painted a lively colour.

Areas likely to carry two-dimensional displays should be of a uniform, neutral colour of matt finish, e.g., moss green, oatmeal, grey, brown, etc. White is currently fashionable in exhibition galleries, but it tends to glare and shows up dirt and marks (a continual hazard in schools). There are many types of textured wall coverings on the market but these are expensive. Other possible textured surface coverings that will hold exhibits are expanded polystyrene tiles, rush matting, or coloured carpet squares. If displays are to be placed on plain, hard surfaces, there are available putty-like adhesive substances such as Blu-Tack (made by Bostik) which may be easily removed when the display is no longer required. The amount of natural or artificial lighting falling upon an area is an important factor in choosing display areas or colour schemes.

The presence of visually distracting wall clocks, cupboards, alarm bells, shelves, etc., can spoil an otherwise potentially suitable display area. Where these cannot be removed or resited they could be 'painted out' in the same colour as the walls. The painting of background surfaces supposes reasonably permanent colour schemes. Where more frequent changes are required coloured backing paper, possibly in the form of 'odd rolls' of wallpaper or fabric can be used. Pin boarding, though excellent for mounting work, has a rather dull natural colour. This disadvantage can be overcome by covering it with lining paper and painting over it in matt emulsion paint to the desired colour.

There are many commercially produced products on the market for mounting two- and three-dimensional displays (Fig. 8.1). However they can be expensive and much can be done through improvisation.

Fig. 8.1 Commercially produced display units. Courtesy of Marler Haley Exposystems Ltd.

For two-dimensional work softboard, hardboard or chipboard sheets can be

(1) attached to wall surfaces,
(2) hung from walls,
(3) made into mobile units,
(4) suspended from the ceiling,
(5) made into concertina screens, or
(6) made into easels.

Backs and sides of cupboards, trellis, or cane screens can be used.

8.5 The Display of Three-Dimensional Work

Three-dimensional exhibits require a lot of viewing space. They are best observed 'in the round' but at the same time exhibits must not be so far apart as to look 'isolated' and unrelated to one another. A display must 'hang together' and the eye spared the effort of scanning spaces to discover exhibits. The display should be given depth by placing some items further forward than others and by grouping them at different levels, including on the floor. (House bricks are useful for this.) When groups of objects

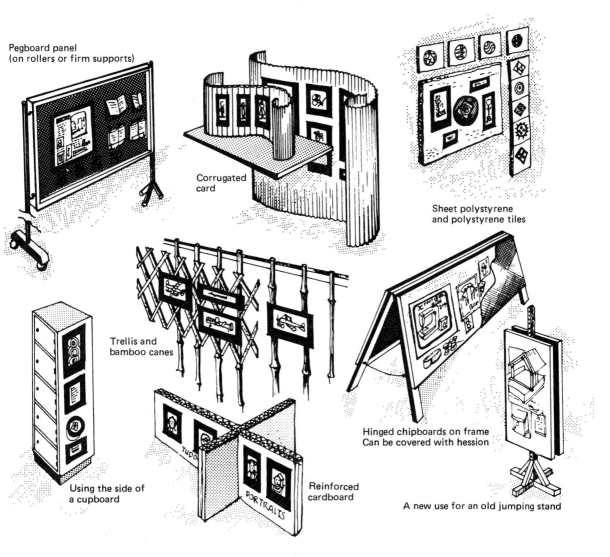

Fig. 8.2   A wide range of display units can be made from readily available sheet materials.

Fig. 8.3 Assymetrical arrangements of standard shelving units offer scope for providing arresting visual impact.

Fig. 8.4 An inexpensive but versatile commercial solution to the provision of a variety of display forms. Courtesy of Berol Ltd.

of different sizes are being arranged at a common level, care should be taken to see that the smallest articles are to the front, ascending in size towards the rear. 'Watch the sight-lines' is a useful motto in display technique.

Shelving can be used in many forms (Fig. 8.3). It can be used as space dividers (Fig. 8.4). The use of a rostrum here and there enables 'island' or 'platform' arrangements to be produced.

8.6 The Mounting and Arrangement of Two-dimensional Work

Display must visually support exhibits. The display technique itself must be a powerful agent in drawing and focusing attention, leading the eye from one subject to another, but it must never rival or dominate the subject itself. This precept must govern important features of technique, e.g., choice of colours, positioning of objects, lighting, and so on.

Two-dimensional work in the form of painting, collages, embroidery, drawings, charts or photographs needs to be mounted if it is to be displayed. A border surrounding a picture serves to contain the subject and isolate it from its surroundings, thus focusing the attention of the observer. The wider it is the more it does so. It might be necessary to trim a drawing or photograph to give the subject a more visually advantageous placing. The colour of the border makes a strong impact upon the subject (Fig. 8.5), a light one making the picture appear smaller than a dark one does. Generally speaking a paler tone of the predominant colour of the picture is a good guide. Strong or bright colours can be effective but must be treated with caution since they can distract from the picture. The colour of the background against which the picture is to be hung

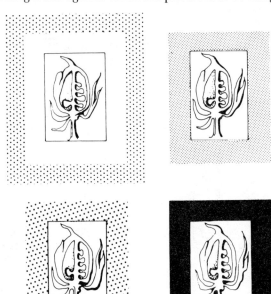

Fig. 8.5 The overall impression given by a picture can be affected by the colour of the border around it.

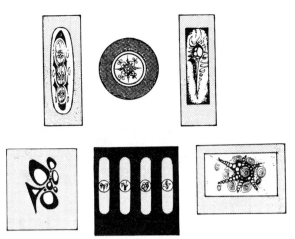

Fig. 8.6 The proportions and shapes of borders can enhance or detract from a picture.

must also be considered. As a general guide, the width of the border is generally the same to the sides and top of the picture, but slightly larger at the bottom. A border is usually the same shape as the picture it mounts, but there are alternatives (Fig. 8.6); selection depends upon the subject matter of the picture.

There are various methods of mounting:

(1) Window mounting. For use with permanent requirements where quality is of importance. The picture is placed between boards, the uppermost having a 'window' or aperture carefully cut into it (Fig. 8.7).

(2) Simple mounting. This method can be employed for temporary requirements, and is quick and simple to achieve.

(3) Double border. This is a variant of (2) but gives a double border which gives a greater emphasis to the picture (Fig. 8.8).

(4) Strip border. When there is a limited supply of backing paper this method can be used, although the results may not be so visually attractive as those above.

(5) Relief mounting. This method is suitable for embroidery, collage or ceramic panels which may have already been stiffened (by the method illustrated in Fig. 8.9). The panel is slightly raised from the backing board (itself of a rigid material, plywood, hardboard, etc., which can have its natural finish, be painted or covered with fabric, hessian) by attaching it to small dowel or wood interspacers. The mounted panels themselves look attractive if

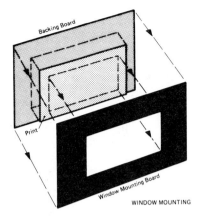

WINDOW MOUNTING

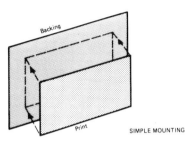

SIMPLE MOUNTING

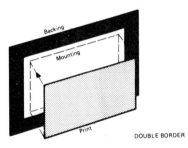

DOUBLE BORDER

Fig. 8.7 Different types of mounting can be employed to suit the degree of permanence and the quality of appearance required.

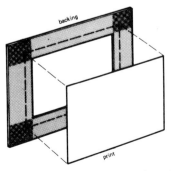

Fig. 8.8 With this form of mounting the strips are stuck together at the corners.

83

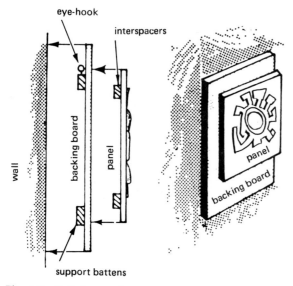

Fig. 8.9   Relief mounting.

Fig. 8.10   Lines drawn around a picture help to focus attention on it.

slightly raised from the background on which they are hung. This can be achieved by attaching strip battens to the reverse side into which screw eye-hooks for hanging can be fixed.

A picture can also be emphasised by drawing fine lines around it with fibre-tip pens (Fig. 8.10).

When a number of predominantly rectangular two-dimensional works are to be arranged on a backing, it is better to form, if possible, continuous

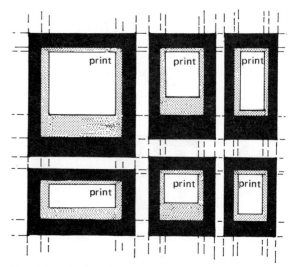

Fig. 8.11   Appropriate mounting provides a balanced layout.

Fig. 8.12   Observation of the principles of pictorial composition materially helps in achieving pleasing displays.

horizontal and vertical lines with the edges of the mounts (Fig. 8.11); this is particularly so around the outside containing rectangle. Displays are visual compositions and exhibits should be arranged to establish order, harmony, balance and contrast. Fig. 8.12 shows how contrast has been achieved in three-dimensional arrangement, by introducing linear and sinuous forms amongst predominantly bulky ones. An observer should not have to expend

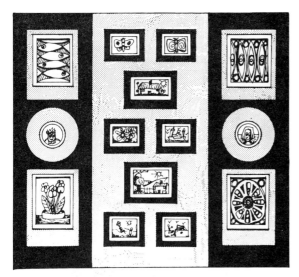

Fig. 8.13 The use of pattern in arrangements.

visual effort in disentangling a jumble of unrelated subject exhibits which have been haphazardly arranged or which are too fussy by the amount and variety they contain. 'Simplicity, unity and clarity' is the essence of successful display.

Similarly shaped but differently sized exhibits can be arranged in the form of patterns (Fig. 8.13).

Although two-dimensional work may be of different sizes it may be required to display several pieces together so that they have continuous horizontal and vertical 'linking lines'. This can be achieved by adjusting the size of the borders for each one.

Colour also plays an important role in two- and three-dimensional display techniques. Exhibits can be visually 'linked' by being of the same colour hue

Fig. 8.14 Strong contrasts produce effective emphasis.

Fig. 8.15 The size of an exhibit should harmonise with the space in which it features—large items in large spaces.

but with tonal differences. Dark objects are best grouped together against a light background (Fig. 8.14) and vice versa.

As stated, backgrounds are better being neutral to dark, but a limited area of bright colour can create a focal point.

Schools contain large surface areas, e.g., walls of assembly halls, entrance halls, stairwells, corridors, against which it might be required to mount a display of a single or a number of items. Very often the normal viewing distance in these places is large, for example, they may be viewed while sitting in the assembly hall and looking towards a back wall or platform, or while coming into or passing through the entrance hall. Exhibits in these circumstances should be large and imposing with an absence of fine detail, e.g., large floral arrangements, murals and large pieces of sculpture (Fig. 8.15). Works of small dimension or concept are 'lost' against broad expanses, but the problem of displaying them against such a background can be overcome by interposing panels which effectively reduce the viewing background (Fig. 8.16). Other similar devices could be employed, e.g., the making of display 'bays' (Fig. 8.17).

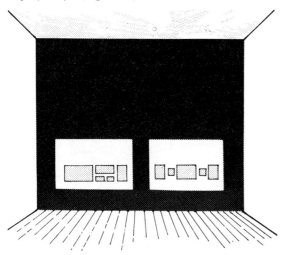

Fig. 8.16 A method of displaying small items against large background areas.

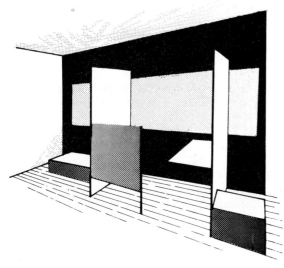

Fig. 8.17 Display bays help to generate a relaxed atmosphere by reducing the apparent size of the exhibition area.

8.7 Fabrics

Fabrics can feature in displays as:

(1) being made up into garments, soft toys, pillows, etc;
(2) Worked as embroidery, batik, tie dye;

Fig. 8.18 The folds, textures and patterns of appropriately draped fabrics provide interest in the framing or setting of exhibitions. Courtesy Sam Robbins Ltd.

(3) as drapery enhancing display, helping to link exhibits together (Fig. 8.18).

Although the context in which fabrics are used largely determines the manner in which they are displayed, they are unsightly if they are creased and dirty, and steps must be taken to avoid this.

Garments are essentially three-dimensional forms and appear lifeless and dull when viewed in two dimensions. Whilst schools may not be able to use the dummy figures that feature in professional displays in stores and clothing shops, much may be achieved by arranging striking poses, by setting limbs at suitable angles, by accentuating certain features (such as waists, shoulders), and taking care with folds in the material. In this way lively and engaging effects may be produced. Similar effects can be produced two-dimensionally by careful arrangement of the garment and the uses of artifices such as invisible thread, tapes and light padding. Nevertheless, garments are better displayed in the round and children can show considerable interest in staging 'fashion' displays.

Drapery is seen to its best with long, flowing, elegant folds that appear to fall naturally. If carefully lit to produce subtle variation of light and shade these are accentuated and further enhance the overall effect. In general, the richer the patterning of the fabric, the fewer folds are required.

Lengths of fabric have a majestic quality and need space around them. If fabrics are used to enhance a display pattern, colour or the amount of folding must be attuned to the exhibits themselves so that they do not visually 'swamp' them or dominate the arrangement as a whole. Curtains may appear an expensive luxury in a school, but they possess an undeniable value in establishing a more comfortable, intimate atmosphere as well as raising the level of attractiveness of surroundings. They also provide convenient means of darkening rooms for film shows and covering unsightly storage areas.

8.8 Lighting

Lighting is possibly the most effective agent in display technique and its potential can be observed by its use in theatre, photography and art galleries. It exercises a strong influence in establishing atmosphere, focusing attention and revealing characteristics of exhibits that otherwise might remain unnoticed.

The priority in schools remains for 'blanket' illumination of spaces, and negligible provision is made for display lighting, not unreasonably for considerations of expense. The onus is thus placed on the schools to improvise, but if electric power can permanently or temporarily be taken to display areas there is a wide variety of lights for this purpose now on the market which can be effectively employed (Fig. 8.19).

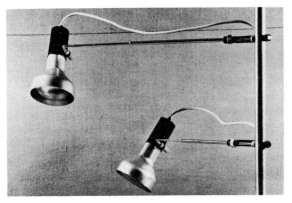

Fig. 8.19 Different lighting effects can be achieved by the use of the wide range of industrial and domestic lighting equipment now available. Courtesy Marler Haley Exposystems Ltd.

Artists such as Rembrandt were alive to the strong visual qualities that can be obtained by throwing pools and obliquely angled beams of light upon subject matter. This is an excellent device for placing emphasis, creating a focus, drawing out characteristics of form and texture or evoking an atmosphere. Exhibitions themselves can be effectively staged in darkened surroundings where the items only are illuminated. Children can be excited by the sinister appearance obtained by lighting the face from beneath in a darkened room. They can be made aware of the variety of effects that can be gained by positioning lights to beam upon a subject and experiment for themselves, possibly by using a selection of the different types of hand lamps now available. Under well-supervised conditions older pupils can play a responsible and imaginative role in lighting displays and dramatic/movement productions with mains equipment. These responsibilities could extend to the projection of films and slides.

8.9 Lettering

Lettering plays an important role in display; it must be of high quality and used with discretion. There are occasions where detailed annotations are necessary to give information or descriptions, but there are others where an exhibit speaks for itself. (There are times when we do not wish to know that the wooden carving on conspicuous display in the entrance hall was made by Charlie Smith; we need to appreciate it for itself, not the person who made it.)

There are very many lettering styles in existence. Some have long established and distinguished histories and, with practice, can be produced by teachers and pupils. Handwriting and calligraphy should form part of a design-based course. Other styles are more recent and have widespread commercial application in advertising, etc. Their distinctive forms usually have a close association with the idea which they wish to symbolise, e.g., security, dignity, modernity, the future, fun, crime, ruggedness, etc. Often a form or style may appear particularly suitable for a title to a subject or theme being displayed. It is therefore an advantage to make a collection of lettering styles from disused magazines, brochures, posters, newspapers, etc. Pupils with graphic skills and time to spare can work from this reference source to produce titles.

Lettering itself is the placing of shapes and

masses on backgrounds, and due care must be taken over details of spacing, margins and arrangement.

The introduction of transfer printing, through 'Letraset', has enabled professional finishes to be brought to lettering and indeed other graphic effects. Although comparatively simple to apply it is rather expensive. Other commercial aids and products are available for lettering.

8.10 Natural Materials

The decorative qualities of flowers, plants and natural materials such as branches, dried flowers, grasses, bark, stones, rocks, seed pods, dried fruit, etc., have been recognised for many years. The art of displaying them has been raised to sophisticated levels. Their qualities of line, texture, colour and shape enable them to be readily incorporated into displays or indeed to form the display themselves.

Natural materials provide effective and 'softening' contrasts to forms which have straight lines and flat surfaces or where geometric shapes are formally arranged (Fig. 8.20). In compositions the characteristics of natural forms must be carefully considered as they cannot successfully be forced into 'unnatural' arrangements. Natural materials are also best viewed in isolation against plain, neutral backgrounds.

Fig. 8.20 The visual 'hardness' of geometrical forms can blend effectively with the 'softness' of natural ones.

8.11 Models

Models have a well-established and important place in display and these should be a common feature in most subject studies. They may be of the variety

Fig. 8.21 Experimental musical instruments made at Finham Park Comprehensive School, Coventry, by pupils aged 13 and 14 years.

produced by manufacturers for teaching purposes, or perhaps more importantly made by the pupils themselves. They may illustrate a specific point, e.g., costume of the Georgian period, the construction of an oil tanker, etc., but models are excellent teaching aids if they actually work; there is great value in operating a model to show the function of a process or system. Pupils may boast the number of gears their bicycles contain but fail to appreciate the mechanical and mathematical principles on which a gear system operates. Science and technology offer a rich source of opportunity to make things in order to learn and apply scientific laws, e.g., electric circuits, periscopes, etc. (see Fig. 8.21). The progress of some continuous process— e.g., the growth of plants and bacteria, the filtration of muddy water, a 'chiming' candle clock, the rusting of nails, etc.—forms a display showing the change of state or condition over a period of time. Sometimes a display needs to show simultaneously different stages of some process such as throwing a pot, making a garment, preparing a meal. Several models of a sequence therefore have to be made, as some children can experience difficulty in projecting back or forth in time: 'How do I go about planing this piece of wood up square and to size?' 'How does a fleece become a piece of fabric?' Within the permissible limits of safety and personal behaviour exhibits can take advantage of the pupils' urge to tinker about to 'see how it works' and to find out 'what happens if . . .'. These are learning experiences.

8.12 Display and the Observer

There is a dialogue between display and observer. Display must therefore address itself to the likely mood or circumstances of the observer. Factors which make for effective communication must therefore be built into display. For example, the observer may be passing through, or in a hurry (in the entrance hall, along the corridor, on the staircase), in which case the display only needs to 'greet' or make a pleasing impression. The observer may be in a contemplative mood, or need transporting into one — in assembly, in the library, listening to music, or discussing personal matters in the Head's study. The effective communicator is one, who having aroused interest, sustains it by offering the prospect of further delights if you stay with him. Rather than being shown all the goods at once in an exhibition, can the observer be taken on a leisurely conducted tour, sampling only a few at a time, possibly displayed in bays or on strategically placed islands? People also prefer individual or small-group identity rather than being a member of an impersonal mass. Does the exhibition or display give a sense of intimacy and 'talk' to the oberserver personally? Should the exhibits induce the observer to come close and examine or stand back to reflect, or witness the 'grand' statement? Has the observer to crane his neck or perform other painful contortions in order to grasp what is being 'said'? Familiarity breeds boredom and ultimately contempt. Exhibits that have been up too long lose their appeal and become a visual nuisance. The value they might once have possessed eventually disappears.

8.13 Tools and Equipment for Display

A convenient range of tools and equipment is an asset in erecting and dismantling displays. A suggested list is as follows:

Large and small guillotines
Staple gun (tacker) and hardwire steel staples
Staple extractor
Large and small (detail) scissors
Cutting knife with replaceable blades
'Slimline' cutting knife with a variety of blades
Pin pusher and pins
Medium-sized screwdriver and small electrical screwdriver
Drawing board, T-square, set squares and compasses
Lettering pens, nibs (of various sizes) and lettering inks
Fibre tip pens
Drawing pins
Small pliers
Variety of adhesives (cow-gum, clear 'Bostik', PVA)
Rolls of 'Sellotape', masking tape and brown sticky tape
1 metre and 300 mm steel rules
Cutting board.

Display may fall to the responsibility of a member of staff or an advisory teacher who can actively assist colleagues. Such a teacher may find it convenient to transport a selection of the above equipment in a tool box.

If design education is to be successful in the middle years of schooling then, amongst other things, it must be *seen* to be so. Excellent display can go a long way in confirming the educational, social, spiritual and personal benefits that can be derived from education through design.

Section C   The Provision of Design Experience in Two and Three Dimensions

Chapter 9   Visual Communication

9.1   Introduction

Man's awareness of his environment is mainly visual. Since design education is concerned with the natural and man-made forms in the physical environment, an important aspect of it should be the education of the visual sense.

Forms in the environment exist in two or three dimensions, i.e., either they are flat or they possess depth, but they are seen through the mechanism of the eye as being two-dimensional. The brain is able to distinguish whether forms are two- or three-dimensional. It is also able to perceive and interpret those forms, but this is a complex mental activity. Perception — 'the process of becoming aware of something' (*Dictionary of Psychology*) — involves the use of some or all of the other senses; touch, smell, hearing and taste. Sight is not always the main agent in transmitting information about the qualities of forms to the brain.

It is artificial to discuss an education of the visual sense separately from an education involving all the senses, and it is just as artificial to discuss two-dimensional experiences or activities separately from those of three dimensions. An education which is concerned with the forms in the environment is one that involves the whole of the body, including the senses, in both two and three dimensions. However, the authors will make these distinctions in the following four chapters, simply because they clarify educational arguments in design education as a whole, and because they make individual facets easier to deal with.

9.2   The Determinants of Visual Form

What an object communicates visually results essentially from the role played by two determinants

(1) Its utilitarian or structural function, i.e., the purpose the object serves.
(2) Its expressive function, i.e., the ideas, information the object conveys or the feelings it evokes.

The motor vehicle is a common example of a man-made three-dimensional form. Its structural function is to transport. Vehicles are made to convey individuals or groups, a family, an invalid. They can transport heavy or bulky loads, or be used for racing and so on. 'Need-factors' dictated by the use to which the vehicle will be put will determine its structural functional design and therefore contribute to its visual appearance. Once a person has seen a vehicle and learns what it does, the image of it becomes part of his visual vocabulary; he will identify its function with its appearance. The same applies to two-dimensional forms, e.g., a notice or label has the function of transmitting information.

There are other factors helping to determine visual form — those representing the expressive function. These are not so easily recognised and are concerned more with perception and subjective interpretation. The ability to sell in the vehicle market is achieved by producing goods which express ideas about status, wealth, comfort, convenience and styling with which customers can identify, as well as factors of structural suitability and reliability. This applies to many other man-made, especially consumer, products. The idea of presenting an appearance to bring about some desired perceptive interpretation occurs also in the natural world, e.g., camouflage protects by the practice of deception.

Both determinants are present in visually observed forms, but the extent to which one or other operates depends mostly on the overall purpose the object serves and what the observer is consciously aware of about it, e.g., in looking at a vehicle one person may 'see' it as a means of conveyance, another a piece of machinery, whilst another a status symbol, etc. It is a matter of what the person 'perceives' in the object.

9.3   Material Technology and Visual Form

Since earliest times man has developed a material

technology to provide for his basic needs of food, water, and protection. Although he has produced forms — artifacts — to help meet these needs, he has been aware of the emotional and spiritual parts of his mental make-up. Through the visual arts man has expressed his urge to unite the spiritual and the material, the physical and emotional. Forms of visual expression were bound up with technology and society and developed together. We see examples of this phenomenon in the decoration which appears on primitive tools and weapons, or is found in cathedrals and temples.

In societies that lacked a written language the visual arts were the only media through which information and ideas could be communicated. Even where literature and language did exist the visual arts were employed to amplify or interpret in ways that writing could not. There are parallels today, especially in multi-racial societies where people with different cultural backgrounds and languages share common services and common employment. For such societies to function there must be a common system of communication. Visual symbols are being preferred to written language.

Another characteristic of contemporary life is speed. Where speed of communication is necessary a visual symbol is interpreted faster than a written or verbal statement, e.g., flashing signs on motorways.

Political, social, economic and technological developments of the nineteenth and twentieth centuries have tended to separate the visual arts from other aspects of life. Life and society are commonly viewed as a collection of unrelated parts, not a balanced organically functioning whole. Whilst for many the material quality of life has improved, the humanising influence of art has often been absent. This has resulted in waste and widespread ugliness in the environment and in the lives of people who inhabit it.

The Bauhaus Movement (1919-33) did much to reconcile traditional values of art and craftmanship to developments in science and technology. The principles and ideas of the movement have subsequently exerted a considerable influence on design, but many visual forms today are mainly determined by economics, convenience (e.g., prefabricated buildings), the function to be performed (cooling towers), or purely scientific or technological considerations (overhead power cables). Scant regard may be paid to the spiritual or emotional needs of human beings, the qualitative impact of the object upon the environment or its role within the context of a delicately balanced ecology. Concessions to feeling or aspirations are at a transitory level and make their appeal to fashion, status, sex, class or power. The well-designed and well-manufactured article presents a visual acceptable article whatever the age.

An education in visual awareness should develop a critical faculty with regard to forms in the environment, by:

(1) Enabling pupils to study why forms are visually as they are. How are they structured or operated? How do they function? Are they appropriate for the purposes they serve? Do they harmonise with other forms? Can they, should they, be modified? Are they necessary?

(2) Offering pupils the opportunity of working in a variety of materials, with a variety of tools employing a variety of constructional and expressive processes. From this experience they will become aware that visual and structural form can be determined partially by choice of material, tool and process.

(3) Preparing pupils for their role in a consumer-orientated society. An abundance and variety of goods are available on the market. They are manufactured and promoted by commercial bodies who employ advertising agencies to help sell their products. Visual techniques play a major role in this process, e.g., TV commercials, advertisements in magazines, etc. Pupils should be helped to understand the process of choice, to interpret the visual imagery employed in advertising, to cultivate a mature but personal sense of taste and quality, and be given wide experience in decision making.

(4) Helping to restore the affinity that man has with the natural world. 'Development' and 'progress' in the nineteenth and twentieth centuries has taken place with an almost total disregard for the natural world and the aesthetic and ecological contributions that it can make to the quality of life. Pollution, urban decay and the unprecedented consumption of natural resources pose a serious threat for the future (see also Chapter 3).

The natural world has a traditional and obvious role in scientific and geographical studies in schools. Many children are fond of animals. What is not often appreciated is that nature can also make a major contribution to the study of structure, form, order and function and the visual properties of colour, shape, texture, balance, pattern and composition. Pupils should be helped to become aware of how natural forms visually influence surroundings, how natural materials and resources can be conserved and replenished, how technology can harmonise with natural ecocycles and how past and present violations of the natural world could have been avoided.

(5) Perpetuating the traditionally accepted role of art and 'art-orientated' crafts in schools and society. It is a habit of our age and society to want everything to serve a practical purpose, but man is also an artist, musician, dancer and poet. In being so he expresses an emotional response to his thoughts and feelings. He also challenges accepted doctrines and explores different ways of seeing and interpreting. In time these may become accepted conventions and find their way into the cultural fabric of a society. People's lives are impoverished without the influence of music, poetry, pictures, sculpture, drama or dance.

In dismissing art, particularly modern art, there is not only a failure to recognise that we are setting a limit upon perceptual horizons and stunting emotional sensitivity, but we are failing to appreciate the degree to which it is manifest in the forms around us. Post-war architecture, for example, had its origins in the explorative innovations of the 1930s, which in turn stemmed from the social analysis of Ruskin and Morris and the 'art' movements of expressionism, futurism, cubism and constructionism. Le Corbusier and Picasso distorted or destroyed form before reassembling it in different ways.

The most important value in 'expressive' art and craft work is in 'doing', but benefit is also derived from looking critically at the work of artists, craftsmen or designers. These can, for example, show the different ways that forms in the environment can be interpreted or how ideas, or information, have been expressed and communicated. Pictures also show how people lived and dressed in different ages or in other countries.

9.4 Communication and the Use of Symbols

Communication (*Oxford Dictionary*) — 'the imparting or exchange of information by message or otherwise' — is an activity performed by social animals to ensure their survival. With man the written and spoken language has been used as the primary vehicle through which thought and feeling can be expressed and information communicated.

But words are symbols and language represents only one such system employed by man to communicate.

In general terms symbols are a substitute for situations, objects and experiences. Reality is simplified to a sign or cypher. Although a symbolic language is convenient and essential, it can have a number of inherent features which can be thought of as advantageous or disadvantageous, depending on the viewpoint of those manipulating the system.

Fig. 9.1 Cattle ahead! — but the sign does not tell the whole story.

(1) The symbol, or word, does not present a total or detailed picture of reality.

The sign, Fig. 9.1, warns the road-user of cattle, but does not tell us if cattle are actually on the road at the time, how many there are, what breed they are, if they have trailed mud with them and so on.

(2) Not all members of the social group have an equal understanding of the system, nor may they be able to operate it with equal proficiency.

(3) Although symbols may be commonly recognised, they can be misinterpreted. No two people perceive or interpret things exactly the same way. If we see the written statement 'I like your new coat', it can be interpreted several ways, depending on emphasis, e.g.:

I like your new coat.	(The writer does but implies others don't.)
I *like* your new coat.	(There is a suggestion that he may dislike it.)
I like *your* new coat.	(That which is yours, not those of others.)
I like your *new* coat.	(A particular one, not necessarily the others.)
I like your new *coat.*	(But not necessarily the new hat, shirt, shoes, etc.)

I like your new coat. (That's the end of the argument.)

I . . . like your new coat. (Which could imply the exact opposite.)

The closer a common understanding between members of a group with respect to the symbol the more effective it becomes as a vehicle of communication.

(4) The system can induce conditioned thought patterns. Written language is expressed in linear forms which, it is thought, develop linear thought patterns, and mental images are constructed. A picture on the other hand presents a totality of subject which a viewer can break down to study its component parts (for example the plans of a house).

People communicate in two and three dimensions. Cultures, past and present, have done so at different levels of sophistication. With some, two-dimensional forms have predominated, with others, three. Some have developed both equally. The conventions that have been established have reflected the way people perceive and interpret. These conventions are peculiar to individual cultures, and people from alien ones might have difficulty in understanding them. Recently problems have been encountered in training students from emergent countries in western technology as they have found difficulty in comprehending the pictorial material and conventions commonly employed for teaching technological processes.

9.5 Visual Communication in Contemporary Society

There are features of contemporary society which suggest the necessity of educating children in visual, as well as verbal, literacy.

(1) Extensive use is made of charts, diagrams, number systems, graphs, plans, and pictures, as well as hours of TV to transmit ideas, information and to instruct. They pervade the man-made environment in places such as schools, streets, offices, public places and in the home. Industry and commerce could not function without them. Can it be assumed that people can 'read' this quantity and variety of material intelligently and critically without some prior form of education in visual interpretation? Such an assumption would not be made with respect to the written word!

(2) It is now easier for the ordinary citizen as well as the politician and business executive to travel further, faster and more frequently than has been possible in the past. International hotels, national capitals, administrative, exhibition and conference centres, rail, air and motorway systems — all these are confluences of many people from many nations 'on the move'. Many of their immediate requirements for help and direction can be and are being provided by the media of sign and symbol.

(3) The tempo of living is fast. Even a well-regulated life style cannot entirely avoid the necessity to absorb and transmit ideas and information at speed. The fastest media of communication is the picture.

(4) There is a greater volume of specialised knowledge being transmitted internationally amongst people who nevertheless have national, cultural and ideological identities. Space technology is a familiar example. A commonly understood language is required.

(5) With the increasing volume of international trade there is a more extensive flow of technological hardware and specialised services which require complex support systems. Even the ordinary home contains technical gadgetry, much of which is likely to be imported. People often need to learn about the operation and maintenance of the products they use. In many cases they can best be instructed by visual means in the absence of personal help.

9.6 Visual Language

Verbal fluency results from a breadth of knowledge and personal experience which enables one to interpret the ideas or information in the arrangement of words. It also depends upon a familiarity with the language itself: which words most accurately describe or express the subject or situation, which form is most suitable for the occasion or context, and how the words ought to be structured to communicate effectively. There are guiding rules and principles governing the use of words. There is a grammar.

What is true for a verbal language applies equally to a visual one. A visual 'vocabulary' and 'grammar' enables children to interpret visual images and make their own personal statements — expressing and communicating — in visual terms.

Visual form can be considered as deriving from six basic elements — line, point, shape, colour, texture, movement — to which may be added the aspects of composition and balance. Visual literacy depends upon an awareness of these elements and of their roles individually or in combination; it also entails the ability to manipulate them. (Chapter 10 offers suggestions for study of these elements by pupils.) Pupils must be made aware that the elements are present in two- and three-dimensional visual forms.

Pupils should observe these elements and use them in visually communicative devices, by studying the forms they see about them, especially in the communications media, and by producing examples that correspond to situations and experiences appropriate to their conceptual level and relevant to their personal experience. Examples of this are (1) the representation of the flow of pupils to and from morning assembly, (2) the representation by graphs of statistical information, (3) diagrams to illustrate the tactical moves in a game of chess or football, and (4) the visual recording of the anatomical details and arrangements discovered in a dissection.

The transmission of ideas and information communicates the 'how, why, where, when and what' of things. Pupils should consider how these questions could be interpreted in visual terms. Under *what* could be considered the following:

What does the object look like physically, or symbolically, or under its skin?
What will happen, or has happened? What is its change of state or being?
What is 'it' made up of? What are its component parts and what is their relationship to one another?
What should be done (in an emergency, or under given circumstances)?

Some questions involving *why* are as follows:
Why do things happen (cause and effect)?
Why must a procedure (not) be adhered to?

Under *where* we might consider:
Where are we going?
Where is the factory?
Where is the boundary of the farmer's land?

For *when* we could be discussing traffic lights:
When does the amber light appear alone? (i.e., after which colour?)

Finally, *how* arises in such questions as:
How do we carry out this process?
How do we organise an outing?
How many are in the class?

How many enjoy football?
How well did I do that?
How does rainfall affect vegetation?
How can we display this artwork to best advantage?

9.7 Sensory Experience in Communication and Learning

Systems of communication between people and between animals employ one, several or all of the senses. Music, dance, drama and sculpture are media of expressive communication, but music, for example, is visually non-dimensional and relies on hearing alone. Dance, drama and sculpture are three-dimensional. The siren is an auditory signal practically devoid of 'expressive' character, but whose message is uncompromising. Hand signals are employed by drivers and for the direction of taxiing aircraft, and so on.

Any one system may be very sophisticated, but it employs only one or a limited range of the senses, so it cannot accurately convey a complete reality of thought or feeling. The blind can communicate through a heightened sense of touch and/or hearing, but total comprehension is denied through the absence of sight. Technical devices have opened up areas of experience and made possible greater social integration, but it is pointless to communicate experience to the blind which is strongly visual in character, because the images lie outside the limits of personal visual experience.

A single or selected number of different modes of communication are more suitable in one context than another. The dance, which can utilise colour, sound and sometimes the tactile element, may evoke a stronger emotional response than sound alone. A pungent smell or loud noise may stimulate immediate reaction, whereas a warning notice may be ignored. A single picture is said to be worth a thousand words, and so on.

The behaviour of babies and young children shows the energy that is expended on using all the senses to explore the environment and to develop concepts. Studies by Piaget and others have influenced the education given to children in their early years. An environment is created and experiences are provided which exploit these innate drives and the use of all the senses for learning and conceptual development. Structural apparatus, the considered use of colour and materials, dance, mime and movement, music, story and uninhibited 'play' activity are features of nursery play-groups and first schools. Although they are present to greater or lesser degree in later education, they tend to be abandoned, along with experience of a 'concrete' nature, in favour of formal traditionally based teaching methods with the primary objectives of making a pupil literate and numerate. Sensory experience — in learning, communicating and expressing — of a continuous nature through the full use of all the senses is subordinated to that which can, or may be, acquired through a verbal or written language. The terms 'literacy' should have a wider connotation and include a facility in visual, auditory and movement skills.

A person who lacks facility in verbal skills not only finds himself with a serious social handicap but is denied the contribution that language and literature can make to a full life and, in social terms, a useful and responsible one. This is recognised by the provision of an education in language which runs right through primary and secondary schools. What is taught and learnt at one stage depends on previous experiences. Efficiency in a verbal language is largely the outcome of a well-structured education spanning an entire school career. What applies to a verbal language applies equally to a visual one. We must think no less of making children visually literate than we would of helping them to become verbally literate.

9.8 Visual Expression and Mental Growth of the Child in the Middle Years

It is recognised in the teaching of reading and number that account must be taken of the patterns of mental growth. Educative activities in schools are structured to develop concepts and skills where that which is taught and learnt follows on sequentially from that which has previously been taught and learnt. The two- and three-dimensional activities of a designed-based course, especially those involving visual communication, must no less relate to patterns of perceptual development, interpretation and representation. These differ from child to child but within this range of variation there are general characteristics of development and behaviour.

The subject is one that has been thoroughly explored. Whilst a great deal of information has been produced this book will not consider in detail that which is described elsewhere. Nevertheless there are features in children's expressive (communicative) work, particularly in two dimensions,

which are common and noteworthy. Those involved in teaching these aspects of design education should be aware of them.

The age range 7-14 is a considerable developmental span in a child's life. Before considering the visually communicative/expressive aspects of development in roughly three stages, i.e., 7-9, 9-12, 12-14, there are phenomena that are generally applicable over the whole period.

(1) The stages in the various aspects of conceptual/expressive development are not clearly defined, nor are they necessarily sequential. Pupils at a certain chronological age may produce work characteristic of earlier or later ages.

(2) Transitional phases can extend over a long period or a comparatively short one.

(3) A number of characteristics indicating several levels of development may be observed in a single piece of work. The picture of the yacht (Fig. 9.2) by a boy of 11 illustrates a level of graphic skill and a regard for detail which is appropriate to his age, but the view of the keel and the symbolic, almost pattern-like representation of the gulls is representative of an earlier stage of development. The well-drawn plan view of a proposed room by a 12-year-old girl (Fig. 9.3) shows certain articles drawn in plan, some in elevation and others in perspective; others could be 'flattened out'.

(4) The visual statements of a child tend to be determined by:

(a) general level of intelligence;
(b) richness or otherwise of stimulation in his cultural background;

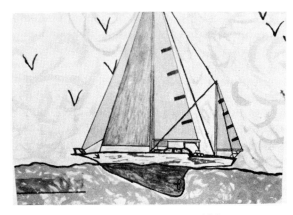

Fig. 9.2 Painting by an eleven-year-old boy.

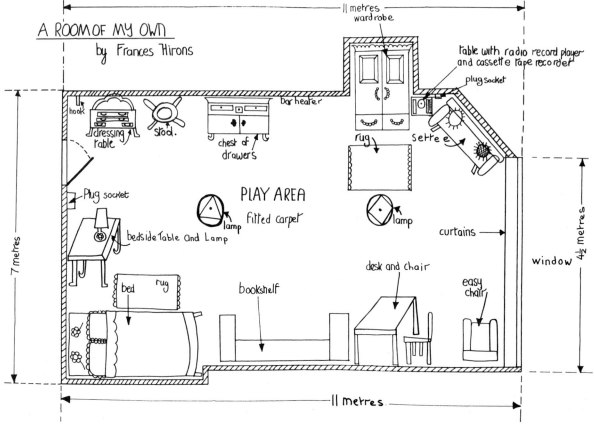

Fig. 9.3   Drawing by a twelve-year-old girl.

(c) the personal way he perceives or 'sees', or interprets a thing or a situation;

(d) what he knows about the thing, e.g., how it is made, its functions, purpose, etc;

(e) what other sensory impressions/experiences he has of the object;

(f) the emotional feelings he experiences towards the object or situation.

Expression from 7 to 9 Years

Concepts are built up over a period of time. We do not acquire a comprehensive knowledge of anyone, anything, or any situation at first acquaintance, nor develop an accomplished skill at the first attempt. Our behaviour and statements relative to the subject at any one time are based on the knowledge, experience and emotional involvement that we possess at that time. Expressive forms are likely to remain static until further knowledge is acquired, or skills developed by experience, or unless there is an emotional incentive. As no two personalities are

exactly alike, neither are the educative experiences of two individuals; hence no two forms of visual expression are identical. Whilst these statements apply in general terms to people they are of particular relevance when considering the two-dimensional (pictorial) expression of younger children.

By about the age of 7 children have achieved a way, or scheme, of representing objects, space and figures in the world about them. This is often referred to as the *schema*. This undergoes progressive modification as the child learns more about things. When a particularly strong impression has been made, e.g., that 'a lady wears red nail varnish' and a 'hat on her head', these features are likely to be stressed by exaggeration in the work of, say, a 7-year-old.

Spatial awareness, during this stage, is mainly concerned with representing two-dimensionally the relationship that things have to one another. Figure 9.4 (by a 7-year-old girl), shows the house on the

Fig. 9.4 House and person. Painting by a seven-year-old girl.

Fig. 9.6 The stylised use of the symbol is repeated in this picture by an eight-year-old girl.

Fig. 9.5 House and person. Picture by an eight-year-old girl.

ground, and the chimney with smoke coming from it is on the roof. Apples are 'in' the tree, arms are attached to the body. The dog is on the ground but is held by a lead which is held in the hand. Flowers are attached to the ground but are at right angles to it.

The ground becomes the child's base of reference and this is familiarly represented in pictorial work by the distinctive 'base-line' which is placed at the bottom of a picture. The ground can be the earth, grass, floor or road, in fact anything on which something, especially the child itself, is standing. Similarly, but not to the same extent, a line, which is usually blue, is drawn at the top of a picture to represent the sky, the ceiling, etc. The intervening objects, people or phenomena relate to ground or sky. Even when the child moves towards a more mature representation of spatial relationships (Fig. 9.5 by an 8-year-old girl), i.e., where the earth and

sky appear to meet, the security of establishing ground and sky line might still be required. The base-line phenomenon is a feature of aspects of primitive pictorial art. At this stage in development little attempt (mainly as a few exploratory lines) is made to represent depth although the child is consciously aware of it.

When the objects are repeated in the picture, e.g., the flowers in the garden, the girls playing hockey (Fig. 9.6), the symbol is basically unchanged. The frequency with which objects are represented in a picture is also indicative of a child's innate feeling for pattern and rhythm.

Through an increase in awareness, the child may wish to state facts about a horizontal surface, as well as a vertical one, together with the relationship that things have to both, e.g., the floor with its coloured tiles (Fig. 9.7 by a boy of 8), the road with its drains or markings, the lines on a football field (Fig. 9.8 by a boy of 11). This problem is resolved by representing vertical and horizontal planes as being 'flattened out'. As the child becomes visually more aware of his surroundings, the representation of the horizontal and vertical relationship can present a problem. The boy drawing the picture of the football field proceeded happily until he came to draw the goals, which he erased and re-drew several times as he wrestled with the problem of a rectangular shaped goal mouth and triangular side-netting. He resolved this (unsatisfactorily in his mind) by a compromise angling of the posts. From there his attention was drawn to the blank spaces, X, where he encountered another problem in 'joining the stands up at the corners'. In the span of a single lesson he had begun to pass through a

97

Fig. 9.7   Picture by an eight-year-old boy.

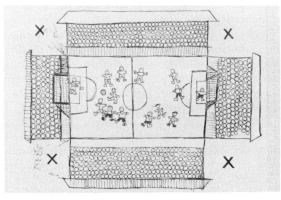

Fig. 9.8   Drawing by an eight-year-old boy. Whilst executing this work the child began to realise that the way he drew things was not as he knew them to be.

transitional phase from one stage of visual representation to another.

At this stage children employ other devices to represent 'what they know', which, strictly speaking, are non-visual in the realistic sense. In Fig. 9.2 the keel of the boat is drawn as though seen through the water. This phenomenon is known as 'X-ray representation' and is also a feature in primitive pictorial art. Plan and elevation of an object can be shown together. Insides of things may also be shown with reference to their exterior, or inside and outside can be mixed together.

The child's use of colour during this stage develops in a similar way to his representation of objects and space. Increasing objectivity, as opposed to a purely emotional response to colour, enables him to associate a particular colour with objects, e.g., the grass is green, fire is red and yellow, the sky blue and apples are red. The first impression that a child has that relates a colour to an object can be a strong one, and the association may remain and be represented even when he knows reality to be somewhat otherwise, e.g., that not all apples are red, and the sky is not always blue. Colour is also used in a schematic fashion and modifications do not occur until experiences consciously make the child aware of differences, e.g., that apples can be red, green or yellow and maybe a mixture, that soil is not always brown, and that clouds can be grey and so on.

Of creative expression Irving Taylor, a social psychologist, identifies five levels. The first 'expressive creativity' is more relevant to the child of pre- and early middle years. It is characterised by complete independence and spontaneity: the child views skills, materials, techniques and the finished product as largely unimportant. There would be little benefit—indeed there could be positive harm—in teaching formal aspects of two-dimensional pictorial expression at this stage. They are adult concepts and children do not have the capacity to understand them.

A design course at this stage should provide subject material that is lively and stimulating and related as far as possible to everyday experience. It should provide opportunity for the pupil to represent various aspects of what he sees: the relationship that objects and people have to one another, different views of an object, and the space-time relationship involved in movement and action (see the section on Movement on p. 104).

However a number of children in this age range could also be operating at what Irving describes as the second 'productively creative stage', i.e., there is a conscious effort to represent things realistically and improve techniques.

Expression from 9 to 12 Years
During this period the child is increasingly aware of the real world about him and this is reflected in visual communicative and expressive work. The terms 'real' and 'natural' are often confused. The latter refers to things as they exist and can be seen by all, in nature. Two- and three-dimensional

representation that is 'naturalistic' is the attempt to render things as they are, i.e., to get a photographic imitation. This is erroneously but not infrequently held to be the criterion of 'good' art and one of the objectives of a visual 'education'. Reality on the other hand is personal and subjective; it is what the individual sees and considers significant in an object. This view of things is influenced by factors of personality, background and emotion. What is expressed visually is not a naturalistic representation of the object or situation itself but the experiences associated with the object.

The energy and curiosity of this age, which are expressed in the desire to 'know', record, collect, distinguish and 'be accurate' lead to a concern for representing detail in visual expression. Subjects produced in two or three dimensions consequently tend to be stiff as detail tends to subordinate a feeling for action (even where the subject itself can be associated with action). The conventions and devices that were formally employed to express, communicate, or represent (e.g., X-ray drawing, fold-over, exaggeration, etc.) are abandoned as inaccurate. Pieces of work at this stage tend to be carefully observed statements of fact.

As the child develops greater visual awareness he gradually moves away from a rigid colour-object association to realise differences and similarities. The green of a bush is not the same as that of the grass, but his awareness is insufficiently advanced to discern or represent the tones and shades of colour of an object.

The symbolism of the base and sky lines are also

Fig. 9.9 Picture by an eleven-year-old boy. Note the increasingly sophisticated relationships between the various parts of the composition.

abandoned as the child discovers more about depth and endeavours to portray it. This perception is also not likely to be fully developed in this stage of growth. In the picture of the hunt (Fig. 9.9) by a 11-year-old boy, the trees are shown to cover the sky and the horizon line is established, but the stream is represented in plan as a band of constant width disappearing abruptly at the horizon. The child at this stage can be conscious of the fact that things overlap and wholly or partially obscure one another. This is a clear indication that he is aware of depth. It is at about the age of 10 to 12 years that some children attempt perspective representation.

The keenness and interest shown by children of this age for the detail of objects, the environment and for why things are as they are provides a suitable starting point for studying the more formalised aspects of visual language, e.g., line, shape, texture, pattern and form, etc.

Expression from 12 to 14 Years
Emphasis is placed on this period as a time of considerable physiological and psychological change in the lives of children. It is at this period in the middle years when the widest range of physical, emotional and intellectual development can be observed. Young people at this time are neither fully adult nor children and, being acutely aware of this, can be very self-conscious. This is expressed behaviourally in many ways as they attempt to resolve in personal terms who they are, what they believe in, what view people and the world have of them and what their role and relationship to both are to be. Consequently they lose the spontaneity and confidence of former years and become increasingly critical of themselves, their products, the environment and the authority of adults in its various forms. Being a time of difficulty and uncertainty, it is not uncommon for the child of these years to vacillate between 'child-like' and adult modes of behaviour. Visual expression tends to lose its uninhibited statement of fact and moves towards a considered treatment of what things are, how they operate, how they are seen and naturalistically represented and how they can alter in form and appearance (e.g., subleties of light, tone and colour).

It becomes possible in this period to discern a spectrum of expressive character in pupils which is closely related to personality. At one end is what is known as the 'visual type' where the individual

Fig. 9.10 'Ships in a storm'. Picture by a 'haptic' type ten-year-old boy. The subject is treated with a marked feeling for atmosphere, movement and the drama inherent in such a situation.

Fig. 9.11 'Ships in a storm'. Picture by a 'visual' type ten-year-old child. Here the treatment of the subject is more restrained, formal and objective.

informs himself of people and the environment through the eyes as an 'observer'. The overall impression is initially formed and constituent parts and their relationship to one another and the whole are thereafter analysed. Even features of a non-visual nature, e.g., those of sound and texture, are translated in visual terms. The visual type is predominantly objective in attitude. At the other extreme is the 'haptic type' (from the Greek *haptus* which means 'laying hold'), who uses tactile and other sensory experiences primarily to inform and express. This type is subjective and tends to relate to people and things emotionally. The young child is primarily haptic, but obviously adolescents and adults cannot arbitrarily be differentiated as belonging to either one or the other category. Most people are placed somewhere between the two ends of the spectrum.

In the representation of space the child of this age can utilise perspective or other depth clues (e.g., overlapping and the reduction of size as objects are situated in the distance). This tends to be an acquired ability and not a 'natural' one. The laws of perspective (a convention of visual expression established in the fifteenth century by the Florentine masters) should only be taught if it is within the intellectual capacity of the individual child to assimilate or is relevant to the work in which he is involved, and not as an exercise in itself.

Physical growth at this stage can be fast. Limbs may therefore lose some of their former co-ordination. The child's natural self-consciousness can be exacerbated by discovering that his hands, feet and body do not respond exactly as the mind directs. This fact must continually be borne in mind and sensitively handled when involving children in design activity.

Chapter 10   Visual Communication: Experience in Two Dimensions

The previous chapter presents an argument for visual education as an important component of a design-based scheme of studies. But what form, in practical terms, might these studies take? How is visual literacy to be achieved?

There follow suggestions which are grouped for purposes of convenience, but the order or form in which they appear in a design-based scheme of work would be influenced mainly by those factors determining the choice and sequence of course activities (see Chapter 5).

The elements of visual language, like those of a verbal one, can be studied as separate entities. 'Texture' can be treated in a similar fashion to the traditional way of teaching spelling, syntax or reading. There may be circumstances in which such an approach is desirable; for example a teacher might feel happier teaching formally or prefer a 'theme-centred' approach (see example of 'Form', pp. 23-8). Alternatively a consideration of textural qualities may arise from a subject being explored, e.g., mosses, buildings, or artifacts being manufactured, e.g., a dress, mosaic, etc. This may stimulate a wider study of the subject. In practice no visual element exists in isolation. A building is seen, or a model is made as a three-dimensional form, where elements of structure, line, pattern, texture, colour and shape, etc. play complementary and interactive roles. Although the nature of an activity may place an emphasis on one specific element or aspect, pupils should be encouraged to discover and appreciate its relationship to other elements.

The majority of activities of a design-based course contain the potential for teaching a visual language which satisfies the following requirements:

(1) It is present in natural and man-made forms that embody, in varying degrees, structural and expressive functions, e.g., colour must be shown to be as important to traffic lights as it is to impressionist painting. Pattern exists in the structural form of an electricity pylon as well as in a length of fabric or the petals of a flower.

(2) It can be expressed in a variety of natural and man-made materials.

(3) It is manifested in two and three dimensions.

(4) It is only part of a total form vocabulary which utilises the other senses, as well as the visual, for communication.

10.1   Elements of Visual Form

Line
The first visual 'words' of a child are expressed in the form of lines. The earliest marks appear as scribbling and drawing. The two-dimensional paintings of young children have a linear quality and from them and successive activities the following properties and qualities of line may be discovered:

(1) That in reality a line does not exist but that it is a man-made convention.

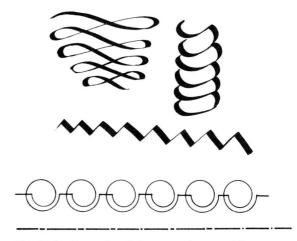

Fig. 10.1   Examples of the expressive use of line.

(2) That, strictly speaking, a line is two-dimensional, i.e., that it covers an area since it has thickness as well as length. Its character, however, is essentially one-dimensional.

(3) It can be employed to indicate boundary, division, direction and movement.

(4) Line can possess an inherently expressive character, or can visually express other verbal and sensory qualities (Fig. 10.1).

(5) Line is not necessarily continuous throughout its length, it can be broken or interrupted, e.g., 'a line of dots'. The eye sees this as a linear form.

(6) Line can represent motion or texture, or express three-dimensional qualities on a two-dimensional plane (Fig. 10.2).

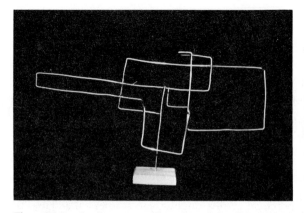

Fig. 10.3 A linear quality in three-dimensional sculpture can be emphasised by using wire in its construction.

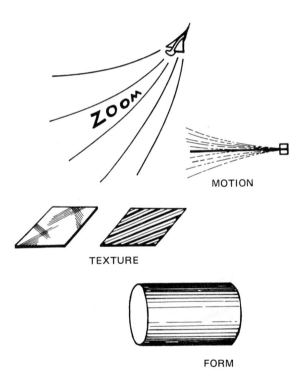

MOTION

TEXTURE

FORM

Fig. 10.2 Lines can be used to express qualities such as motion, texture or form.

In using or exploring line, pupils should be encouraged to use a variety of instruments, e.g., brushes and ink nibs of different widths, wax and pastel crayons, fingers, widths of foam sponge attached to the end of a stick, and so on. Line can be applied to or incised into, a variety of materials. Experience of line must also include its movement

in a three-dimensional space, creating and defining volume as in wire sculpture (Fig. 10.3).

Point

Dots are also a feature of children's early graphic 'words', made by jabbing a marking instrument into or onto surfaces. Theoretically a point is non-dimensional and when describing 'the point of focus' a point, as a concrete visual phenomenon, does not necessarily have to exist. Point, in an abstract or concrete, form can serve as a visual centre to which the eye is drawn.

As a visual element point can, for example, be employed to express qualities such as density or texture (Fig. 10.4).

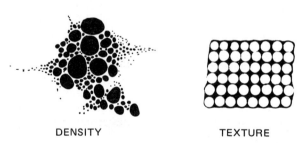

DENSITY   TEXTURE

Fig. 10.4 Here the use of 'point' expresses qualities of density and texture.

Shape

The schema (see Chapter 9, p. 96) is employed by the young child to make symbolic representations of what he knows. Many of these symbols are in the form of shapes and correspond closely to the understanding of the term, i.e., that shape is a two-dimensional area defined by real or imaginary lines and occupying a flat space. Initially the repertoire of shapes is limited, but as powers of perception and graphic skills develop the repertoire increases.

The collection, observation and recording of natural and man-made shapes and their inclusion in pictorial work, together with their use as a stimulus in creative/expressive design work, should form part of a pupil's experience of shape.

Use is frequently made in society of signs, book illustrations, advertisements, manuals, etc. which rely heavily on shapes to communicate information. Symbolism, by using simple shapes in a sophisticated manner is employed to represent things, objects or situations. Since pupils will be required to 'read' and understand this form of communication, activities should be included in the course which encourage this particular use of shape. Signs and notices to be used about the school, or suggested for use in society, could be made. Pupils will inevitably include detail in their pictures which, in this context, may be irrelevant and detract from the simplicity which is necessary in making the statement and creating a strong visual impact. In this situation they should be encouraged to see that effectiveness is obtained through an economic use of means.

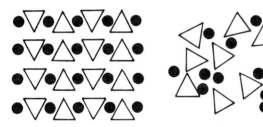

Fig. 10.5 Regular and irregular patterns. Pupils should be encouraged to identify both types of pattern within their own environment.

Fig. 10.6 Shapes arranged to form a visual 'composition'. The background itself is a shape whose value as an important element in the composition cannot be ignored.

Shapes in the natural and man-made environment do not always exist in isolation. They may be grouped in order (Fig. 10.5) forming 'regular' patterns, or disorder, forming 'irregular' patterns.

Shapes may not be exactly the same yet collectively may possess common characteristics. They are said to be 'related', and lines can be similarly related. Shapes and lines can be combined in visual compositions (Fig. 10.6).

Pupils can become so intensely preoccupied with the arrangement of shapes within an area that they can ignore the fact that the background itself is a shape exercising an influence in the overall composition. Experience in the arrangement and composition of shapes inevitably leads to a consideration of visual harmony, balance, contrast, etc.

Experience in composition that involves the overlapping of shapes (where the shapes may also have different tonal values), should be included in two-dimensional studies, as it enables the pupil to explore and develop the visual concept of recession and depth in pictorial representation.

Colour

The effective use of colour requires a certain amount of the theoretical knowledge associated with it, but this can be obtained in the middle years through links with science supported by a range of lively practical activities.

A child's reaction to colour at the different stages of development has been outlined in Chapter 9, but activities and studies over a period of years can, without lapsing into sterile exercises, aim at the following results. To:

(1) Acquaint pupils with basic colour theory and an understanding at their own levels, of the terms 'primary', 'secondary', 'tertiary' with respect to colours generally and 'intensity', 'temperature' and 'tone', as describing qualities of a single colour, or hue.

(2) Give experience in simple colour mixing.

(3) Illustrate the behaviour of colours when juxtaposed or otherwise combined together, or when subjected to different intensities of light.

(4) Study the strong influence that colour can have upon emotional responses. People interpret colours in different ways largely depending upon personality, the context in which the colours appear and the particular association regarding them. In this sense colour has a strong influence upon man and the environment in which he lives.

(5) Provide decision-making activities involving the choice of colour, e.g., making a garment, weaving, painting a toy, etc.

(6) Study the role and uses of colour in man-made and natural environments and objects, e.g., traffic lights, advertising, camouflage, etc., assessing its effectiveness or otherwise.

(7) Develop a personal colour sense. A sensitivity towards colour is likely to be achieved through the studies and activities suggested and not by the imposition of arbitrary standards or what is currently fashionable.

Texture

Texture describes the quality of a surface. It is essentially a quality that is most accurately determined by touch but which can be visually appreciated. An emotional association can be linked with visual/tactile experiences. The look and feeling of thick carpeting can convey an impression of comfort and possibly a sense of quality, wealth, homeliness, etc. Manufacturers are alive to this type of effect and produce many materials that look like something else; for example, printed wood-grained and natural stone wallpapers, imitation crocodile skin, synthetic 'fur' and 'velvet', chromium plated metals, and so on.

The explorative stages of development in the early years enable a child to build up an initial body of tactile experiences but this must be extended in the middle years. A design-based course should enable a pupil to experience something of the variety and richness of textures that exist in his surroundings. Many of these can:

(1) be collected and classified (for example, as being natural or man-made);

(2) be recorded by photographing, 'rubbing', drawing or by the collection of photographs or illustrations;

(3) be reproduced, created or employed in two- and three-dimensional work.

Movement

Children enjoy and are excited by movement; they swing, climb, slide, jump, run, etc. Kinetic experiences involving themselves, objects and motion in a situation, together with other associated sensory stimuli, have a strong appeal, e.g., playing football, nursing a doll, having a fight, squirting water, throwing snowballs, dancing to 'pop' music, etc. They are alive to the expressive/

qualitative character of movement. A baby is able to interpret the expression on its mother's face. Children enjoy making faces and performing body gestures to mimic, or to insult. A design education should help children develop social and communicative skills through the refined and controlled use of body movements; the art of conversation depends on the interpretation of visually perceived 'body-language' as much as on the use of words.

Movement is 'a continuous change of position'. The only permanent record of its having taken place is by visual evidence. But this evidence is meaningful to a viewer only if he is able to interpret it from his own experiences. We may take as an example sets of footprints being left in the sand. Here the visual sense enables us to make certain statements and speculate about certain phenomena which involves the element of time. Sensations regarding movement are being evoked although actual movement is not taking place, neither is the cause of the evidence present. This device is frequently employed by commercial advertisers.

Fig. 10.7 Change or movement is inferred by this 'before and after' approach. Courtesy Sperry Remington Consumer Products.

Another example of visual symbols evoking responses which involve the element of time is the musical score.

Movements in plants and animals is a highly developed response mechanism. Plants react by movement to changes in the environment, e.g., the turning of leaves and flowers to a light source. Similarly with animals and man movement can be of an involuntary nature, e.g., a reaction to danger, as well as of a voluntary origin, e.g., dancing.

Humans experience movement in basically three ways:

(1) the movements that they make themselves,
(2) the movements that they observe, and
(3) the evidence of the movement they produce.

A visual language incorporates all of these elements.

When he scribbles the young child makes marks which are graphic representations of the body movements which have produced them. This is not peculiar to young children. At a more conscious level the 'action' painting of recent times is quite similar.

The uninhibited approach of children in the early middle years enables them to be totally absorbed in much of their pictorial work and visual expression. But being involved in a movement experience they can remain unconscious of a time differentiation. A boy painting a 'war' picture started to narrate the battle as the events took place in his mind and as he recorded them; 'guns shoot-shells — that fly through the air — and then explode'. A litle girl carefully 'dressed' a painting of herself by superimposing one layer of clothes upon another, completing the operation by 'putting on a blue coat'. The result was a visual 'mess' in adult eyes, but she was satisfied with the result. For her the painting had served its purpose.

The phenomenon of the 'multiple-image' is not uncommon in the pictorial work of young children. A single person can be represented as doing different things at the same time but in a common situation, usually the home. The sun shines brightly with the moon, the washing is 'hung out' at the same time as people are going to bed.

Children gradually learn to represent the dimension of time in their pictures by 'freezing' the action of the subject. For example, the goalkeeper dives for the ball as it travels from the head of the striker, or the boxer falls as the punch is received on the chin. In choosing the subject matter for visually expressive and communicative activities in two and three dimensions, the teacher should bear in mind the need to help pupils to pass through this transitional phase in time representation. The problem of making clear that something has taken place, or is taking place, or is about to take place can be resolved by presenting images which provide time clues, e.g., there *has been* an accident, the

police *have* arrived, the ambulance *is coming* to the scene and *will*, presumably, take someone away, and someone *is* running away to spread the news. The images express apparent motion.

A design-based course should also include opportunities to observe, record and analyse the relationship between time, movement and state or form; for example the spinning colour wheel, the drawing out of forms on the potter's wheel, chemical reactions, things burning or having been burnt, the growth of plants and animals including the human body, the process of decay, the seasonal changes in the natural environment and so on.

The ubiquitous comic-strip and the fascination of 'flick-books' should not be discouraged as they are popular aids in enabling children to break down the development of a story or happening into a sequence of pictures. The time factor is thus represented by the passage from one visual image to the next. The visual image can also be related to specific words. Foreign language courses in schools make particular use of this device, as do many instruction manuals, etc. (Fig. 10.8). Pupils should be encouraged to present a story or describe a procedure in this manner, e.g., making a cup of tea, mending a puncture, preparing a simple dish, loading a camera, etc. Attention must again be drawn to the fact that they might include extraneous detail, which must be avoided.

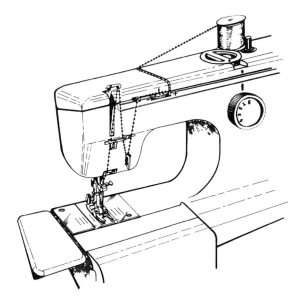

Fig. 10.8   Directions given in pictorial form — threading a sewing machine. Courtesy of Frister and Rossman Ltd.

A single picture or diagram using a symbolic approach can be employed in other contexts to convey information or give instructions which cover a longer time span, e.g., recording a flow of traffic or people in a physical situation, or the sequence of relative moves in an operational situation, e.g., a game of chess or a movement in dancing.

10.2 The Organisation of Two-dimensional Space

Destructuring and Restructuring
The square, rectangle, triangle and circle can be taken as starting points in developing knowledge and skill in the use of two-dimensional space. The examples in Fig. 10.9 show how these forms can be transformed by sub-division and rearrangement into new ones, and how parts of the original can be brought into new relationships (Fig. 10.9).

Fig. 10.9 Sub-division into parts and their re-arrangement. Simple geometrical two-dimensional shapes.

This activity can be extended to enable pupils to develop their visual vocabulary as shapes can be arranged to express*

(1) direction,
(2) rhythm,
(3) focus,
(4) growth/extension, and
(5) positive/negative relationships.

Unlimited freedom is not a prerequisite to original creative work. Examples of excellent creative expression have frequently been conceived and executed under the most adverse and limiting

*For further interpretation of this theme see Rottger, E., *Creative Paper Craft*, Batsford.

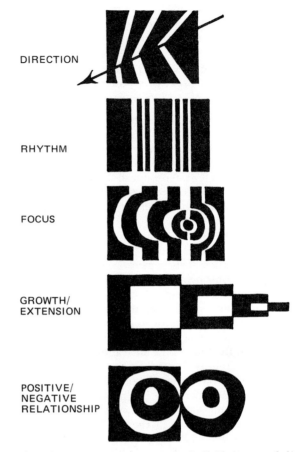

DIRECTION

RHYTHM

FOCUS

GROWTH/
EXTENSION

POSITIVE/
NEGATIVE
RELATIONSHIP

Fig. 10.10 Re-arrangement of sub-divided parts of the square to express visual qualities—direction, forms, growth/extension and the positive/negative relationship.

of circumstances. The mind most likely to produce arresting and original ideas is one that has been trained to see the potentialities that are contained within the limitations of certain constraints, or to work with restricted terms of reference. This applies in visual expression, where an economy of means can enhance aesthetic and communicative qualities, e.g., simplicity, clarity, impact and elegance. By imposing clearly defined constraints in a design brief (see Chapter 2) the pupils can be taught to

(1) develop a creative imagination by focusing the attention yet at the same time directing the intellect to explore possibilities beyond the immediate and the obvious, and
(2) realise the potential of specific tools and materials.

Through this type of activity pupils are likely to develop those aspects of the vocabulary and articulation of two-dimensional space mentioned above (direction, rhythm, etc.). Possible constraints might be that 'nothing of the original shape be taken away', that 'lines of the cut(s) are straight or curved', that 'a representational image be produced', e.g., a face, flower, bird, or that 'black and white or two colours of paper or card be used', etc.

Sub-division of Two-dimensional Space

The division of a shape into a number of smaller component parts is an important aspect in the organisation of two-dimensional area. Puzzles fascinate pupils in the early middle years. By posing the question 'How many rectangles or (How many diamond shapes) are there in each of the diagrams shown (Fig. 10.11)?' this interest can be used to stimulate an awareness of sub-division.

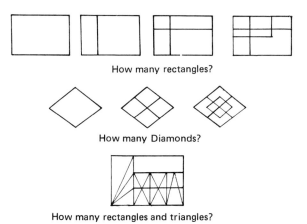

How many rectangles?

How many Diamonds?

How many rectangles and triangles?

Fig. 10.11   How many shapes?

Pupils can create their own arrangements using combinations of similar or dissimilar shapes.

For older pupils, the examination of a wide variety of examples of sub-division is an extension to this activity. Artists, designers and architects construct arrangements of shapes in two dimensions to convey an impression, evoke a response, or create balanced, harmonious compositions. The painters of seventeenth century Dutch interiors, such as Vermeer, relied on compositions having horizontals and verticals. This arrangement gives a sense of stability and quiet dignity which epitomised the attitudes of the middle-class burghers of those times

in that society. The same device is recurrent in architectural designs from the Parthenon onwards.

The triangle is also used to sub-divide space. Structurally, in three dimensions, it is recognised as a stable framework, e.g., girder bridges, scaffolding, pylons. This is also true of two-dimensional arrangements, as may be seen, for example, in certain works of the early Renaissance and later artists, e.g., Giotto and Cézanne. It is used today in two- and three-dimensional compositions, e.g., flower arranging and window dressing.

Other geometric shapes, e.g., the circle, are also employed, and arrangements may contain elaborate frameworks composed of several basic shapes within which the subject is presented.

The Golden Section

The 'golden section' has its origins in antiquity and evolved as a result of man's efforts to resolve visual beauty by the arrangement of shapes, lines and colours according to a series of laws in much the same way as they were discovering laws in mathematics. The golden section has been applied by artists, architects and craftsmen in their organisation of space. Pythagoras proved that the proportions of the human body were based on it, the Greeks used it in their sculpture, painting and pottery, and it was shown to exist in the proportions of natural forms such as plants, snowflakes and shells. The medieval cathedral builders used it as a foundation for their designs and believed it came from God.

The golden section can be defined thus:
The division of a line in which the smaller part is in the same proportion to the greater as the greater part is to the whole.

$$A \qquad\qquad B \qquad\qquad\qquad\qquad C$$

Thus, in the diagram, $AB/BC = BC/AC$. The point of intersection B lies about 0.382 of the distance AC from A.

Taking the sub-division of a rectangle (Fig. 10.12) $ABCD$ and drawing lines KL, IJ, EF, GH to the golden section (from either ends of the lines AB, BC, CD, and DA) points of intersection at X are given. These are the best places to situate a focus of interest or subject in two-dimensional compositions.

The theory and application of the golden section, particularly with its close mathematical and geometrical associations, is well within the scope of understanding and appreciation of pupils in their later middle years or at Piaget's stage of 'concrete

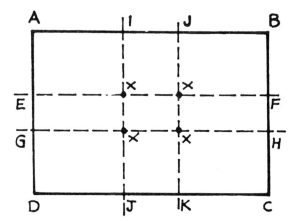

Fig. 10.12 The Golden Section applied to the rectangle, determining the most suitable points for visual focus.

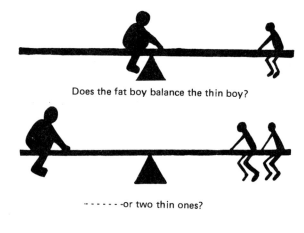

Does the fat boy balance the thin boy?

- - - - - -or two thin ones?

Is △ in the right place? If not, where should it be put?

Fig. 10.13 The 'see-saw' as used in play or as mathematics apparatus is a familiar object to children. It can be used to develop the concept of visual balance as the questions indicate.

operations', although it is best taught with positive reference to actual examples that preferably arise from their own experience.

Balance

Where children have enjoyed a varied play experience 'balance' is understood through physical experience involving objects and the whole body. This concept is developed through the more refined and controlled physical activity in PE and is applied in mathematics in which, through the structural 'see-saw' apparatus (Fig. 10.13) pupils begin to develop an understanding of equality. Having this experience behind them, pupils will be receptive to the introduction of 'visual balance' which is an important aspect of two-dimensional composition.

Initially the presentation of the idea can take a simple form related to common personal experience, e.g., possibly as a question and answer activity.

'Does the fat boy balance the thin boy?'

'. . . or the two thin ones?'

After this, work may move towards the abstract, involving shapes as symbols.

'Is the fulcrum in the right place to balance the two squares?'

'If not, where should it be put?'

Three other lines can be included to establish a two-dimensional plane and the question asked, 'How many smaller squares could be used and where might they be situated to establish a visual balance?' (Fig. 10.14).

The fulcrum could then be moved up into the

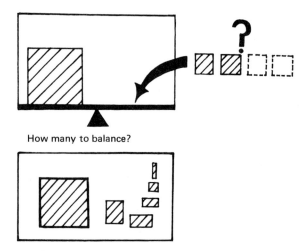

How many to balance?

A balanced arrangement?

Fig. 10.14 Visual balance should be exemplified by reference to natural and man-made objects and situations, e.g. a landscape or good (and bad) architectural features.

two-dimensional picture plane and organised to give what pupils feel to be a 'balanced' arrangement.

If the treatment of two-dimensional organisation outlined above appears too formal and academic, it must be reiterated that it forms a theoretical foundation upon which many practical applications are based. As suggested, pupils may respond to either method of instruction, i.e., working from theory to application or be introduced to the principles through two-dimensional activities. In Home Economics, for example, the planning layout, and decoration of the home and the making of garments, etc., offers wide scope, as does picture or poster making, and so on.

Size of Two-dimensional Work

Uninhibited drawing on walls, pavements and sandy beaches illustrates children's capacity to execute graphic work on a large scale; at the other extreme, drawings and doodles on hands and fingernails show an equal facility with small areas.

Before two-dimensional work is carried out, questions need to be asked by pupil and teacher alike regarding the size and shape of the surface:

(1) What purpose is the drawing, picture, design, etc., going to serve? Is it for public display or personal record? Is it a means to an end, e.g., a sketch or an explanatory drawing, or an end in itself, e.g., a mural, scenery, a picture?

(2) What size would be appropriate? For example, would it be large enough to enter on to it all the detail that might be required? Would the poster or sign be large enough to capture attention? Would the diagram, picture, etc., be small enough to fit alongside other work, on to a display panel, in a project folder or book? Does the theme, title or subject suggest a shape?

(3) What are the limitations or potentialities of facilities, materials, work areas or spaces in the situation

   (a) for the execution of work, and
   (b) for its final presentation?

   It might be convenient to work on the corridor floor or wall, but at regular intervals the corridor carries the tide of school traffic. Perhaps one could 'work large', but where could the results be stored? Is it possible to 'put it together, or mount it' after school hours, and so on?

(4) The personal preferences of the pupil. Some may prefer to work large and others meticulously, with detail, on a small scale.

Pupil attitudes towards size also tend to be conditioned by a number of factors. Pictures of subjects are made by them to a certain size simply because they appear that size in books, on the TV screen or in the comic. Reality must be expressed as reality is ('I'm drawing a leaf this size because it actually is this size—but I can't draw all the veins in'). Very often the home or school environment has not permitted expression on different, particularly large, scales. Standard-sized exercise books, drawing paper, etc., tend to be issued to children with the unconscious implication that it establishes the area to be 'worked on' or 'filled up' for the job in hand.

Pupils benefit from an inversion of their normal perspective of viewing the size of things. The microscope and telescope enlarge that which is normally viewed as being small, whilst a view through the reverse end gives a different view of things. A fascinating activity in this respect is to construct 35 mm slides which carry small compositions made from a varied assortment of materials such as sugar, crystals, scraps of nylon, mesh, coloured tissue, feathers, leaf skeletons, oil, coloured inks, etc., and project them. This and similar activities can provide a stimulus for creative work as well as broadening the concept of size.

Design activities should equip pupils with the simpler techniques of reproducing a two-dimensional subject to the same, larger or smaller size. The principle of scale, with its links to mathematics, is necessary, for example, in producing or reading maps, technical drawings, plans, dress patterns, etc. The pantograph remains a useful instrument for this purpose.

Scaling up or down can also be achieved by the 'grid method' (as described in Chapter 5, pp. 57-8).

The advantages of large two-dimensional pieces of work are that they offer better scope for group activity and breadth of subject treatment than is the case on a smaller scale. A child who lacks personal confidence can benefit by contributing to an overall presentation, since his efforts will not be judged in isolation (and possibly unfavourably) but rather in the context of the whole group effort. At the same time he can experience a satisfaction and pride in his 'bit'. This is also true of dramatic productions where the aim is to include maximum pupil involvement. Children do not like being 'left out'.

10.3 Expression in Two Dimensions

As mentioned in Chapter 9 there are basically two components to visual form:

(1) that which serves a utilitarian function, and
(2) that which serves an expressive function.

Both are present in any piece of work, but rarely in equal amounts. In making a map a pupil is primarily concerned with the former, but painting a picture of, say, 'The Fantastic House' calls for treatment that is subjective, imaginative, and personal. A design-based scheme of work must ensure a well-balanced blend of subject matter across the objective-subjective spectrum.

It is often supposed that children can spontaneously express themselves creatively in two and three dimensions. They have the subject, they discover the means, and they execute it unaided. Whilst this can happen, the assumption that it is widespread is incorrect. The child probably has the subject as a result of experiences associated with it and about which he has the urge to make a statement. He has the means because he knows what tools and materials will 'do' but he looks towards teachers for guidance and help in broadening his horizons. It follows that two-dimensional activities in schools usually require a stimulus which the school or teacher provides. The scheme of design activities should include a rich and varied content of subject material. For example the more expressive themes could develop from

(1) stories, fables, legends,
(2) music and sounds,
(3) seasons, festivals, and celebrations,
(4) work activities, e.g., 'mending the road',
(5) reactions to sensory experiences such as watching a dance/drama, subject 'The Dancers', and
(6) poems.

Themes and subjects are many and are suggested in books and magazines that deal more specifically with this aspect of design work in school. Bibliography).

Reference has already been made (p. 38) to the advisability of a preparative phase prior to the execution of two-dimensional activities. To this can be added the need to enter into some discussions with pupils individually or as groups, before, during or after the execution of their work. Verbalisation of ideas, and reactions regarding subject, materials or techniques can enrich and develop visual expression as the reverse holds true for verbal expression.

The responsibility of the teacher is to offer stimulus and guidance to the pupil so that he can progress in visual expression, yet the pace must not be forced and the child must be allowed to work and develop at his own pace.

10.4 Two-dimensional Techniques and Skills

There is a wide range of techniques and skills associated with working in two dimensions. They are practised at all ages and levels of sophistication and a large amount of published material is available on their specialised aspects (see the Bibliography). Recent developments in science and technology have produced a wide range of new materials and associated techniques, e.g., chipboard, expanded polystyrene, acrylic paints, metal alloys and synthetic fibres. These have supplemented the more traditional ones used in two-dimensional activities. Many of these can be safely employed in schools, but careful note must be taken of instructional information produced by suppliers or manufacturers. Design education should attempt to introduce pupils to as broad a range of two-dimensional skills and techniques as possible, as they provide part of the resources or 'means' of achieving success in design/problem-solving situations and aid effective visual communication. The following offer some suggestions of the more basic skills/techniques that should come within the compass of design education in the middle years.

(1) Drawing

Drawing remains a basic and necessary skill and one that is universally employed for effective communication by those engaged in design activity. It is convenient and versatile. Whilst disapproving of those former teaching methods which tended to equate drawing 'skill' with the ability to represent objects and scenes realistically in two dimensions, the discipline afforded by this activity in focusing the attention, training the eye and co-ordinating it with the hand must be recognised.

Like all design-based skills it is one that can be taught and, as such, must conform to the same educational principles upon which their teaching is based, i.e., awareness of developmental stages in concept formation and graphic expression, individual personality and growth factors, and the provision of a well-devised sequence of experiences

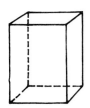

Fig. 10.15 'Drawing' can express qualities of line and area, texture and form.

with defined objectives. With regard to the latter the definition of 'drawing' is not wholly clear. Although it has strong linear associations (Fig. 10.15), it can also be used to represent area, surface texture or form.

Many design-based activities require the use of drawing, e.g., tracing, geometry, batik, dress-making, etc. Activities must be included in the course with the specific aim of developing the skill. In considering the role of drawing in design education the following suggestions are made:

(1) That the drawing skills associated with technical, mathematical and scientific subjects (i.e., formal uses) must be taught in addition to those employed expressively. This involves the use of drawing instruments, e.g., compasses, set-square, T-square, ruler, etc.
(2) That pupils have a broad range of experience with a variety of mark-making materials. Suggestions are:

pencil, charcoal, fibre-tip, felt-tip, ball-point, knibbed pen, brush, chalk, dry pastel, oil pastel, wax pastel, coloured pencil.

From their personal collection pupils can choose appropriately for the effects they wish to achieve.
(3) That examples of a variety of drawing techniques and styles employed by artists, designers, technical illustrators and others engaged in design-based occupations be examined and compared.

(2) Painting
Success in painting depends upon a disciplined use of the paint medium and a sound practice of technique as much as any natural ability as a painter. Technique largely depends on a knowledge and appreciation of the properties and qualities of the medium being used and a design course should teach these through demonstration and practical experience.

Paints commonly used in schools are as follows:
powder colour, solid tempera blocks, PVA/acrylic, water colours.
Others which are less commonly employed are:
oils, emulsion, enamel, gouache, stains.

A number of points need to be noted in connection with painting in school, as they contribute to success, prevent frustration and help to maintain equipment and materials in good order.

(1) Pupils must be made aware that many people use the paints and materials that are supplied. 'Leave as you would expect to find' is a helpful motto for the efficient running of the studio or workshop in school. Furthermore, materials are expensive and wasteful practices are to be avoided.
(2) Keep the work area clean by covering surroundings with old newspaper, polythene sheets, etc. Pupils should also protect their clothes by wearing aprons, smocks, old shirts, etc.
(3) When the colours are to be mixed this should be done separately in a mixing tray, palette or dish, *not* in the container holding the pigment.
(4) Select the right size and type of brush before using another colour, and wash it out thoroughly after use (turpentine, substitute or white spirit may be necessary for certain paints).
(5) Pupils should be encouraged to judge:
    (a) The amount of water required on the brush and palette for 'wet' and 'dry' painting techniques. Thicker consistencies can be obtained by using PVA or cellulose adhesives in the mixing medium.
    (b) How much paint is required on the brush. The dipping of the brush into paint or water as opposed to plunging is to be encouraged, as is the draining off of any excess on the edge of the container.
    (c) Painting one colour over another is to be avoided unless manufacturers suggest the possibility of doing this. It is sometimes successful with certain types of medium and with dark colours over lighter ones.

(3) Printing
Block printing. This technique of printing is capable of considerable sophistication but the principle upon which it is based is simple and can

be introduced to pupils at an early age. Experience will have taught them that pressing an object on to a surface can leave an impression, e.g., the wet foot on a dry floor, the dirty hand on a clean surface.

The fundamental parts of the process are:

(1) The block, i.e., that which is going to be printed (Fig. 10.16). Virtually any object is printable.
(2) The medium, i.e., that which is applied to the block and is transferred from it to the printing surface, leaving an impression.
(3) The surface which is to be printed on.
(4) The force that brings the block and printing surface together.

The simple placing of a paint-covered hand upon a sheet of paper can be the point of departure for the introduction of progressively more sophisticated materials, equipment and techniques in block printing which can be introduced throughout the design course (see the Bibliography).

Screen Printing. The main visual element of block printing is texture, but with screen printing it is shape.

The starting point for screen printing is stencilling, where pupils can be introduced to the principle that a shape can be painted on to a surface by applying the medium over a stencil which effectively masks out the areas not to be painted. There is a positive/negative relationship between stencil and print, i.e., the shape that is required is the one that is cut *out* from the stencil.

With screen printing the stencil adheres to, or is part of a permeable material (usually nylon) stretched taut across a frame. A thin film of medium (usually ink) is drawn over the material with a 'squeegee'. In so doing it passes through the fine mesh of the material on to the surface that is being printed, over those areas that have not been masked off by the stencil (Fig. 10.17).

Like block printing the principle of screen printing is simple but can be practised in schools at more advanced levels (see the Bibliography).

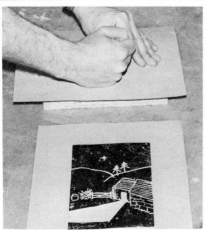

Fig. 10.16 (a) Inking the block, (b) burnishing by pressing the block against the surface to be printed.

Fig. 10.17 The Screen Printing process. (a) The screen and squeegee, and (b) a stencil can be cut from newsprint. Whilst cheap and freely available, newsprint allows only a limited number of prints to be 'pulled'.

(4) Collage

Collage as a two-dimensional technique is the rendering of a subject, pattern or design by the application of materials on to a supporting surface. The range and diversity of materials that can be employed is considerable, e.g.:

Fabrics: hessian, felt, wool, silk, corduroy, scrim, carpeting;
Fibres: string, sisal, rope, thread, nylon, canvas;
Wood: offcuts, bark, shavings, sawdust, blockboard.

Other possibilities are lentils, beads, stones, glass, sequins, and practically anything that will stick onto a surface or provide such a surface.

Fig. 10.18 A wide variety and mixture of materials can be employed in collage. Here string is used, a linear material interestingly applied to a two-dimensional situation.

The skill in collage lies not so much in the technique of applying materials to the surface as in carefully choosing and arranging the materials which are sympathetic to the subject. Elements of texture, line, shape and general composition are important in this respect. The materials themselves can provide the stimulus for the subject or for the way it is treated.

(5) Mosaic

Mosaic is an ancient art form which reached its zenith in the Byzantine period, but which has been practised continually since then. It is a permanent form of surface treatment which retains its colour and can easily be cleaned.

In principle mosaic is simply the execution of a two-dimensional design by the building up of areas from the juxtaposition of small pieces or 'tesserae' such as glass, stone, etc., but it is capable of wide adaptation (see the Bibliography).

Simplified versions of the technique can be used in schools but selection for use by pupils depends on a number of factors:

(1) The techniques are relatively slow, laborious and time consuming. They require patience, a competent degree of fine finger control and a mind that will persevere.

(2) The size of the subject and the area to be covered must be matched to organisational method (individual or group working) and the pupils' ability. Mosaics can range from small, individual pieces of work to a mural involving the whole of the school.

(3) The materials for mosaic. Whilst the setting of predominantly flat rectangular stone tesserae in plaster is the traditional technique, it is one that is better suited to pupils in the upper middle years. 'Pebble' mosaics can provide a suitable introduction to this technique. 'Pebbles' can be widely interpreted as small stones, chips of ceramic tile, coal, broken (coloured) glass, crockery, granite chippings, etc. These can be set into slow-drying plaster or cement mix laid on to a backing material in the form of a shallow tray.

Tesserae may also be attached to a backing material using strong adhesive. This method extends the range of materials that can be used, e.g., shells, beads, buttons, beans, dried peas, lentils, felt and coloured paper. Different materials could also be used for backing purposes, e.g., cardboard, papier mâché, etc.

Another practice is to cement the tesserae to a supporting base and then fill in the spaces between them with a thin mix of plaster 'filler' by spreading it over the surface. When almost set the excess plaster is wiped away.

The production of a mosaic is not necessarily a direct activity. The design to be executed can initially be drafted out on to the working surface in simple, large shapes and strong lines. Colour areas in mosaic are mainly flat, without graduations of tone, except when such graduations are achieved by painting cardboard tesserae and carefully placing them together to achieve this effect. Naturalism is not a feature of mosaic and should not be attempted. Subject matter, or patterns, should be

113

Fig. 10.19 Appliqué. Work typically produced by an older pupil.

simple to be striking. When a design has been developed in a sketch it can be transferred to the backing material.

(6) Fabrics
Fabrics are materials that can be used both two- and three-dimensionally (e.g., wall hangings, cushions, etc.). Several skills are associated with them:

appliqué (Fig. 10.19), batik, tie-dye, embroidery, screen and block printing.

It is not unusual to find examples of work in fabric where several of these skills have been brought together.

Appliqué is an extension of collage with certain similarities to mosaic. A design is executed by

Fig. 10.20 To produce batik pictures in several colours requires careful forethought as wax must be applied, and/or withdrawn for successive dye applications depending on the desired effect. In learning this process children can find it helpful to prepare the picture or pattern, with its listed sequence of operations.

means of applying areas of plain or patterned fabric to a backing (also usually of fabric) using adhesives or by stitching. The design can be developed by use of plain or decorative stitches.

Batik and tie-dye are methods of dyeing a design into cloth by the principles of resist, i.e., preventing the dye from reaching selected parts of the fabric.

With batik the resist is achieved by applying clear molten wax to those areas which must not be dyed by using a traditional molten wax applicator (tjanting tool) or a brush. The wax is soaked into the threads of the weave and when cooled and hardened prevents the penetration of the liquid dye into which the fabric is immersed. The wax is later removed. Colour mixing can be achieved by dyeing one colour over another (Fig. 10.20).

In tie-dye the penetration of the dye is prevented by tying up the fabric, by knotting, or by sewing and drawing up the threads (tritik) (Fig. 10.21).

Single designs having different colours can be obtained by dyeing several times.

Batik and tie-dye are capable of elaboration but are within the scope and appeal of pupils throughout the middle years (see the Bibliography).

(7) Embroidery
In the past embroidery was mainly understood in terms of stitchery. Traditional education in the skill mainly focused on developing the pupil's proficiency in a multiplicity of different stitches. Technique was all important and tended to dominate the design of the article.

Today the situation has altered and the emphasis is on design as a means of personal expression. There is available a wide variety of stitches and a selection of fabrics and threads, and these provide the means and inspiration for interpreting and developing the subject. This itself is mainly conceived in terms of shape, line, texture, colour, composition, etc. (Fig. 10.22). The range of subjects for embroidery is limitless (see the Bibliography) and the craft possesses an excellent scope for creative two-dimensional design development.

A design department should carry a wide collection of materials, threads and worked samples of the more commonly used stitches as these are valuable aids in assisting pupils to develop design ideas (see the Bibliography). Modern embroidery is virtually inseparable from the techniques of appliqué, can be used in conjunction with the fabric skills listed above, and extend to aspects of tapestry work and weaving.

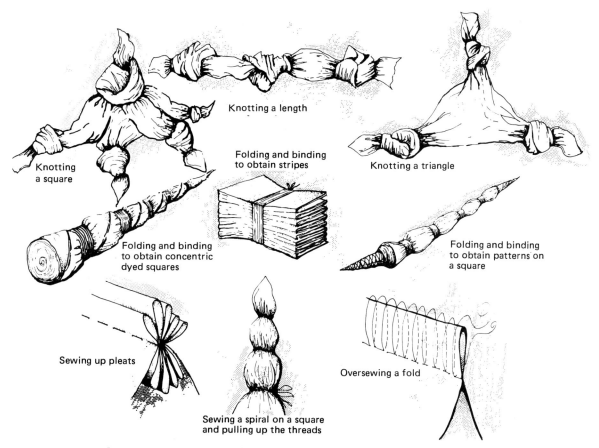

Knotting a length

Knotting a square

Folding and binding to obtain stripes

Knotting a triangle

Folding and binding to obtain concentric dyed squares

Folding and binding to obtain patterns on a square

Sewing up pleats

Sewing a spiral on a square and pulling up the threads

Oversewing a fold

Fig. 10.21   Methods of achieving tie/dye effects by folding, knotting, tieing and sewing.

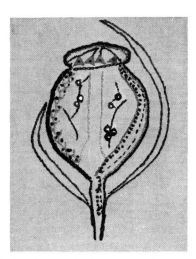

Fig. 10.22   Where possible, pupils should be encouraged to develop their own ideas from a variety of sources and stimuli before attempting to interpret them as embroidery. (Published material provides clear illustra- tions of the shapes of stitches and the scope of their expressive qualities. These may be selected and incorporated into the finished work.)

115

10.5   The Relationship between Two and Three Dimensions

From early childhood onwards people in most societies look at pictures which exist mainly in two-dimensional form. Many people are concerned in producing them, e.g., artists, draughtsmen, photographers. The subjects of these pictures are mainly three-dimensional. Although there is a considerable variation in the style of interpretation and representation of subject matter the majority of people wish to recognise and identify what they see. The enquiry, 'But what does it mean?', especially when the viewer is looking at the more abstract interpretations, indicates:

(1) how strong the urge amongst people is to recognise and identify.
(2) how much picture making in its many forms is a cultural convention. Something that cannot be recognised is something of which the individual has not previously been aware.
(3) the facility to interpret, in both making the statement and looking at it, is a learned one. As an important element in visual communication the ability to interpret is a social necessity.

Thus one of the main objectives of design education should be to develop the facility of:

(1) being able to represent in two dimensions three-dimensional phenomena, ranging in treatment from the purely subjective or expressive type to the formal type that follows universally agreed standards, conventions and terminology (e.g., ordnance survey maps, electrical wiring diagrams, geometrical or technical drawings). The pupil should also be able to produce two-dimensional pictures from ideas, specifications or a model, i.e., working from the abstract to the concrete.

A proportion of design activity in the middle years usually is devoted to picture making based on subjective/expressive themes, but the following are suggested as a few of the many activities (not in any pre-determined order), that could help pupils develop an understanding of the relationship between two- and three-dimensional work:

(1) Asking the pupil to roughly sketch out ideas that are in his 'mind's eye' of something he wishes to make — how something looks, or how it operates: 'Show me how you see your go-kart . . . or your pot'.
(2) Making 'mock-ups' in card or expanded polystyrene and then drawing different views.
(3) Producing geometric solids from 'nets', e.g., cuboid, cylinder, tetrahedron, hexahedron, octahedron, dodecahedron.
(4) Building clay slab pots of rectangular or cylindrical forms around cardboard mock-ups.
(5) Teaching the standard plan-elevation drawing convention for the representation of solid objects. Children in the later middle years should experience little difficulty with this concept although initially it might be an advantage to work directly from concrete examples that they can handle and view from different angles.
(6) Garment and soft-toy making working from simple two-dimensional patterns.
     General experience in working directly from plans and drawings, e.g., aero-modelling, 'Lego'.
(7) Paper sculpture. Modelling paper into three-dimensional forms of a representational abstract, decorative or functional nature.
(8) Map-making. Constructing a model in relief, illustrating the concept of contour levels and the adding of physical details, e.g., roads, buildings, trees, boundaries. Drawing the same model two-dimensionally using symbolic conventions.
(9) Papier mâché modelling by pasting paper on to a relief or three-dimensional mould (of clay or plasticine) and then withdrawing the mould. A two-dimensional material, i.e., paper, has then been used to make a three-dimensional form.

Chapter 11   Experience in Three Dimensions

As well as experience in two-dimensional work (see Chapters 9 and 10), children need to develop an awareness of three-dimensional space, and to gain a facility in its use and in the manipulation and application of three-dimensional media.

Further, it is vital to cultivate their awareness of the three-dimensional environment so that their attitudes to the physical form of their surroundings becomes less egocentric. From a concern with their own personal and immediate needs, they need to progress towards a more mature concern for the environment, the way society treats it, and the conservation of its resources (see also Chapter 3).

Four closely related areas of three-dimensional experience should be provided by the curriculum, each of them having an identifiable relationship with or function within design education in the middle years. These four areas are dealt with in Sections 11.1-4.

11.1   Wide-ranging Exploration of Volumetric Space

This is aimed at developing spatial perception — the ability to think in three dimensions.

Piaget and others concerned with the study of child development have drawn attention to phases in this development, through which all children pass.

While in early pre-school years, children soon come to appreciate that they are not at the centre of the universe. Determining their particular place within it even in very basic terms of physical relationships, takes much longer. The growing child needs to be able to establish his position relative to his environment (immediate and total) and also the spatial relationships which exist between other objects and himself within it.

From nursery age right through the middle years of schooling pupils need a great deal and variety of experience of spatial relationships so that rudimentary three-dimensional awareness is translated through involvement into knowledge of composition, balance, simple perspective, relative dimensions, proportion and so on. In addition, the relevance and importance of the space-time relationship should be absorbed by participation in those forms of activity in which it is critical: for example, drama, dance, sports and many physically demanding pastimes.

Such activities which involve the body as a whole help the child establish his physical relationship with the immediate surroundings and his associates.

To this end, for instance, dance and drama 'in the round' provides more valuable experience than similar work carried out on a conventional stage, with its proscenium arch framing what tends to become visually a two-dimensional activity. Young children performing on a conventional stage tend towards straight-line groupings, all of them facing their audience, and the use of the available space is either limited or contrived. Arena-type settings on the other hand more naturally provide opportunities for movement and action, (a) at different levels, (b) in irregular groupings, (c) to different positions within a defined three-dimensional space. Three-dimensional scenery, or settings — even if they are only simple steps and box structures — facilitate movement around the stage for the actors or dancers, who are playing to an audience on three or four sides. Thus they become aware of the need to know what is happening throughout the three-dimensional volume of the stage and scenery, as well as the small portion they are facing at any one time.

Such activities, carried on with or without an audience, help the child to develop an emotional 'feel' for space and his use of it to express mood or movement.

Team games such as football, hockey, netball or volley ball (involving position play) offer experience of being one unit amongst many, all of which move relative to one another in a space-time-direction relationship.

The relationship between actual and apparent sizes is one which calls for practical consideration, as does that between actual and apparent speed. The apparently small size and slow speed of an aircraft or approaching car (often a direct cause of accidents) calls for explanations involving the relationship between time, space and size.

There are many ways of providing such explanations. A study of the solar system involves considerations of scale too difficult even for many adults to comprehend, but the production of models of it, even if sadly lacking in accuracy, provides experience in the relationships between space, distance and time.

As an indication of children's limited ability to visualise three-dimensional space, an average ability group of 11-year-olds was asked to say how many cuts would be required to convert a cube into eight smaller cubes. Only about 10% were able to offer the correct answer.

When asked how many sides of one of the eight small cubes would touch the others (when stacked to make one large cube), again many children gave the incorrect answer.

A similar age-group was asked to 'draw six cubed' after spending some time studying volume and cubic values. Amongst other devices the concept had been illustrated by using structural apparatus, i.e., wooden blocks, and the pupils were allowed to use these to help them draw six cubed if they felt they needed this assistance. Fig. 11.1 illustrates the variety in response given by a group of boys and girls having approximately the same level of measurable intelligence (slightly above average).

Figure 11.2 shows how a pupil can easily misunderstand what he is being taught. The drawings tend to disprove the case for traditional 'chalk and talk—all do the same' methods for mixed-ability groupings, in which there are such wide variations in intelligence and perception.

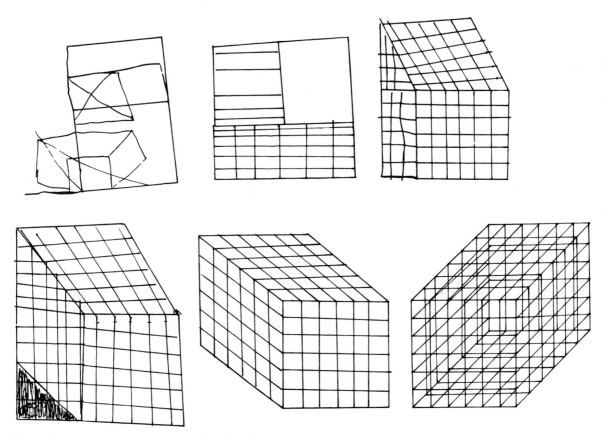

Fig. 11.1   Attempts by eleven-year-old pupils of mixed ability to draw 'six cubed'.

118

Fig. 11.2 An example of pupil error caused by misunderstanding of 'six cubed'.

The pupils were also asked to answer a series of questions regarding their three-dimensional experiences, e.g., climbing trees, dancing, playing sports, making camps, playing with dolls' houses, model-making, etc. Although such a questionnaire cannot evaluate on a scientific or a carefully controlled basis, the results indicated a correlation between wide-ranging three-dimensional kinetic experiences (involving both the whole body and the hands) and a higher level of three-dimensional perception.

Even greater problems arise when young children attempt to represent three-dimensional forms in two dimensions. In an attempt to 'see all round', several views of the subject are sometimes combined.

In one interesting activity a group of 11-year-olds were 'designing' a house. Problems arose in diagrammatically 'going upstairs'. Representing the relationship between different floor levels brought about some unusual solutions (Fig. 11.3).

Early practical work in mathematics, where activities involve concepts of mass and volume, is important, particularly when changes of shape and of volume do not go together. Later the building of structures using building bricks ('Lego'), light wooden strips and other repeating units such as 'Meccano' and similar apparatus further develops the organisation of volume and the importance of volumetric economy.

Patterns in space, the aesthetic relationships which exist between three-dimensional shapes and the spaces which separate them are of equal importance. In this field of intellectual and emotional growth, meaningful experiences can be provided by the purposeful study of the environment to be found outside school. Objects for such study

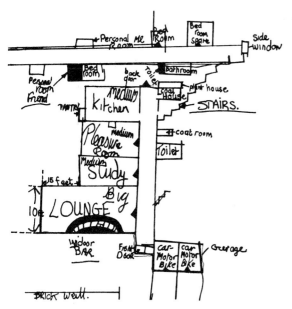

Fig. 11.3 A ten-year-old's interpretation of a plan view of ground and first floors of a house.

Fig. 11.4 A paper sculpture sited so that its three-dimensional effect is enhanced by light and shadow.

Fig. 11.5 The three-dimensional lattice of an electricity pylon provides an insight into aesthetic as well as functional spatial relationships.

might include subjects as diverse as the spatial composition of arcades in a modern shopping centre, the three-dimensional patterns provided by the buttressing of a cathedral wall, a suspension bridge or electricity pylon (see Section 10.1, the part headed 'Shape'). Similarly, but on a smaller scale, the arrangement of the switches and knobs on a hi-fi set, or the components of a machine, provide starting points for such a study. Naturally occurring subjects, in which the patterns of spaces and elements can be compared, include plants and shells, the branches of trees in winter or sectioned fruits and the flight patterns of flocks of migrating birds.

The activity of arranging things for exhibition or display further promotes the awareness of spatial relationships in both two and three dimensions, but more than this, such activities assist in the learning of specifics such as composition, proportion, balance, grouping, focal points and lines of direction. (See also the series of publications on visual education by Kurt Rowlands.)

11.2 Design in the Environment

The pupil's environment, his surroundings at school, at play, at home and in his neighbourhood, provides a context within which a good deal of

direct and indirect experience in three-dimensional design activity can take place. Here the accent is upon using specific examples of design in the environment as starting points for three-dimensional investigation and activity. Environmental models can be made ranging from simple measured models of the classroom (this has links with practical arithmetic), the playing field or the park (involving a geographical survey), the ruined castle (history), to the town, real or imaginary, and its component buildings and structures (social design) (see Chapter 3).

Fig. 11.6 This model of fourteenth-sixteenth century Coventry was created over a period of about six weeks by 81 9-11-year-old pupils at Christopher Cash Junior School, Coventry.

In all this, scale is a dominant factor, not only in terms of physical dimensions and relationships, e.g., the home, street, field, neighbourhood, town, etc., but also the increasing complexity of the environment, which in the urban situation appears to grow as the size of the unit increases. Scale in this sense can be increased or decreased to range from molecular structures — or at least structures which can be discerned only through a magnifying glass or microscope — to models of great structures such as the universe.

Added to these activities is three-dimensional work associated with technology, transport, archaeology and so on. To make realistic models, the older pupil needs to undertake widespread study and research of the chosen topic. This may involve finding photographs and diagrams culled from literature, the pupil's own sketches, paintings and maybe photographs of sites and buildings, visits to planning offices and libraries, etc., which will precede or supplement the three-dimensional work which follows.

Patterns of spaces provided by tubular steel scaffolding on a building site can be related directly to simple work on structures for either aesthetic or primarily functional purposes. An open staircase or display area in a modern department store may become the starting point for compositions where the patterns of spaces are considered far more important than the solid materials which produce them. At another time when the work in hand is concerned with the relationship of form and function, the sheer bulk of a building or structure, or its purpose, may itself provide stimulation for architectural modelling in materials such as expanded polystyrene (polyphenylethene).

Fig. 11.8 Collections serve to focus attention on particular topics or areas of human activity.

Fig. 11.7 The massive structure of a mediaeval castle is faithfully simulated in this model made of expanded polystyrene (polyphenylethene).

11.3 The Study of Natural Objects and Artifacts

To look is not necessarily to see, and the close study of both natural and man-made objects complements the pupil's direct physical experience of manipulating and using materials which are capable of three-dimensional form (see Section 11.4).

Many young children are avid collectors of 'things', and collections of many kinds can be brought together in the classroom or studio/ workshop, to be arranged and displayed. Such activity provides scope for direct investigation, not only of spatial relationships on a micro rather than a macro scale, but also for observation and reasoned discussion about similarities and variations among superficially identical objects or classes of objects.

Fig. 11.9 Technological awareness and functional relationships, albeit at elementary levels, can be brought about and enhanced through practical handling of commonplace objects.

Handling and discussing items as diverse and as commonplace as flower heads and hand tools, bicycle wheels, toys and saucepans may appear at first sight to be prosaic and uninteresting, but in all these pupils can be helped to appreciate their purpose, to note and describe their feel, shape, structure and function, and their relationships to other objects or to their surroundings (see also Chapters 9 and 10).

In presenting specific objects for discussion, starting points for investigation and creative work, it is important that the teacher himself has clear objectives in mind. Interest is not always self-generating, and particular teaching points need to be clearly defined before introduction to the class.

The production of a list of appropriate questions

is a useful preparation, e.g. — of a set of three gear wheels — with a class of ten-year-old pupils:

Where do we find wheels like this?
What do they do?
Why do they have teeth around the edge?
Does the size of wheel matter? Or the size of tooth? Why?
Do they all turn the same way if we rotate one of them? Do they all turn at the same rate?
What are these gear wheels made of? and why?
What else do you think you could use these gear wheels for? etc.

This is just one way in which pupils can be helped to look — and *see*. Above all we need to develop in our pupils a sense of questing — and questioning — awareness.

Activities of this nature spread quite naturally across disciplinary boundaries, the example given above having positive reference and relevance to mathematics, physics, geography, history, art and to basic engineering principles and practice. All these disciplines in this way can provide additional opportunities for the development of a critical awareness.

11.4 Manipulating and using Materials of a Three-dimensional Nature

The utilisation of materials to 'make' things is, in a sense, a rather facile answer to that most basic of questions about design education, i.e., 'What do the children *do*?'

An activity may be of an investigatory or experimental nature, or it may lead to an end product or artifact, but in either case it must be considered with regard to the overall and specific course objectives, though not inflexibly so, as new objectives may arise as the work develops. In this context the teacher must always be prepared to review his attitudes towards activities in progress so as to avoid the possibility of stultifying growing points for further worthwhile pupil experience.

Young children at play use, almost indiscriminately, any materials or objects on hand to satisfy the creative needs of the moment.

It is particularly interesting to note the recurring activity of camp or den making in which nearly all young children indulge. Adventure playgrounds, where children are permitted to play unhindered by adult intervention, often centre upon camp building as a major activity (see Lambert, J. and Pearson J. *Adventure Playgrounds*). As stated in Chapter 2, however, subtle but far reaching changes of attitude have begun to occur before the young child reaches the teens. Realism then begins to assert its dominance over the highly imaginative play of the young child. The child of seven or eight can endow his product with any character or property within his imagination. The child of twelve or thirteen lives more in the world of the actual, and the properties of his artifact as he visualises it stem largely from the properties of the materials from which he made it.

Coming to terms with both the aesthetic and engineering properties of materials is thus a logical development which should parallel the pupil's natural maturation. The reader is referred to the Schools Council Science 5-13 Project publications, in particular *Working with Wood*, *Metals* and *Children and Plastics*, which offer a good deal of detailed guidance and pupil activity material in this field.

Before children arrive at this stage of development, where their questions are more probing and their personal experience requirements more explicit, a great deal of experience is called for in handling and arranging 'things', so that grouping under various headings is possible, whether it be through form or structure, function or properties, source, natural or synthetic, or any other possible method of classification.

Pupil involvement with 'found' objects, whatever their source, progresses naturally from aggregation and arrangement to manipulation and conscious tooling in an attempt to modify or change the original form. Such activity appears almost instinctive as can be witnessed in the carvings, often of a highly imaginative order, of primitive or so-called 'uncivilised' tribesmen. Such activities should not be closely channelled so as to result in programmed skills training for its own sake. Rather the emphasis should be upon developing a conscious awareness of form and spatial relationships associated with natural and man-made or modified materials.

While school playgrounds and facilities do not extend to the possibilities of the adventure playgrounds mentioned above, the making of large-scale models on a group basis appeals to many children. Whilst the model can never provide the innate sense of purpose which the construction of a 'den' appears to promote, large environmental models offer scope for the imaginative use of a wide

Fig. 11.10 A first attempt at free form 'carving' in expanded polystyrene (polyphenylethene) by a nine-year-old girl.

Fig. 11.11 Working clay provides experience in and awareness of spatial and dimensional relationships.

range of media such as wood, plaster, cardboard, etc. Possibly because of their relationship to life outside school, models relating to real situations often stimulate pupil involvement to a greater degree than do models which have little or no social connotations.

Two further concepts should be noted in connection with three-dimensional design activity.

(1) Volumetric form can be created
   (a) by enclosing a space (producing a structure),
   (b) by subtraction from a given form, or
   (c) by a combination of (a) and (b). Such a concept will emerge through pupil involvement in design realisation across the whole range of materials.
(2) The relationship of 'inside and outside'. Though many kinds of activity assist the growth of this concept, the relationship can be positively experienced through manipulative activities initially involving clay. Simple pot making is an excellent example of such activity, since wall thickness must be gauged by tactile as well as visual senses — by 'seeing through the fingers'. Later work, for example utilising thermoplastic sheet in conjunction with male and female moulds or simple press tools, will reinforce the concept (see Fig. 12.11).

Architecture and the study of structures, especially from a technological viewpoint, provides another area of activity which relates directly to this concept, thus linking it to the topic of volumetric space detailed at the beginning of this chapter.

Chapter 12   Constructional Techniques for the Middle Years

While Chapter 11 refers to three-dimensional experiences appropriate to pupils in this age and ability range, this chapter is concerned with the methodology of teaching children to manipulate, with confidence and increasing competence, the more resistant materials, particularly those which call for:

(1) the use of specific hand tools to cut, shape and form them, and
(2) specific techniques to enable them to be assembled or joined together.

Reference is made in this chapter to a number of topics about which the reader may lack detailed knowledge or experience. It is not the purpose of this publication to give explicit instruction in craft techniques as such; references may be made to appropriate literature (see the Bibliography). Nevertheless it goes without further comment that before attempting possibly hazardous tool techniques with his pupils, the teacher himself must become thoroughly acquainted with them by receiving adequate professional instruction and guidance followed by personal experience and practice until competence is achieved. When teachers have only partial responsibility for the teaching of tool skills and techniques, when acting in the capacity of assistant to a teacher-co-ordinator or specialist trained teacher, appropriate 'on the spot' assistance with specific activities can often be provided by a local co-ordinating, semi-specialist or specialist trained teacher.

As suggested elsewhere, children's awareness of individual materials and their properties varies from minimal to extensive, as does their experience in the use of appropriate tools and techniques to manipulate them.

The authors suggest that, initially at least, for pupils in this age range the teacher should concentrate on using methods and approaches to marking out, cutting and shaping which are common to wood, light gauge sheet metal and plastics, rather than on treating them as very specialised materials, each needing to be worked by its own particular methods.

Thus a pupil will not learn woodwork or plastics or dressmaking in isolation, but will come to employ tools and techniques appropriate to the basic working properties of any material he meets.

Hardness or brittleness are not properties exclusive to any one material or range of materials, but through an appreciation of such properties on a comparative basis pupils can soon correctly associate the use of certain tools with certain materials, e.g., a tenon saw is excellent for cutting wood but not for mild steel — obvious! But which saw should be used to cut thick acrylic sheet — and why?

12.1   Marking Out

The marking out of sheet materials, card, plywood, tinplate, etc., almost always follows one basic rule, i.e., mark out from one edge of the sheet only so that its basic rectangular shape is thereafter maintained. Pupils left to their own devices have been known to cut a piece from the centre of a sheet, or end up with a sheet looking rather like Fig. 12.1.

Basic instruction in the use of rule, try-square and means of drawing clear lines with pencil, felt pen or scriber should be given as required. Some experience will be gained in related practical mathematics activities, but unless these are carefully planned and closely co-ordinated, they will not replace clear precise instruction and practice in the workshop which will reinforce or anticipate them. No budget can withstand the ravages of the exclusive use of 'discovery' methods at this stage of the proceedings.

Similarly, whilst the concepts of right angle, square, rectangle, parallel, etc., appear in

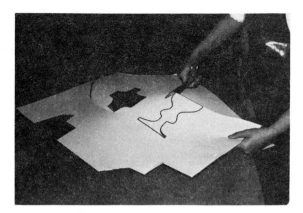

Fig. 12.1   Wasteful reduction of sheet material is to be avoided!

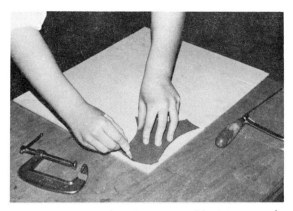

Fig. 12.2   Using a template as an aid to economy in sheet material.

mathematics teaching, much tactile as well as visual experience of such shapes is called for to enable children in the early middle years of schooling to grasp their importance.

This experience can be provided both by the two- and three-dimensional shapes they attempt to produce themselves, and by the physical experience of assembling such shapes into cohesive units, e.g., building blocks, cut-out shapes, etc. There are many such areas of concept development in which close liaison and interdisciplinary activity can play a vital role to the obvious advantage of pupil and teacher.

As a preliminary to marking or setting out shapes on sheet materials from which parts or objects are to be cut and fabricated, it is often advisable for pupils first to draw and cut out paper templates (patterns) which can be checked for accuracy of shape and dimensions before the actual material is cut. Young girls may be *au fait* with the use of tissue patterns in dressmaking, but quite probably neither they nor the boys will initially appreciate the positive advantage of such an approach to cutting shapes in materials other than fabrics. Considerable practice in simple arithmetic and basic geometry can be provided by this activity.

Other points to be noted are:

(1)   The degree of unavoidable wastage incurred. When marking out, an allowance must be made for sawing and 'cleaning up'. With a piece of hardboard, for example, how much is a reasonable amount to add on? Certainly not the 3 or 4 cm many enthusiastic young pupils would suggest.

(2)   The degree of accuracy required for a particular piece of work is often unappreciated by young inexperienced pupils. Their work is either wildly inaccurate or far more accurate than necessary. Only when two or more mating parts are fitted together can many pupils in the lower half of this age range appreciate the need for accuracy in marking out, or indeed, at any stage during construction. The concept of accuracy or 'fit', particularly when related to three-dimensional perception, generally appears to develop only after a period of concrete experience, initially of the 'hit and miss' variety.

(3)   The physical inability, through lack of adequate neuro-muscular control, of younger pupils to cut to a line—with consequent potential wastage of valuable stock. Thus for work with young or less able pupils it is often advisable for the teacher either to reduce large sheets of material to more manageable sizes before distribution to pupils, or to cut the shape prepared by the pupil from the large sheet for him, if only to avoid consequent waste production. Further difficulties in cutting, caused by either the physical problem of managing large pieces of material or by attempting to manipulate materials that are too difficult as yet, bring with them considerable frustration. This again is likely to lead to a high degree of waste.

Strip materials such as pre-planed softwood are much easier (than large boards) for young pupils to handle. The correct use of rule, try-square, and pencil or marking knife should be insisted on, as slipshod techniques will ultimately hamper and

Fig. 12.3 The use of correct techniques and sound practice in marking out is essential to ensure success.

restrict progress rather than promote it.

It must be emphasised yet again how much variation will be found in levels of development between pupils of similar age, not only in intellectual ability and physical size but, equally important, in neuro-muscular control and co-ordination.

12.2   Cutting to Shape (outlines)

At an early stage pupils should understand that scissors, snips and knives can produce an accurate finished outline from the first cut when employed on thin sheet material, but when saws are used, whatever the type and whatever the material, further shaping, cleaning up or trueing up of the sawn edges will be required.

The choice of saw for use on thicker sheet or slab stock depends on:

(1) the material itself, whether hard or soft, and
(2) the shape of the cut to be produced, whether straight or curved.

It is unfortunate that the hacksaw is so named because hacking at the material is exactly what it should *not* be used for. Pupils possessing sufficient manual dexterity and physical strength can control saws of appropriate dimensions at a relatively early age. However, to expect a 9-year-old to use an adult-sized rip saw is to court inevitable disaster!

All this may seem very obvious to the adult reader, but unless children at home or elsewhere have had an opportunity to watch the skilled use of such tools, a progressive introduction to saws, such as coping saws, junior and standard hacksaws, tenon saws (200 mm or 250 mm) and small cross cut saws (not longer than about 500-525 mm) is necessary. Recognition of saw shape and name, as with other tools, can be assisted by colouring in the silhouette of each tool and printing its name on the tool cupboard or rack in which it is stored. Frequent repetition of tool and equipment names by teacher and pupils also leads to increasing familiarity.

At quite an early stage children soon master the use of scissors, providing the scissors are of appropriate shape and size, that they are sharp and correctly adjusted. They are thus able to control the outline of cut paper, card, fabrics and thin flexible plastics sheet. Cutting convex curves sometimes presents difficulties for young pupils who tend to cut them as a series of straight lines. Movement of the work in conjunction with the scissor action to cure this fault calls for quite a high degree of co-ordination. They are however often defeated when attempting to cut thin sheet metal (aluminium or tin-plate) with hand shears (tin snips). One arm of the shears can be held in the vice jaws thus giving the pupil greater control over the cutting action.

Bench shears of the traditional type are potentially very dangerous and should be used only by teachers and experienced older pupils under direct supervision.

A different type of sheet cutter, the 'Gabro' works by 'nibbling' a 3.2 mm wide slot instead of shearing the material (Fig. 12.4). It can be used to cut hardboard and non-brittle plastics in addition to metals and will also cut 3.2 mm wide slot type joints. This versatility of application suggests that serious consideration be given to the provision of such a piece of equipment in the craft workshop/studio for pupils in their middle years. When not in use the lever arm of either type of shears should be padlocked in the closed position to prevent access by pupils.

Small hand-held cutters working on a similar principle are also worth consideration, especially for cutting curves, though they are not so easy to use.

Modern cutting knives with their well-shaped handles and shielded blades have minimised some of the hazards inherent in the use of such tools.

Cutting expanded polystyrene calls for a unique

126

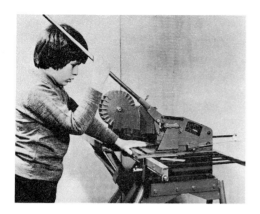

Fig. 12.4 A 'Gabro' sheet cutter in use. Such equipment facilitates the safe and efficient cutting and slotting of sheet material. Courtesy Gale Bros (Engineers) Ltd.

Fig. 12.5 Hot wire cutters can be made in a range of sizes but should be operated only at black heat and from a low-voltage supply.

technique, that of melting away the material with a heated wire. Expanded polystrene (polyphenylene) being a thermoplastic of pith-like consistency does not lend itself to cutting with saws or knives because it readily crumbles under tool pressure.

Hot-wire cutters, either of the portable or bench type (Fig. 12.5) work by passing a current at low voltage (not more than 6 volts) through a wire possessing high electrical resistance, e.g., 'Nichrome'. It is imperative that the wire should be heated only to black heat, just hot enough to melt through the material without producing smoke or fumes. When worked at the correct wire temperature expanded polystyrene (polyphenylethene), can be 'cut' without forcing or straining the wire in any way. *It is totally wrong* to use a red-hot wire heated in a gas flame or to use a converted electric soldering iron over which no real temperature

control can be maintained (see BS 4163:1975, *Health and Safety in Workshops of Schools and Colleges*).

The tendency for children to lower the face very close to the work in progress should be resisted as this proximity to the melting material can more easily lead to inhalation of any fumes. Adequate through ventilation must always be provided to avoid such hazards.

N.B. This technique is suitable for use only with expanded polystyrene (polyphenylethene) and with *no other* foamed or cellular plastic materials!

12.3 Shaping

Shaping by Modelling

Shaping plastic materials such as clay, plasticine and papier mâché by modelling is in itself not over-demanding physically, yet at the same time it provides opportunities for much manipulation and self expression by young children. The direct shaping of the material by the fingers rather than via the use of tools of varying degrees of complexity carries with it an immediacy of effect which cannot be matched when less easily shaped materials are employed (Fig. 12.6).

Fig. 12.6 Models in clay have the advantage that they can be made permanent by 'firing'.

Shaping by Removal of Surplus Material

Three-dimensional materials (slab or block) as opposed to sheet materials provide pupils with rather different problems in their manipulation.

Given a rectangular block to start with most children appear reticent or unable to physically

Fig. 12.7 A 'stiff' shape resulting from the causes suggested below.

Fig. 12.8 Basic outlines are usually best produced by first sawing to shape.

alter its form to any appreciable extent, with the result that free-form work originating from slab stock sometimes appears rigid or geometrical in overall effect (Fig. 12.7).

Three likely reasons for this are:

(1) The child possesses little preconception of the form he wishes to achieve. This difficulty can be reduced by a tactile as well as a visual study of naturally occurring shapes and forms, which, snowflakes and crystals apart, are rarely exactly geometric in structure.

Much early experience of breaking down and building up structures from building blocks, containers and sand helps in the development of this ability.

(2) Rectangular blocks in all but the softest of rigid materials present difficulty in the removal of surplus material. For this reason alone much prior and concurrent experience with clay and expanded polystyrene is called for so that the pupil may provide himself with a model or prototype form toward which he is striving.

Left to their own devices unskilled children usually attempt to produce a rounded shape from a block of wood by whittling or *surforming* away the corners and edges instead of using the carver's technique of first cutting out silhouette shapes in two planes using appropriate saws (Fig. 12.8). If the latter technique is used rounding out can be carried out much more quickly and effectively using edge tools, surforms, rasps, files and abrasives.

It is possible that the early attempts at rounding off to produce three-dimensional forms may be a developmental stage through which all children must go. Squeezing mud pies or clay through the

Fig. 12.9 Branches, by their shape, suggest interesting forms which can be developed by the inexpert wood-carver.

fingers or pressing together wet sand is a popular activity with children younger than junior school age, which itself may suggest an even earlier stage.

If free-form work in wood is to be attempted, it is often better for the teacher to provide material cut from branches, where a degree of prior shape or form already exists (Fig. 12.9). Such natural flowing shapes or outlines can be more easily taken as starting points by pupils in the upper part of this age range than can rectangular blocks of wood, which initially may exhibit little character of their own. Adequate and effective means of holding such irregular shapes or of fixing them to the bench top must be provided. Such methods include the use of bench 'holdfasts', small leather or canvas band clamps or soft-jawed vices.

Children, like many amateur wood and soft-stone

'carvers' are too often anxious to use abrasives such as glasspaper in order to complete the shaping. They must be helped to appreciate that such abrasives are of real value only in the finishing or smoothing of surfaces and not in the actual shaping process itself.

(3) Inadequate development of spatial perception prevents many children from projecting their own mental three-dimensional 'picture' of the completed form. As discussed in Chapter 11 (three-dimensional studies), a good deal of complementary study is called for, but natural rates of development cannot be forced. Whereas considerable research work has been carried out in the field of two-dimensional activities in children, it seems that much less has been correspondingly ascertained for three-dimensional activities. Personal observation, however, suggests that a development along Piaget-type lines is likely. In this, early experience in dance and movement provides growth points for the development of the concept of volumetric space, as does much play associated with the filling of one shaped container with the contents of another of different shape. Again there is an early relationship with experience of mathematical concepts.

Shaping by Fabrication

Three-dimensional forms are often more easily and quickly produced, by children in particular, by bending, folding and joining together sheet material rather than by the removal of surplus material from a block or slab. Fabrication can be taken a stage further by combining a number of such units, e.g., assembling box-like forms and then combining them in architectural arrangements.

To the well-known traditional techniques associated with producing paper sculptures, card and papier mâché models, all of which produce artifacts of a temporary nature, may be added the newer but simple methods of heat-forming thermoplastic sheet such as acrylic, PVC (polychloroethene), and polystyrene (polyphenylethene). These modern materials are easy to cut using ordinary hand tools, and once the edges are smoothed or quickly hand polished, can be made into permanent articles such as racks and containers. The bending is carried out by heating for a few minutes over a strip heater and then allowing to cool to shape in a simple jig. (Fig. 12.10).

More experienced pupils of 12-13 years can take

Fig. 12.10 The use of strip heaters makes possible the straight-line bending of thermoplastic sheet.

Fig. 12.11 Shaping heated thermoplastic sheet by the use of simple wooden press-tools enables compound curves to be produced.

this technique further. If the thermoplastic sheet is heated in an oven to between 110°C and 170°C, depending on the type of plastics, it softens and can be draped over a former or 'pressed', using wooden press tools made by pupils. Thus one material (wood/chipboard) is used to help form another (Fig. 12.11).

Vacuum forming using basically do-it-yourself equipment can be considered as the most sophisticated method of shaping thermoplastic sheet. If suitable equipment can be made available, children of about 12 years upwards can use the technique very effectively in the solution of many constructional design problems (Fig. 12.12).

Such experience is often found more rewarding than too much early work with sheet metal. The 'built-in' colour and ease of manipulation of these materials enable unskilled pupils more easily to produce artifacts and effects which are attractive and utilitarian by any standards.

129

Fig. 12.12 An easily made vacuum-former. (*N.B.* All electrical wiring on such equipment should be carried out and regularly checked by a competent electrician.)

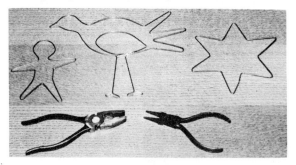

Fig. 12.13 Pliers of different types can be used to bend light metal strip and wire.

Fig. 12.14 'Horns' bent from mild steel enable smooth curves or scrolls to be produced with little difficulty.

Ferrous and non-ferrous strip metal and wire of small cross-section can be bent to shape by using pliers (occasionally in conjunction with a small metal worker's vice) (Fig. 12.13). An alternative method is to use a pair of 'horns', an elongated U shape bent up from 10-12 mm dia. mild steel. With

this crude but effective piece of equipment simple curves and scroll shapes can be produced after just a few minutes' practice (Fig. 12.14).

The major pupil difficulties here are concerned not with the methods of forming involved, but with adequate assembly of the various parts of the structure (see Section 12.5).

Traditional woodworking in schools is based largely on the ability of the maturing pupil to be able to join one piece of wood to another (see Shaw, D. M., *Woodwork design and practice*, Hodder and Stoughton, 1973). For all but the older and more able pupils in the middle years of schooling only limited joining techniques are possible and indeed appropriate. Thus, in this context 'working with wood' does not correlate particularly closely with 'woodworking' as generally perceived.

Shaping by Casting
Although metal casting such as is practised in many secondary schools is inappropriate for pupils in the middle years, they are quite capable of casting (moulding) in plaster of paris, sand, and cement (older pupils) and, under supervision, in polyester resin (Fig. 12.15).

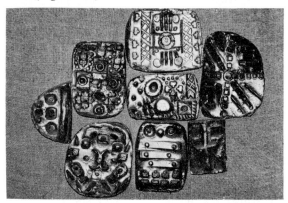

Fig. 12.15 Cold casting in plaster of paris, sand and cement or polyester resin offers scope for the production of decorative and sometimes functional forms.

The moulds themselves can be made from a variety of materials either rigid or flexible, and ingenuity is called for rather than a great deal of skill. The output of such activity will in the main be ornamental rather than functional, but understanding of the processes involved is of interest not only for its own sake but because it will lay a foundation for work at a later stage of development.

12.4 Surface Treatment

As mentioned in Chapter 10, the surface treatment of two- and three-dimensional work may arise in one of two ways.

(1) As a direct result of the essential tooling required to produce the form, e.g., chisel or gouge cuts or facets from a planishing hammer.
(2) As a design decision to enrich an otherwise nondescript surface, e.g., the use of colour and/or of decorative tooling (Fig. 12.16).

The surface of aluminium, for example, is capable of taking a wide range of surface textures and finishes ranging from stamped or embossed detail to brushed, polished or coloured effects.

Fig. 12.16   A decorative panel produced by deforming or heating small squares of aluminium sheet.

12.5   Joining Things Together

One of the most difficult decisions facing young pupils — and for that matter many adults too — is how to join together the various parts of the artifact he is making.

Many methods of joining together a wide range of materials are available, but because of pupils' limitations in skills and techniques, the teacher is advised initially to select and teach a relatively small number of joining methods which are applicable to a variety of situations.

For convenience and consideration these may be loosely classified as follows. Note that some methods can be listed under more than one heading.

(1) Joints involving metal fasteners, e.g., nails, wood screws, self-tapping sheet metal screws, nuts and bolts, pop rivets.
(2) Self-locating joints, e.g., cross-halving and bridle joints in wood, dowelled joints.

Fig. 12.17   Display boards such as this provide a useful reminder and can be used to stimulate interest in a particular topic.

(3) Joints involving adhesives, e.g., gluing sheet materials (paper, card, plywood, expanded polystyrene, thermoplastic and laminated plastic sheet, metal), mounting jewellery.
(4) Joints involving thread, e.g., fabrics, leather, macramé.
(5) Metalworking joints involving molten metal, e.g., soft soldering, hard (silver) soldering and brazing.

(1)   Joints Involving Fasteners

Numerous types of inexpensive metal fasteners are available which, according to type, are suitable for temporary or permanent fixing of wood and wood products, metals of various thicknesses and certain plastics.

Quite young children have often had experience outside school of using hammer and nails and of assembling 'Meccano' or similar constructional kits using nuts and bolts. However, such experience, gained on an *ad hoc* basis, generally lacks width or selectivity. Thus clear demonstrations of technique and adequate discussion of appropriateapplications is called for, e.g., relating the type, length and diameter of a nail to the load it will be expected to bear calls for both logic and experience. However, even when introducing or systematising previous experiences in basic skills and techniques such as those associated with hammer and nails, the physical stage of development of the child must not be overlooked, nor can his mental age be ignored. There are no hard and fast rules to guide the teacher as to the right moment for such introductions to new techniques. Each pupil's combination of developmental stages (intellectual,

Fig. 12.18 Self-tapping screws and 'pop' rivets are widely used in industry. They can be used to help solve many jointing problems in sheet metal.

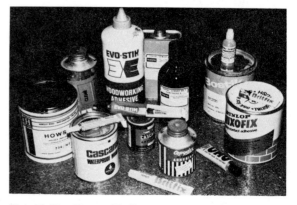

Fig. 12.19 Many adhesives are available but must be closely matched to the materials to be joined.

emotional and physical) must be assessed individually so as to match experience to the particular stage of development. The use of self-tapping screws and pop rivets (Fig. 12.18) adequately solves many problems associated with locating and joining thin sheet metal, and once pupils are able to bore a hole using a wheelbrace and twist drill, the actual fitting of the screw or pop rivet is very easy indeed.

(2) Self-locating Joints

Most woodworking joints are of the self-locating type (i.e., their position is fixed by the interlocking of the two parts of the joint). The degree of precision and tool skill called for in such work is beyond most children up to the age of about 12 years, and it is a mistake to attempt to force pupils to attempt such work before either their physical ability and mental/emotional attitudes will enable them to cope with it.

The teacher can produce simple jigs which will greatly assist in sawing joints straight and 'square', and such do-it-yourself equipment does on occasion prove most valuable. Wooden dowels fitted into pre-drilled holes are probably among the easiest methods of fixing wooden members together. Dowelling as a method of jointing calls for little more than careful setting out and alignment of the hole centres. The use of a stand-mounted drill ensures that holes are bored square to the face of the work. If a hand-held drill is used, a try-square clamped to the face of the work will act as a sighting guide. Here too the use of simple drilling jigs may prove advantageous.

(3) Joints Involving Adhesives

Currently very many adhesives (most of which are based on plastics) are available (Fig. 12.19). The difficulty for teacher and pupil is in using an appropriate adhesive in each case, as the use of

incorrect adhesives can have disastrous effects, or at least lead to disappointing failure. For example, the use of conventional impact adhesives dissolves expanded polystyrene (polyphenylethene) instead of gluing pieces of it together. It is essential when using modern adhesives to follow closely the manufacturer's instructions, but prior consideration will clarify many of the problems likely to arise, e.g., 'Is the joint to be a flexible one such as fixing felt or hessian in a collage, or a rigid one such as sticking acrylic sheet together?' 'Does the adhesive need to be waterproof as when building a model boat, or is a water-soluble adhesive acceptable as when making a cardboard model?' 'Must the adhesive be solvent free as when gluing non-porous materials, such as polished stones and metal in costume jewellery? Many of the so called 'cements' sold in tubes, e.g., 'balsa' 'PVC' or 'polystyrene' cements, contain solvents which are both flammable and toxic. Attention is drawn to the considerable health hazard of allowing children to inhale such solvent type adhesives. See BS 4163: 1975, *Health and Safety in Workshops of Schools and Colleges.* Epoxy-based adhesives can cause skin irritation leading to dermatitis, so that such adhesives should be used by children only under close supervision.

Some adhesives, particularly certain wood glues, while possessing excellent adhesive qualities, are rather slow to set, and this, with younger pupils, may lead through impatience to frustration.

Despite the difficulties mentioned above, appropriate adhesives correctly applied help to solve many of the constructional problems likely to be encountered by pupils in the middle years and beyond.

A wall chart can be drawn up showing compatibility of adhesives with materials. Indeed the production of such a chart should be the outcome of technological investigation by the children rather than the teacher.

Many test situations can be set up to compare effectiveness not only of adhesives but of other methods of fixing one material to another.

(4) Joints Involving Thread

Sewing is every bit as important a method of joining materials — usually but not exclusively fabrics — as any other. Clothes made from one piece of material without seams are not the most practical for our modern way of life! Despite the occasional use of adhesives (bonding), needle and thread, whether hand or machine operated, is without doubt the most effective way of joining fabrics or leather edge to edge.

In this general context boys as well as girls should be taught how to carry out simple hand- and machine-sewing techniques. It is most important, however, that the teacher employs considerable imagination in the application of such techniques, whether for utilitarian or decorative processes. Boys of 11 do not usually take kindly to making pinafores. Dressing dolls may be for girls, but producing clothes for a puppet theatre or making sails for a model yacht *can* be man's work! Providing appropriate safeguards are observed, most pupils of 10 years and upwards can safely use a straight stitch hand-operated sewing machine, though the use of a power-driven decorative stitch machine often appeals to older boys as well as girls. Such machines (being precision tools) are both very expensive and rather delicate and will not withstand misuse.

Leather, now being a generally scarce and expensive commodity, is unlikely to be available in the classroom or workshop, but PVC coated cotton, as used for car upholstery, is easily come by and has wide application.

As an indication of how 'sewing' can be related to scientific experiment, pupils can compare the qualities and performance of natural and synthetic sewing threads. The practical problems arising from using cotton thread for sewing synthetic fabrics — such as nylon, polyester or acrylic — are understood by too few teachers let alone their young pupils (Fig. 12.20).

Possibly the most primitive form of fixing by the use of fibrous materials is that of 'lashing'. Despite a rather unfair and quaint 'Boy Scout' image the simple technique involved in lashing together sticks, poles, metal tubes, etc., can offer a wide variety of

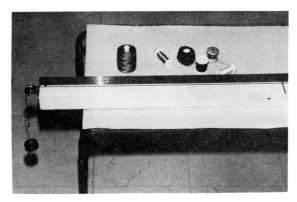

Fig. 12.20   Testing threads for 'stretch'.

interesting yet economical experiences in 'man-sized' work on structures of many kinds.

(5) Metal Joints Involving Molten Metal

Joining metal by fusing the two mating surfaces with a second molten metal or alloy is known variously as soft soldering, hard (silver) soldering and brazing (hard soldering using brass).

While the high temperatures involved (600-850°C) and the equipment used generally precludes the use of the latter techniques by children under the age of 12 years, pupils of about 10 years and upwards can, under close supervision, carry out soft soldering using an electric soldering iron and (preferably) resin-cored soft solder.

Two potential hazards with the use of electric soldering irons are:

(1) Burning the flex, with consequent danger of electrocution. Providing that hot electric soldering irons are supported in a suitable stand or rack when not being used, to prevent rolling along the bench, etc., it is unlikely that the cable will be damaged by contact with the heated bit. See also Chapter 7 regarding the provision of appropriate working surfaces. As stated elsewhere, the use of 110 volt mains supply and equipment, where the supply is passed through a centre-tapped 1 : 1 ratio transformer, will minimise the posibility of electric shock in the unlikely event of an accident of that nature (see also BS 4163 : 1975).

(2) 'Flicking'. Children should never be permitted to remove surplus soft solder from a heated bit by flicking the soldering iron, as molten solder particles are likely to fly upwards and possibly into the eyes. Pupils must be taught that surplus molten soft solder should always and only be removed by wiping the bit with thick dry rag.

Safe procedures must be followed at all times.

Bibliography

Key Readership T = Teacher
                 P = Pupil
     Subject matter D = Design education
                     C = Design context
                     M = Materials/methods

Aberloff, N. de	*Designing with Natural Forms*	M.P.T.	Batsford
Andretti, M.	*Ceramics*	M.T.P.	Nelson
Aylward, B. (ed.)	*Design Education in Schools*	D.T.	Evans Bros. (1973)
Baines, J. D.	*The Environment*	C.T.P.	Batsford (1974)
	'Past to Present' series		
Baynes, K.	*About Design*	D.T.	Lund Humphries
	Attitudes in Design Education	D.T.	Lund Humphries (1969)
	Industrial Design in the Community	C.T.	Lund Humphries
Bjorn, A.	*Exploring Fire and Clay*	M.P.T.	Van Nostrand Reinhold (1970)
Bono, E. de	*C.O.R.T. Thinking Course*	C.P.	Direct Educational Services
	Children Solve Problems	C.T.	Penguin Education
	Thinking Course for Juniors	C.P.T.	Direct Educational Services
	Think Links	C.P.T.	Direct Educational Services
Butler, A. and French, B.	*Practice of Collage*	M.T.P.	Mills and Boon
Brockman, O.	*Good or Bad Design?*	T.P.C.	Studio Vista/Van Nostrand Reinhold
Butler, W.	*Needlework*	M.T.P.	Pan Books
Cuff, P. and Cartwright, P.	*Screen Printing*	M.T.P.	Nelson (1975)
Design Council	*Design Resources for Teachers*	T.	Design Council
Dix, D.	*Filography: Introduction to Thread Sculpture*	M.T.P.	Pan Books (1975)
Eggleston, J.	*Developments in Design Education*	D.T.	Open Books
English Sewing Ltd.	*Learning about Sewing with Dewhurst Threads* (Scheme)	M.T.P.	English Sewing Ltd.
Farnworth, W.	*Clay in the Primary School*	T.M.	Batsford
Gentille, T.	*Jewellery*	M.T.P.	Pan Books (1973)
Green, D.	*Experimenting with Pottery*	M.T.P.	Faber
	Pottery: Materials and Techniques	M.T.P.	Faber (1967)
Green, P.	*Design Education: Problem Solving and Visual Experience*	D.T.	Batsford (1974)

Gundrey, E. A.	Collecting Things	P.C.	Pan Books (1974)
	Joining Things	P.M.	Pan Books
Harding, D. W. and Griffiths, L.	Materials (Physics Topics)	P.T.C.	Longmans (1969)
Harrison, M.	Homes	P.C.	Ernest Benn (1973)
Hayward, C. H.	The Junior Woodworker	P.C.	Evans (1973)
Hopward, R.	Science Model Making	P.C.	Murray
Howard, C.	Inspiration for Embroidery	P.T.M.	Batsford (1967)
Institute of Craft Education	Proceedings of the 1976 Conference	T.D.	Batsford
Jones, J. C.	Design Methods — Seeds of Human Futures	T.C.	Wiley (1970)
Lloyd, A., Mitchell, C. and Thomas, N.	Making and Flying Kites	T.P.M.	John Murray (1975)
Maile, A.	Tie and Dye Made Easy	T.P.M.	Mills and Boon (1971)
Marshall, A. R. (ed.)	School Technology in Action	D.T.	EUP (1974)
Matthews, J.	The Stanley Book of Sculpture with the Surform Tool	P.T.M.	Edward Arnold
	Creative Light Woodcarving	P.T.M.	Edward Arnold
	Further Creative Light Woodcarving	P.T.M.	Edward Arnold
Matthews, J.	Introductory Woodwork Projects	P.M.	Macmillan Education (1972)
Michaelson, S. (ed.)	Jewellery	P.T.M.	Nelson (1975)
Norris, T.	Photography	P.T.M.	Nelson (1975)
Paladin (publishers)	How Things Work (2 vols.)	T.C.	Paladin (1972)
Portchmouth, J.	Creative Crafts for Today	T.P.M.	Studio Vista (1969)
Read, H.	Art and Industry	C.T.	Faber (1966)
Redmayne, P.	The Changing Shape of Things	T.C.	Murray
Richmond, P. G.	An Introduction to Piaget	T.C.	Routledge and Kegan Paul (1970)
Roberts, R.	Musical Instruments Made to be Played	T.M.	Reeves Dryad (1976)
Robinson, S. and Robinson, P.	Exploring Fabric Printing	T.M.	Mills and Boon (1970)
Rottger, E.	Creative Drawing — Point and Line	T.P.M.	Batsford
	Creative Woodcraft	T.P.M.	Batsford (1961)
	Creative Claycraft	T.P.M.	Batsford
	Creative Papercraft	T.P.M.	Batsford (1973)
Rowland, K.	Learning to See (series)	T.P.C.M.	Ginn (1968-71)
	Looking and Seeing (series)	T.P.C.M.	Ginn

Schools Council Projects:

    Science 5 to 13 (series) — T.P.C. — Macdonald Educational

    Design and Craft Education Project

Education through Design	T.D.	Edward Arnold (1975)
Materials and Design	T.D.	Edward Arnold (1974)
Design for Today	T.D.	Edward Arnold (1974)
You are a Designer	P.C.	Edward Arnold (1974)
Connections and Constructions	P.C.	Edward Arnold (1975)

    Looking at Design (filmstrip book and filmstrips. Series) — T.D. — Edward Arnold

    Art and Craft Education Project. 8-13

Children's Growth through Creative Experience	T.D.C.	Van Nostrand Reinhold (1974)

Using Natural Materials		T.C.	Van Nostrand Reinhold (1974)
Using Resistant Materials		T.C.	Van Nostrand Reinhold
Using Objects: Visual Learning and Visual Awareness in the Museum and Classroom		T.C.	Van Nostrand Reinhold (1974)
Working Paper No. 26. Education through the use of Materials		T.C.	Evans/Methuen Educational (1969)
Schumacher, E. F.	*Small is Beautiful*	T.C.	Abacus Books (1974)
Scott, J. and Fisher, E.	*Approaches to Clay Modelling*	M.P.T.	Evans Bros. (1975)
Semper, E.	*The Steering Wheel of Destiny*	T.D.C.	National Centre for Schools Technology
Slade, R.	*Patterns in Space*	T.P.C.	Faber (1969)
Sparkes, R.	*Exploring Materials with Young Children*	T.C.	Batsford (1975)
Stokes, P.	*Looking at Materials*	T.P.M.	Nelson
	Working with Materials	T.P.M.	Nelson
Thomson, R.	*Design and the Environment* (2 books)	T.P.C.	Holmes McDougall (1973, 1974)
Thring, M. W.	*Man, Machines and Tomorrow*	T.C.	Routledge and Kegan Paul (1973)
Ullrich, H. and Klante, D.	*Creative Metal Crafts*	P.T.M.	Batsford (1971)
Vouge	*Vouge Guide to Macrame*	T.P.M.	Collins
Wainwright, J.	*Discovering Lapidary Work*	T.P.M.	Mills and Boon
Wallis, A. W. and Naylor, R.	*An Introduction to Creative Metalwork*	P.T.M.	Edward Arnold
Ward, B. and Dubos, R.	*Only one Earth*	T.C.	Penguin (1972)
Windmill Press/ World's Work (series)	*Concrete* Childrens' University series	P.C.	Windmill Press
Yarwood, A.	*An Introduction to Technical Drawing*	P.T.M.	Nelson
	Plastics — Design and Craft	P.T.M.	Nelson
Zanker	*Foundation of Design in Wood*	T.C.M.	Dryad
Znamierowski, N.	*Weaving*	T.M.P.	Pan Books

Periodicals

Art and Craft in Education	Evans Bros.
Schools Technology	NCST Trent Polytechnic, Burton Street, Nottingham, NG1 4BU
Studies in Design Education and Craft	Studies in Education Ltd., Nafferton, Driffield, N. Humberside, YO25 0JL
Practical Education	Institute of Craft Education, Editor, 30 Endcliffe Glen Road, Sheffield, S11 8RW
The Stanley Link in Design and Craft Education	Stanley Tools Ltd., Woodside, Sheffield, S3 9PD
Craft Teachers' News	Elliot Publishers Ltd., 9 Queen Victoria Street, Reading, RG11 SY
Design	Design Council, 28 Haymarket, London, SW1Y 4SU
Housecraft	Association of Teachers of Domestic Science, Hamilton House, Mabledon Place, London, WC1H 9BB

Organisations Connected with Design

Design Council	28 Haymarket, London, SW1Y 4SU
National Association for Design Education	29 Park Crescent, Oadby, Leicester, LE2 5YJ
National Society for Art Education	37a East Street, Havant, Hants, PO9 1AA
The Plastics and Rubber Institute	c/o Department of Creative Design, University of Technology, Loughborough, Leicestershire
The Institute of Craft Education	General Secretary, 24 Elm Road, Kingswood, Bristol, BS15 2ST

Additional List

Beaney, J.	*The Young Embroiderer*	P.M.	Nicholas Kaye
Berry, J.	*Making Mosaics*	T.P.M.	Studio Vista
Bowman, W.	*Graphic Communication*	T.M.	Wiley, New York
Daniels, H. and Turner, S.	*Simple Printmaking with Children*	T.M.	Von Nostrand Reinhold
Geary, K.	*Make and Find Out* (series)	T.P.C.	Macmillan
Harris, M.	*Environmental Studies*	T.P.C.	Macmillan
Hodgett, C.	*Stage Crafts*	T.C.	Black
Hudson, Rev. V. D.	*Technology*	T.P.C.	SCH Press
Jameson, K.	*Pre-School and Infant Art* *Junior School Art*	T.D.	Studio Vista
Lambert, J. and Pearson, J.	*Adventure Playgrounds*	T.C.	Penguin
Lowenfeld, V. and Brittain, L.	*Creative and Mental Growth*	T.C.	Collier-Macmillan
Macqueen, S.	*Encyclopaedia of Flower Arranging*	T.M.	Faber
Maurice, G.	*Arranging Flowers*	T.M.	Studio Vista
Portchmouth, J.	*Secondary School Art*	T.D.	Studio Vista (1973)
Puckrose, H.	*Creative Themes*	T.C.	Murray
Schools' Council	*Industrial Archeology for Schools*	T.C.	Heinemann
Seyd, M.	*Designing with String*	T.P.M.	Batsford
Shaw, D.	*Woodwork—Design and Practice*	T.P.M.	Hodder and Stoughton
Tanner, R.	*Children's Work in Block Printing*	T.M.	Dryad

Summary Index

Note Topics are grouped under appropriate general headings.

Course Construction   Chapter 5
The need for structure   49
The teacher-co-ordinator   49-50
Factors affecting choice of course activities   50-1
Sources of activities   51-2
Equating activities and objectives — a monitoring technique
   52-3
Teacher activity cards   57-8

Course Planning   Chapter 4
Production and classification of objectives   35-7, 43-8
Materials   37-8, 46
Visual communication   38-9, 46
Personal expression   39-40
Tool skills   40-2
Project work and problem solving   7-15, 16-27
Technology   42-3, 33-4

Design as a Social Study   Chapter 3
Health, the physical and cultural environments as contexts for
   design-based learning   30-4
Home economics as a contributing discipline   30
Architectural studies   33
Technological studies   33-4

Design Education in Schools   Chapter 1
A definition   1
Design education in relation to contemporary Western culture
   and technology   1-2
The central, core and supporting roles of design education in
   the middle years of schooling   2-6, 54-7

Display Techniques   Chapter 8
Educational uses of display   78-9
Display material   79-80
Space and colour in display; two- and three-dimensional
   displays   80-6
Fabrics; lighting; lettering; natural materials; models   86-8
Display and observer attitude   89
Basic tools and equipment for display   89

Experience in Three Dimensions   Chapter 11
Exploration and appreciation of volumetric space   117-20
Design in the environment   120-1
The study of natural objects and artifacts   121-2
Manipulating and using three-dimensional materials   122-3

Recording and Evaluation of Pupil Performance   Chapter 6
Purpose of record keeping   59
Pupil coverage of course-work   59-61
Recording and analysis   61-7
Measurement of pupil performance — factors involved   67-9
Recording pupil achievement   69-70

Resources for Design Education   Chapter 7
Roles of teaching staff   71
Provision and organisation of work-space and equipment   71-2
Types of accommodation   72-3
Workshop provision and conditions   73-5
Timetabling and the provision of a balanced range of activities
   75-7

Scope of Design Education in Schools   Chapter 2
Design/problem-solving approaches, 'linear' and 'lateral'   7-8
Stages in the linear design process   9-16
Case histories: a school directional system, an abacus, study of
   form   16-28

Teaching Materials Manipulation   Chapter 12
Marking out; cutting to shape   124-7
Shaping: by modelling, removal of surplus material, by
   fabrication and by casting   127-130
Surface treatment   131
Joints involving fasteners; self-locating joints; joints involving
   adhesives; joints involving thread; metal joints involving
   molten metal   131-3

Two-dimensional Experiences   Chapter 10
Elements of visual form; line, point, shape, colour, texture and
   movement   101-6
Organisation of two-dimensional space   106
Sub-division of two-dimensional space   107
The Golden section   107-8
Balance; size; expression in two dimensions; drawing;
   painting; printing; screen-printing   108-112
Collage; mosaic; fabrics and embroidery   113-5
The relationship between two and three dimensions   115-6

Visual Communication   Chapter 9
Implications of visual communication   90
Determinants of visual form   90
Materials technology and visual form   90-2
Communication and the use of symbols   92-3
Visual communication in contemporary society   93
Visual language   93-4
Sensory experience in communication and learning   94-5
Visual expression and mental growth   95-100